The

New-Time Religion

*

PRENTICE-HALL, INC. *Englewood Cliffs, N.J.*

*

THE

New-Time

Religion

*

CLAIRE COX

*

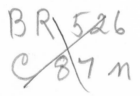

To Max
with love

Table of Contents

Acknowledgments

How can one say "thank you" to the person who has gone with socks undarned, meals uncooked and house uncleaned, who has been disturbed by night and tormented by day by the typewriter clatter that finally has produced a book? My husband, Max L. Lowenthal Jr., not only has had to endure those indignities; he also has been subjected to the further cruel and unusual treatment of reading the manuscript. He applied all his skills as a copy editor to unsplitting my infinitives and making many constructive suggestions, most of which, as an obedient wife, I gratefully accepted. I could not have written this book without his encouragement or his patience.

Many persons have contributed information and advice. I could not begin to mention all of them here, but there are some whose names must be noted. My thanks then go to J. Arthur Lazell, who while still a member of the staff of the National Council of Churches gave much helpful advice and read an important segment of the book; to Fletcher Coates, Meryl Ruoss, G. Paul Musselman, Duncan Burnside and Charles Estus, also of the National Council; to Ralph Stoody, director of information of the Methodist Church; Everett C. Parker, Stoody's counterpart in the headquarters of the United Church of Christ, and the publicity experts of the American and Southern Baptist Conventions, respectively, Faith Pomponio and W. C. Fields. Erik Modean of the National Lutheran Council and Charles C. Hushaw of the United Lutheran Church in America have been most helpful, as has been Bluford B. Hestir of the Presbyterian Church in Southern United States. Rabbi Marc Tannenbaum generously interrupted a busy schedule to share with me his observations on religious activities. My old friend Rabbi Bernard Lander also shared his expert knowledge.

Earl Minderman provided the necessary data on the Mormon Church; Stanley Rowland, on the United Presbyterian Church in the U.S.A., and Douglas A. Bushy, on the Protestant Episcopal Church. My thanks also to Dr. William Douglas of the Boston University School of Theology for reading the chapter on ministers' wives and for his useful comments. The Rev. John E. Kelly, director of public relations of the National Catholic Welfare Conference, was an invaluable help in guiding me to material on the Roman Catholics.

I would like to express my special gratitude to Earl J. Johnson, vice-president and editor of United Press International, for his interest in the project and his permission to draw upon the religion columns I have written weekly for UPI for the last few years. And to John Tiffany Elliott, my agent, a word of thanks for his advice and always helpful criticism.

C.C.

1

"In God We Trust"

THERE IS a new-time religion in the land.

It has made the church more popular and prosperous than ever before.

It also has made the church less pious.

The upsurge of religion has turned churches into recreation areas, nurseries, social service agencies and psychological clinics, as well as places in which to pray, meditate and worship.

It has brought sharp new contours to the nation's skylines, catchy new words to the American language and worldly ideas to the pulpit.

Churches have tennis courts, bowling alleys, swimming pools and barbecues along with traditional choir lofts, study rooms and sanctuaries. Parking lots have become as important as pews in filling churches on Sunday.

New jazz liturgical music, new air-conditioned comfort, new artistic beauty, and even readable new versions of the Scriptures in 20th Century English are making it easier for Americans to get the new-time religion.

Sermons and prayers are shorter, pews are softer, the lighting is easier on the eyes.

Religion is moving forward spectacularly, there is no doubt. Where it stands spiritually in the age of rockets to the moon is causing considerable concern to thoughtful clergymen, who sometimes fear they have been caught up in a theological numbers game where the head count is the most important thing. But sociologically speaking, religion never has been so widely accepted or so "respectable" as it is in the United States today. The Organization Man, the Man in the Gray Flannel Suit, the White Collar Girl, the Working Mother, the Suburban Housewife, the Farmer, the Retired Bank Clerk, the Factory Hand, the Widow, the Status Seeker, the Egghead, all are four-square behind the upsurge in religious interest.

The wave has rolled across America with the help of the President of the United States, Henry Luce, Billy Graham, Norman Vincent Peale, Bishop Fulton J. Sheen, Madison Avenue advertising slogans and the wistful yearnings of frightened millions who have rushed into spiritual togetherness in a sometimes frantic search for security in a world of atom bombs, sputniks, Communist truculence and worries that business won't be so good forever.

What this religious phenomenon is no one is exactly sure. Many a churchman has spent painful hours pondering the question. There is no doubt about the heightened religious interest, for it is reflected in almost every phase of life in America—from the lighted crosses on Wall Street towers of commerce at Christmas time to the spotlights that bathe New England church spires every night of the year. But the religious upsurge appears against a dismal backdrop of payola, television quiz show "fixes," police scandals, increasing rape, murder, robbery and embezzlement, and rising rates of juvenile delinquency, alcoholism and divorce.

Some call the stimulated church activity statistical prosperity. Some say that the crest of the wave was reached in 1955 or 1956, and that there has been a subsidence since. Others say a plateau has been reached. A few are convinced that the best is yet to come. But all agree that times generally are good for the new-time religion.

Nowhere else is religion prospering as in America. Moslems, Buddhists and Hindus are on the march abroad, but without the help of public-relations experts, advertising campaigns, television and color movies. In West Germany and the Low Countries, there has been a resurgence of Protestantism, but quietly, almost silently, in intellectual circles. Only in America are there "ranch-house" style churches, with baby-sitting services for worshipping mothers and machines to total the attendance. Only in America is there a Jane Russell to found an organization called the Hollywood Christian Group and to extol God as "a livin' doll," and a Pat Boone to sing his way to the top of a teen-age church-goers' poll for being a Good Christian as well as a talented entertainer.

The upsurge has been called many things by the clergy who watch over the larger flocks. It has been labeled a "revival," a "renewal of interest," "an upsurge of piety," "a spiritual aspirin tablet," "religiosity," "corporateness," "a cult of reassurance," "faith in faith" and even a 20th Century reformation.

Whatever "it" is, religion is fashionable beyond a doubt. Whether a person goes to church or not, whether he has any religious convictions, when he is asked to state his religious *preference,* he is likely to *say* he has one.

"In God We Trust" has been adopted as the country's official motto, and "Pray for Peace" has been imprinted on millions of letters with Post Office cancellation machines. The Boy Scouts of America claimed the honor of inspiring the first use of the word "God" in a mail cancellation when, in 1960, the Post Office issued a stamp commemorating the 50th anniversary of scouting in America. A special cancellation featuring the Scout emblem and slogan "For God and Country" was imprinted on an estimated one million first-day covers at the Washington, D.C. Post Office.

The unpopularity of avowed atheists is at a peak. In World War II, there were no atheists in foxholes. Now there are no atheists in suburbia, where sparkling new churches, built in a variety of modernistic, geometric, glass-walled shapes and surrounded by parking lots, play areas and picnic grounds, are providing seven-day-a-week community centers as well as sanctuaries, and contributing, among other things, two new verbs to the American language—"to fellowship" and "to church."

Atheism—or at least public avowals of it—is frowned on in business and industry. A man's church attendance is watched by some big employers as carefully as his selling skills and the club activities of his wife. The subliminal appeals of the spiritual have the full endorsement of such industrial giants as General Motors and IBM, and the boss may spend as much time at church taking inventory of his subordinates in attendance as he does peering into the hymnal.

"There is a big difference in religion between now and 30 years ago," says the Rev. Dr. Eugene Carson Blake, chief administrative officer of the United Presbyterian Church in the U.S.A. and a former president of the National Council of Churches. "Religion is popular now. People don't ask any more, 'Is there really a God?' Now the question is, 'What is God like?' There is the quality of today's religion."

Probably no two more unlike persons point up the status of religion with greater clarity than Miss America and the President of the United States. The girl chosen today as the epitome of American femininity is more likely to be a choir singer than a chorine. To her, a bathing suit is strictly for swimming. At a Miss America Pageant, one finalist made a brief religious commentary, while others discussed their boy friends. Lynda Lee Mead of Mississippi, Miss America of 1960, has credited her Episcopalian upbringing for her success, saying, "Faith gives a reason for living. Your relationship with God is the most important thing in your life." Miss Universe of the same year, Linda Bement of Salt Lake City, was crowned on a Saturday night and gave her prayerful thanks in church the following morning. Miss Bement, a Mormon, prayed every night of the contest, but she assured her public that "I didn't exactly ask to win. I just gave thanks for getting as far as I did each time."

At the top of the American success spectrum, the White House, we find the President of the United States—any President of the United States—setting the pace for religious prestige. It is almost mandatory for the President and just about every other political candidate to be not only a member of the American Legion but also an avowed churchgoer. Election campaigns feature frequent mention of the deity. During the 1960 pre-election debate over the merits of a Roman Catholic for President, the then Vice-President, Richard M. Nixon, declared that a candidate's religion should not be an issue—"unless he has none."

Once elected, the President takes the oath of office with his right hand not on the United States Constitution but on the Holy

Bible. After his inauguration, he is expected to attend church every Sunday, whether that was his practice before he entered the White House and whether it will be his practice after he leaves it. No one says he *must* do this. He *may* be doing it because he wants to, but whatever his preference, it is tacitly expected of him, and when he does not appear at church, public notice is taken of his absence.

Nothing expresses quite so adequately the status of religion in America today as the fact that when President Dwight D. Eisenhower flew off to the ill-starred Paris summit meeting of May, 1960, the capital bade him "bon voyage" with a mass pealing of church bells. And when the critical talks with the atheistic Communists failed before they ever really began, what did the President of the United States do? He visited two of France's most famous churches.

The following fall, when the Soviet Premier, Nikita S. Khrushchev, arrived in America to disrupt the United Nations General Assembly "summit meeting," church bells tolled and congregations across the land were summoned to pray for the easing of world tensions. In 1961, Eisenhower ended 50 years of public service with a farewell address he concluded with a prayer.

Never has religion had it so good, to reword an election campaign slogan used successfully by President Eisenhower. Never has religion been so institutionalized, so conspicuous, so public. Never has churchgoing been so acceptable, so much "the thing to do," whether it involves attending a fellowship supper, bingo games, a Bible brunch, choir practice, hi-fi fellowship, ladies' sewing circle, the Wednesday night bowling tournament, Thursday prayer meeting or Sunday worship service.

The church has turned to the layman for support as never before. Laymen appear as substitute preachers in pulpits and in December, 1960, a layman was chosen for American Protestantism's biggest job. J. Irwin Miller, a Columbus, Ind., businessman and industrialist, was elected President of the National Council of Churches, the first layman to fill the post in the council's 10-year history. Miller accepted the post as a leading lay member of the Disciples of Christ denomination and a firm believer that the church should participate in every phase of life.

This new-time religion has taken its shape since World War II. Between World Wars, most congregations were satisfied largely to go to church once a week, perhaps attend a pot-luck supper now and then and send the children to Sunday school regularly. Now there is a ferment, a seeking of ideas that was not present 20 or 30 years ago. People ask questions, instead of merely listening, although the element of spectatoritis still prevails to such an extent that a minister often is hard-pressed when it comes to persuading his congregation to join him in saying "Amen."

Howard E. Butt Jr. of Corpus Christi, Texas, a millionaire supermarket operator and lay evangelist of the Southern Baptist Convention, is one of those who believes that spectatoritis is "the blight of our religion today. When a person's religion consists in coming to a service and listening to someone else perform, that person's religion is paralyzed."

D. Elton Trueblood, professor of theology at Earlham College, calls churchgoing "America's biggest spectator sport." Writing in *The Christian Herald*, he decried what he called "audience Christianity," in which a congregation watches and listens almost as it would at a theater or concert.

There are other commentaries. Some clergymen credit Tennessee Williams' sordid, morbid and often bizarre dramas with preaching more eloquently than the most silver-tongued pulpit orator and therefore drawing more attentive audiences. Williams, to these men, is delineating the problems of contemporary society with frankness and clarity while some ministers are mouthing empty phrases or are getting their Sunday messages from books containing sermons prepared by someone else.

Dr. Joseph Sittler Jr., professor of theology at the University of Chicago and chairman of the North American Commission on Worship of the World Council of Churches, believes that the TV drama "Gunsmoke" may penetrate the ambiguities of man's daily life and thinking much more clearly than do many preachers.

Just by saying this, Sittler himself clearly shows how much the church has become part of the everyday world and how much weekday life has penetrated the realm of religion.

Churches have public-relations departments today to send out announcements that used to be read from the pulpit. Direct-mail publicity is saving much of the shoe leather of pastors who used to call at newcomers' homes to invite them to church. Laymen are helping ministers make pastoral calls. Finance committees conducting large-scale money-raising campaigns are making Sunday collections in many churches only token sources of income. The old-fashioned ministerial study has been replaced by a business-like office.

The differences between the old and new religions are as many and as sharp as the contrast between the imposing old Gothic cathedrals and the flashy new glass-walled tepee churches. Twenty years ago, the chief functions of women in the church were to sew for the poor and cook church suppers. Now they spurn drudgery in the church as they do at home. They conduct community campaigns for housing, migrant workers and schools. Church dinners—gourmet style—still come under their supervision, but professional cateresses often are employed to do the cooking and there are machines to wash the dishes afterwards.

In earlier generations, the church was a place to go mainly for worship. Most churches were dark and their doors were locked during the week. Now the church operates on a seven-day basis; the appeal remains spiritual, but it is expressed in laymen's terms.

There are woodworking and ceramic shops in many a church basement. Diapers, toys and cribs for church nurseries have become as important in retaining members as the ample distribution of Biblical coloring kits and comic books to Sunday school children.

Only a few decades ago, children were forbidden to enter bowling alleys, for fear they would be turned into juvenile delinquents on the spot. Now hundreds of churches have their own bowling alleys, complete with pin-setting machines.

Superlatives are almost endless when it comes to describing the big boom in religion. Roman Catholics, Protestants and Jews alike report record memberships, record contributions, record church building programs, record radio, television, publishing and public-relations efforts.

The Bible still is way out front as a global best seller and church investments on Wall Street and in real estate are soaring. The best Hollywood film of 1960—in the opinion of the Motion Picture Academy—was the biblically inspired Ben Hur, which won a handful of Oscars. No movie maker has yet been able, with or without the help of Marilyn Monroe or Lassie, to match the success achieved by the late Cecil B. De Mille and a "cast of thousands" with his life of Christ.

The Rev. Dr. Norman Vincent Peale was for 186 weeks the most famous name on best-seller lists with his inspirational book, "The Power of Positive Thinking." This book was published in 1952, just 10 years after the all-time fiction winner, "The Robe," a religious novel by Lloyd C. Douglas, appeared on the list, where it remained for what at that time was a record of 178 weeks. The distribution of Gideon Bibles in hotel and motel rooms continues apace, but Conrad Hilton has taken the modern approach to spirituality by placing in every one of his far-flung hotel rooms, from Beverly Hills to Istanbul, current copies of Peale's "Guidepost" magazine. He considers it handier for the traveler than the traditional Gideon version of the Scriptures.

Campaigns to "Put Christ in Christmas" have brought large-scale manufacture of appropriate gifts with religious themes. There was a time when about the only church-connected gifts were Bibles, rosaries or St. Christopher medals. Now there is something for almost every taste and pocketbook, ranging from bracelet charms engraved with the Lord's Prayer to a $35 Tiffany portrait bust of Pope Pius XII. There are family games such as "Going to Bethlehem" or "Bible Picture Lotto" and nonbreakable dolls in the form of an infant Jesus and a nun.

Such merchandise has the full endorsement of religious organizations. It is advertised in church publications and sometimes manufactured under church auspices. Gifts of a religious nature are accepted as seriously as are a newspaper comic strip and a television soap opera with ministers for heroes. The popularization and humanization of religion are all to the good, many churchmen say. They feel they really are getting their message across when they see that the church has become a part of the everyday world.

A rather extreme example of this philosophy was provided in California, where considerable clerical consternation was voiced when a group of promoters jumped on the religion bandwagon with blueprints for a $15,000,000, 220-acre amusement park at Cucamonga, designed as a sort of Biblical Disneyland. "Rides" were to include a "buzz" up to heaven for an introduction to St. Peter, a visit to the Garden of Eden, a quick tour of Hell and a cruise through the innards of Jonah's whale as a variation of the old tunnel-of-love in the traditional amusement park.

The plans called for a park laid out in the shape of a heart, as a symbol of God's love. A huge cross, the Star of David and a Shrine of Faith were included as features, with attractions ranging from chariot races in Rome, a King Tut Tomb ride in Egypt and a Noah's Ark merry-go-round in Israel to a Cecil B. De Mille Memorial theater.

When Southern California ministers rose in protest, the sponsors of the project hastily arranged a meeting, which produced a peaceful compromise. Heaven, Hell and the Garden of Eden were eliminated and Dr. Forrest Weir, executive director of the Church Federation of Los Angeles, agreed to serve as a consultant to the amusement park to help the promoters assemble a board of advisers from the Protestant, Catholic and Jewish faiths.

As finally drawn, the plans received the approval of churchmen. It is highly unlikely this would have occurred 20 years ago—but it also is unlikely that anyone would have concocted such a plan for an amusement park in the 1930's or 1940's.

This is the world going to the church—and the church moving out into the world. In reaching out, clergymen are speaking up on serious matters as well as some that might be regarded as frivolous. Ministers frequently testify before Congressional committees on non-theological matters. The Methodist Church, for example, spearheaded a campaign to try to persuade Congress to outlaw the consumption of alcoholic beverages on all airliners, and clergymen frequently are on the lists of witnesses who testify about aid to underdeveloped countries and other such matters of moment.

One of the most fervent ministerial campaigns has been conducted to promote safe driving. Pastors regard the reckless driver as a social menace of deep concern to the Christian. One clergyman practiced what he preached so well that he was named 1960 National Driver of the Year by the American Trucking Association. The Rev. Russell R. Brown, a Baptist preacher of Mount Pleasant, Tex., who drove a truck so he could afford to be a minister and still support his wife and four children, was honored for driving nearly 900,000 miles in 14 years without a chargeable accident.

Another minister reached into the world with a pair of bar bells. The Rev. Hanford L. King Jr., rector of St. James' Church in Bozeman, Mont., was chosen Mr. Montana of 1960 for his skill as a weight lifter. He also was Montana commissioner of weight lifting for the Amateur Athletic Union.

Magic is the medium used by First Lt. Robert Anderson, an army chaplain. Once thought the work of the devil, magic was taught at Northern Baptist Seminary when Anderson was a student there. The subject was called "gospel magic" informally. On the official academic schedule, it was part of a course called "audio-visual aids in religious education."

Anderson said he had found that magic created an interest in the program of the church by serving as an ice breaker in introducing a pastor and new groups to one another. It also is useful, he said, in illustrating Bible stories for children. Enough ministers agree with him to have formed a Fellowship of Christian magicians, with headquarters in Chicago.

Examples of the mingling of the world and the church are endless. Successful commercial plays have been presented in church sanctuaries. Ministers are taking active roles in politics. Housewives are holding prayer meetings in their homes. More and more businessmen are tithing.

The status of religion in America today can be pointed up in many ways, but perhaps the nuclear age has provided the sharpest picture through a government agency of nationwide scope and a single small southern city. Both are creatures of the nuclear age —one a cause, the other an effect.

Without any hint of a threat to the doctrine of separation of church and state, the National Civil Defense Organization has set up a section devoted to developing emergency measures to be taken on the spiritual level in the event of an enemy attack. This section is making plans for the services of clergymen in a nuclear crisis, just as other sections are supervising civil defense preparedness for schools, hospitals, office buildings and homes.

"The worshipper who carries in his soul an incorruptible faith will not so easily panic," a Civil Defense official reasoned.

On the local level, nuclear-age religion is dramatized by Oak Ridge, Tenn., which is deeply involved in the spiritual resurgence and yet helped to launch the atomic era and trigger the chain reaction of fears that brought development of the Civil Defense ministerial corps.

Oak Ridge was created in 1943 as a one-industry town. The industry was the manufacture of atomic bombs. A few weeks after the first scientists and technicians went to work, a handful of the pioneer "settlers" held a meeting to establish the town's first church. Interdenominational services were held first in a school cafeteria and later in the government-built Chapel On The Hill. The Presbyterians were the first to build their own sanctuary. Other denominations followed.

Today, in Oak Ridge, still a one-industry town, there are 31,000 persons and 42 congregations, most of them with their own churches. Of the 17,000 adults in the town, about 11,000 belong to a church. This is a far higher proportion of church-goers than is to be found in most of the rest of the nation.

2

A Matter of Mathematics

ORGANIZED RELIGION in America has a mathematical problem
that not even UNIVAC could solve: How many persons are
affiliated with churches and synagogues?

There is no doubt of record religious activity. An estimated
60 million Americans turn up in church on any given Sunday, and
that is a lot of people to be doing the same thing at approximately
the same time.

But where are the 120 million other Americans when weekly
worship time rolls around?

So far as statisticians are concerned, anywhere from 60 to 100
million of these people are unchurched—meaning they have no
association with organized religion. The rest are simply AWOL.

While talk has been rife of a spiritual upsurge in the United
States since World War II, the ranks of the unchurched also have
been swelling, quietly, steadily and at a rate estimated to exceed
the rate of the population explosion.

It is known that a majority of Americans come from Protestant
backgrounds—but most of this majority stay away from church.

Nearly a third of the baptized Roman Catholics in this country
are estimated to have strayed from the fold.

The number of synagogue members apparently is only a fraction
of all the persons with Jewish backgrounds.

While all of this is true, it also is true that more Americans
are flocking to more houses of worship than ever before; that the
nation has been resounding to highly publicized declarations of

religiosity since the end of World War II. It is true as well that church building has become a major industry in the race to keep pace with the demands for more and larger houses of worship.

The big boom in religion is here, but there is a boom also in what some call paganism. It has led Roman Catholics to declare that this no longer is a predominantly Protestant nation. "Gentile" is the way some persons describe America today.

Being unorganized, the unchurched millions have no voice and therefore no influence. The churched millions constitute the largest body of organized persons in America. Being highly organized, they speak out loud and clear, through their leaders, on many issues, lay and clerical, while the unorganized and unled remain silent and therefore impotent.

It was just this situation that prompted the Federal Civil Defense organization to set up a religion bureau geared to rush into action in the event of a nuclear holocaust or other emergency. In mobilizing for a crisis, Civil Defense officials turned to the one segment of society occupied by the largest number of persons.

This does not gainsay the existence of a statistical quandary in organized religion. Clergymen and other religious leaders have been aware of this situation for a long time. They fear that the number of strays may increase by 10 million in the next decade. Their apprehensions are fed by the fact that some denominations take in thousands of new members a year, while nearly as many slip out the back door. Some groups are just barely keeping up with their own birth rates; others are lagging behind.

In the course of a reappraisal of the religious upsurge since World War II, clergymen have gone on a statistical spree in which they have learned just about everything about their members except exactly how many of them there are. Nearly every religious organization has a statistical department that tries to keep track of members, contributions, construction, investments and other such vital data. The statisticians, teaming with inveterate pollsters, have turned up an amazing conglomeration of data about the churched—where they live, how much education they have had, what books they read, how much money they earn, whether they like to see their pastors in clerical vestments, their attitudes toward God and their professional aptitudes.

They know all these things—and more, too—but quite frankly they admit they do not have any reliable idea how many persons actually are affiliated with organized religion.

The best figures available are those rounded up each year by the National Council of Churches. As of 1960, here generally is how the various religious groups stood in the council's computations, based entirely on information supplied by the individual denominations:

Protestant—62,543,502
Roman Catholic—40,871,302
Jewish—5,500,000
Eastern Orthodox—2,807,612

The addition of others brought the grand total to around 112,-000,000 out of the nation's population of 180,000,000 claimed as members by the 254 bodies that reported to the Council. But even some officials of the Council did not really regard these figures as having much significance. They noted that even if the computation was correct, it still meant a substantial bloc of persons were not on any religious rolls.

How were the official figures arrived at? Here is the Yearbook of American Churches' explanation:

"The Roman Catholics count all baptized persons, including infants. The Jews regard as members all Jews in communities having congregations. The Eastern Orthodox churches include all persons in their nationality or cultural groups. Most Protestant bodies count only the persons who have attained full membership, and previous estimates have indicated that all but a small minority of these are over 13 years of age. However, many Lutheran bodies and the Protestant Episcopal Church now report all baptized persons, and not only those confirmed."

Thus, in the case of the Lutherans, for example, of the 2,387,292 members of the Lutheran Church-Missouri Synod, in 1960, nearly 800,000 were children. About the same number of the United Lutheran Church in America's 2,477,012 members also were children. But the Methodist Church, largest single Protestant body in the United States, claimed nearly 10,000,000 members—not including well over 1,500,000 children.

While the National Council's figures therefore admittedly are inaccurate in any given year, they indicate a trend over a period of several years. If figures rise continuously, it means that the upsurge is continuing. When, and if, they ever drop several years in a row, organized religion will have to pause and take stock.

One trend that emerged from figures announced by the Council late in 1960 was that the rate of growth of Roman Catholicism was outstripping that of the Protestant churches. In 1959, the Council reported, the Protestant growth rate trailed the population rise slightly, while the Catholic increase was considerably ahead of the birth rate.

The increase in Protestant church membership reported for the year was 1.7 per cent over that for the preceding year. The Catholics reported an increase of 3.4 per cent. The population of the United States rose by an estimated 1.8 per cent.

For statistical purposes, Catholic churches include all persons within parish boundaries who have been baptized in the faith.

The official Roman Catholic figures for 1960, compiled by P. J. Kenedy and Sons of New York for the Official Catholic Directory, which weighed in at seven pounds, showed a growth of 1,365,827 over the preceding year and a 10-year increase of 13,105,161, or 47.2 per cent in 10 years. Two million of these members were accounted for by the inclusion for the first time of all Roman Catholic servicemen and their families and all Catholics in government overseas. This two million also swelled the National Council of Churches' grand total.

"Every statistic for the individual dioceses are given to us by the chancery office of each diocese, and to that extent can be considered absolutely official," explained J. Louis Meyer, business manager of the directory. "Over the years, of course, everyone realizes that our figures for the total number of Catholics is undoubtedly substantially lower than the actual number of communicants, largely because we might consider that the pastors of individual parishes are prone to be rather moderate in estimating the number of Catholics in their charge."

A dissenting note on the Catholic figures has been sounded by a Catholic priest, the Rev. Joseph H. Fichter, chairman of the sociology department at Loyola University of the South in New Orleans, in a report on "Social Relations in the Urban Parish" (published by the University of Chicago Press). He said studies have shown that approximately one-third of the white baptized Catholics in this country must be considered "dormant," meaning unchurched. One study he cited estimated that about 36 per cent of the infants baptized in the church never were brought back.

Fichter said that the number of persons received into the church was recorded carefully each year but that there were no complete studies providing accurate statistics on the number or rate of Catholics leaving the church.

A Protestant leader also complained about Catholic computations. Richard A. Meyers, executive director of the Bureau of Research and Planning of the Church Federation of Greater Chicago, said that Roman Catholics report all baptized persons, including babies, in their figures and then compare the total with predominantly adult Protestant membership. The country may not be quite so Protestant as it used to be, he said, but it is more so than the Catholics maintain.

"Thus, in our studies, we've tried to make the Protestant figures comparable by adding affiliated persons, which in reality would be the children of our member families, and it is a better comparison to use with the Roman Catholic figures than are church membership figures alone that count persons mainly above the age of 12 or 13."

One of the most extensive studies ever made of religious affiliation was conducted by the Catholic Digest, and the results were published in its monthly issues over a three-year period that ended in 1954. Answers to 186 questions brought declarations from 99 per cent of those polled that they believed in a God and statements from 95 per cent of a religious *preference*—not an affiliation, but a preference. The survey concluded that about a third of those with preferences did not attend church at all, about a third attended only sometimes and the rest went to church every Sunday.

According to the preferences stated, two out of every three persons 14 or over regarded themselves as Protestant; one out of every four as Roman Catholic and slightly over three per 100 as Jewish. These figures gave no clue to actual membership, however.

The American Jewish Year Book of 1960 estimated the Jewish population in the U.S. in 1959 at 5,357,000—slightly under the figure used by the National Council of Churches. The Year Book editors explained that their estimate was reached through question-naires to member communities of the Council of Jewish Federa-tions or Welfare Funds. The files of the United Jewish Appeal were reviewed for other communities. The estimates for New York City, which has the largest concentration of Jews in America, were a projection of a sample study taken in 1952 by the Health Insurance Plan of Greater New York. For suburban communities in the Greater New York area, replies to special questionnaires in 1957 gave the number of Jewish households. These were multiplied by 3.5 to give an estimate of the total number of individuals.

Nowhere in the computations was there an indication that sta-tistics had been based on actual synagogue attendance. Two other techniques are mentioned frequently, however, in Jewish computa-tions—the death-record and Yom Kippur methods.

In one, the number of Jewish deaths in a community is com-puted by consulting Jewish cemeteries and undertakers' records or by searching health department files for "typical" Jewish names. The number of Jews then is estimated on the basis of the general ratio between deaths and population.

In the other, the number of school children absent on Yom Kippur is obtained. All are assumed to be Jewish. The total Jew-ish population in each community is then estimated by using the known ratio between all children in school-age brackets and the general population and assuming the same ratio exists between the Jewish school age population and the Jewish population.

It is anybody's guess, actually, how many Jews there are in the United States. Because of their autonomy, individual synagogues are not required to send their membership figures to a central office. What the grand total of their statistics would be no one can say. It is a certainty, however, that if Jews are no more loyal than Protestants in participating in worship services, there must be far fewer than 5,000,000 Jews on synagogue rolls.

From all sources, Protestant, Catholic and Jewish, it is easy to see that the total figures given for membership in various religious organizations do not reflect actual participation in the lives of the churches and synagogues. Labels are claimed by individuals or are parceled out to them on a wholesale basis.

A survey made by the Southern Baptist Home Missions Board on the east coast of Florida from Key West to Palm Beach disclosed that nearly 75 per cent of approximately 1,400,000 persons questioned had no active church membership. The proportion of unchurched was described as about twice that of most large cities. More than 400,000 of those questioned had no church affiliation. About the same number claimed membership in church organizations but did not belong to any local congregations. Many of the latter were in the retirement age bracket and in all likelihood still were listed as members of congregations in cities they had left.

The Rev. Meryl Ruoss, executive director of the department of the urban church of the National Council of Churches, reported that research in urban neighborhoods seemed to indicate that about 50 per cent of the people who identified themselves as Protestants actually were not affiliated with a local church. In many instances, they did not even know the name or location of a Protestant church.

"These same surveys indicate," he said, "that about 65 per cent of the self-identified Jews are those in ethnic heritage only. About 35 per cent of the self-identified Roman Catholics do not accept the services of any local parish.

"Such percentages would reveal a total of about 33 million persons identifying themselves in one or another major religious category as being essentially unchurched. If we add to this the approximately 70 million persons unclaimed by any religious body, according to our annual church membership data, we see that the Protestant church faces a staggering evangelistic challenge of 100 million souls in America at any given moment.

"The great bulk of this evangelistic potential are pagans—the second, third or fourth generation outside the nurture of any religious institution. These are not just the 'eggheads,' or the artists, or the Bohemians. They are your neighbors and mine, and the people who live around every one of our churches.

"The challenge for expansion to Protestantism in the second half of this century is to evangelize these multitudes. The serious question our churches, our seminaries and our denominational bodies must ask themselves is, 'Are we equipped for and oriented to such evangelism?'"

Individual denominations also are asking such questions. The larger the denomination, the more problems it has. The American Baptist Convention found itself in the position of having no idea at all exactly how many churches were affiliated with it or how many members these churches had. It conducted a painstaking person-by-person, church-by-church count, completed late in 1960, which cheered denominational officials who had feared the worst but raised a major question about the value of such a census.

Before the American Baptists sent denominational census takers to every church and to call on a representative cross-section of individual members, there was considerable pessimism both inside and outside the denomination. It was widely believed that this was a dying denomination. The strength of the Baptist movement had been in rural areas; with the mass migrations to the city, it was feared that the membership had slumped.

The census, as tabulated by Baptist officials with the aid of IBM machines, gave a total of 1,548,795 members, as compared with 1,491,048 five years before. It also turned up a total of 6,180 churches, more than denominational officials had thought there were. Of these, 65 per cent were built before 1900, but 729 had been started since 1940. The median size of the congregations was 159.7 members.

The question that must be raised stems from the fact that the grand total of more than 1,500,000 American Baptists tallied included inactive as well as active members. That meant the inclusion of persons whose names still were on church rolls but who never attended services and had stopped contributing. For all practical purposes, they were non-members.

Denominational officials figured that about 1 out of every 6 persons counted as members was inactive. That would mean a total of about 250,000 had strayed.

When asked about this situation, a Baptist official said the survey had been made in such a way that the inactive members *could* be separated from the active list so that active members *could* be studied as a group. He added the rather startling bit of information that many of the inactive members had been found to know more about the Bible and religion in general than a large number of those who regularly went to church.

The Southern Baptists reported at about the same time that 1960 had brought them downward trends in offerings, baptisms and commitments of young people to church service. W. Douglas Hudgins of Jackson, Miss., a former vice-president of the convention, questioned whether his denomination was slowing down or merely catching its breath after a decade of phenomenal growth. He called for a reemphasis on worship as a possible means of ending the slump.

Another major denomination that has been going through a period of intense self-examination is The Methodist Church. It began taking stock when it found itself in a statistical revolving door in which it accepted 1,881,609 new members between 1956 and 1960 but at the same time lost 1,389,428. The net membership gain therefore failed to keep pace with U.S. population growth. The annual Methodist rate was 1.3 per cent, while the population as a whole went up at a slightly higher rate.

"We have not been keeping enough of our members," an official Methodist report said. "We have had to receive nearly four persons to keep one. We have been letting too many members get out the back door through inactivity and through being lost sight of."

An example of how far statistical introspection can go was provided by the Methodists in a searching three-year self-study that produced the first detailed profile of their membership ever drawn.

The Board of Social and Economic Relations of the church and the Boston University School of Theology conducted the survey, the results of which were published in four volumes. Here are some of the facts they unearthed:

Most Methodists are members of the upper middle class. The denomination is failing largely to reach laborers, poor families and persons of lower attainment.

The children of Methodists have three times more chance of graduating from college than the average American.

There are three times more professional men and women in the Methodist Church than in the general population.

The denomination has 25 per cent fewer service workers and

laborers than the national population; 75 per cent fewer private household workers and 20 per cent fewer craftsmen.

The median age of Methodists is about 34½ years.

Eleven out of every 20 Methodists are female; eight out of every 10 Methodists at least 25 years old are married.

Only one Methodist in 100 is divorced, as compared with two in every 100 in the total population.

The largest Methodist church is the 8,718-member Highland Park Church in Dallas. The average has 400 members.

Although the Methodist Church absolutely forbids the use of alcohol, only 54.2 per cent of the members say they abstain.

What does all this add up to? That is what the Rev. Albert C. Hoover, editor of the Methodist Fact Book, asked.

"We have nine and three-quarters million members—who are they?" he inquired. "We received 380,204 on profession of faith—do they stay? We have over seven million in church schools with a 3,734,881 average attendance at Sunday school—what do they learn?"

The Lutherans have joined in the running discussion of church mathematics, with some leaders expressing alarm and others optimism.

The Rev. Dr. Donald L. Houser, executive secretary of the Board of American Missions of the United Lutheran Church in America, estimated that more than half the total population in 24 states had no church affiliation and that more than 80 per cent of the people in 110 counties were unchurched.

He told the denomination's 1960 convention that every year an additional million persons were joining the ranks of Americans with no church home.

"All the efforts of all the churches in the United States and Canada are unable to gain on this vast army," Houser said with a warning that if the present trend continues it will bring about a "post-Christian era" in North America.

"The church no longer receives a welcome reception as it enters a new community," he said.

"Church attendance is no longer popular. Only by recapturing the sense of urgency to carry out our mission and allowing the Holy Ghost to compel response can the tide be turned."

The Rev. Dr. Franklin Clark Fry, president of the denomination and often referred to as "Mr. Protestant," has tried to calm such worried outbursts and statistical concerns with the admonition that "my great concern is never the percentage of the population related to the church but the percentage of the individual who is really involved in his religion. I believe there is a large number of persons intelligently and actively involved in the life of the church, in thinking and action."

But even as Fry was making this point, Houser was putting the finishing touches on his report decrying the number of unchurched and the denomination's statisticians were preparing an annual membership report boasting that the United Lutheran Church still was the largest Lutheran body in North America.

In friendly rivalry, the Lutheran Church-Missouri Synod had pointed out earlier that *it* was the largest Lutheran church in the *Western Hemisphere*.

One of the chief worriers about where the church stands in society has been the Rev. Dr. G. Paul Musselman, director of the National Council of Churches' evangelism department. He would like to see an end put to speculation and an effort on the part of the churches to find out where they really are.

"A definite audit of church membership statistics would reveal a most abysmal state of affairs," he said. "People are always reluctant to sever connections with a church. As a result, statistics deal with a sentimental or social desire to stay on. It inflates the figures. It contrasts with the number who support or attend.

"In any church where an attempt is made to audit these lists on which we have to work, a shrinkage has resulted. In no cases have there been more. The shrinkage is absolutely phenomenal."

Musselman said that in one church, an audit of members reduced its official roll from a claimed 2,400 to an actual 485. Another church had claimed between 2,300 and 2,500 members but found it had 1,200.

"I don't know of anyplace where the percentage has been less than 20 per cent discounted," he said.

Inadvertently, a false picture of the church in America has been given. The optimism inherent in Christianity may be partly responsible for this. But on a more practical level, the responsibility can be pinned on the complete absence of any pretense of a scientific approach to numbers.

The churches must face the fact that they are flourishing in a statistics-minded society, in which machines chart the course of big business and compute the population increase down to the last birth in any hour. Huge electronic brains can tell man in a moment how many days it will take him to get to the moon, but when it comes to determining how many persons are affiliated with religious organizations, statisticians might just as well be counting on their fingers.

What useful purpose do the figures as now computed serve? Is there any point in issuing announcements every year boasting of a big religious surge in America if no one really knows how many persons are involved?

If the churches wish to continue putting out statistical figures every year, they should either get together and agree on a uniform system for counting heads or ask the Federal Government to do the job for them in the next regular census.

The Census Bureau conducted a sample poll in 1957 in which it found that 96 per cent of those questioned had a religious *preference*. Suggestions that this be done in the 1960 census were opposed as threats to the constitutional freedom of worship. This left religious bodies to continue limping along on an abacus basis in the UNIVAC age.

If a business or government agency were to issue a report based on such haphazard statistical methods, it would not last very long. Everyone would benefit by a scientific poll of religious affiliations of all Americans, with the key question being "Do you belong to a church and if so which one?" rather than, "Do you have a religious *preference?*" Almost anyone will state a preference, whether he has any affiliation or not.

To those who fear for their religious freedom as a result of such a census, it can only be said that there would be no likelihood of repercussions from stating "I am a Protestant," "I am a Catholic," "I am a Jew" or "I have no religious affiliation." Few persons keep their religious preferences secret in the course of their daily lives and there should be nothing to risk in confiding such information to a census taker.

Religious organizations would have everything to gain from this, principally the satisfaction of knowing they no longer were involved in a spiritual numbers game.

3

Sheep—Lost, Strayed, Stolen

Sheep counting is an age-old remedy for insomnia, but not when it comes to clergymen. It only serves to keep them wide awake.

Many a clergyman has been spending sleepless nights counting sheep that are gone from his flock—lost, strayed, stolen, or possibly out shopping for another place to worship.

In an era of record church membership and attendance and general institutional prosperity, the competition between denominations, or even various branches of a single denomination, is keen. And the more they have competed, the more alike they have become, until today there is a sort of homogenized Protestantism, with the difference between denominations diminishing all the time.

In any local church there is a hard core of loyal old-timers and enthusiastic newer members who form the nucleus for a permanent organization. But on the edges are the jumpers, strayers and shoppers and those whose convictions are so weak that they can be lured away.

Many churches openly engage in courting membership through proselytizing—"sheep stealing," some call it.

Others concentrate on gathering in the strays, the lost sheep.

More engage in evangelizing their own members, just to keep the status quo.

Shopping for a church grew out of the competition between individuals for status and out of the nomadic culture that has been produced by a people constantly in motion. In flitting like so many gadflies from one church and denomination to another, in looking before they light, many Americans hope to improve their standing in society through the "right" religious affiliation. This is a sort of fringe benefit that has accompanied stimulated religiosity.

One thing that makes this possible is the ease with which one may become a church member in most denominations today. Generations ago, a person had to study and be tested before he was accepted in a church. Today, membership often is solicited and requirements are easy. It is possible to belong to some denominations without knowing very much about *what* one actually belongs to.

Churches have been in ferment in America for 15 years, largely because of the peripatetic propensity of the sheep.

First, there is "sheep stealing."

The Church of Jesus Christ of Latter-Day Saints (Mormons) frankly states that it proselytizes. Every young man in the church devotes at least two years of his life to seeking converts, and at his own expense. In 1958, 11,446 of these volunteer missionaries converted more than 33,000 persons, nearly 9,000 of them in the United States.

The Southern Baptists are conducting a multi-million-dollar evangelizing campaign that has seen not only individual members but whole churches switch allegiance lock, stock and pipe organ from the largely northern American Baptist Convention. In some instances, the Southerners' powers of persuasion did not "take," and the churches returned to the northern fold.

American Baptists are represented by a handful of evangelists in the South, sent there to give spiritual aid and comfort to any southern individual or group wishing to join the northern body, but mainly to help displaced Northerners find church fellowship in Dixie.

The Southern Baptists have evangelized so widely and so well that they have more churches in the northernmost state of Alaska than any other denomination. The numerical strength of the Congregationalists, first Christian church to send missionaries to the Hawaiian Islands, is being threatened in the 50th state by the Southern Baptists.

The biggest threat of all in Hawaii, however, is from the east—

the Far East. Christianity has been losing out in Hawaii to Buddhism, which with 160,000 members in 1959 was the largest single religious group in the islands.

Roman Catholics, in their turn, like to talk about conversions— sheep stealing—from Protestantism. They would like, in fact, to bring every Protestant into their fold in what they would regard as a "homecoming." Wide publicity is given to many conversions to the Catholic faith. Clare Boothe Luce was one of the most celebrated converts; Helen Hayes made news when she returned to the church.

Then there is sheep straying.

More important to the pastoral head count than stealing is straying. This is a chronic cause for sleeplessness among the clergy. Many persons join a church but do not stay. They tarry for a while, perhaps, and then drop out of religious activity entirely. It has been estimated that about half of all persons who join churches drop by the wayside in the first six months.

The sheep stray for many reasons. Perhaps they did not like the minister. Perhaps the congregation was not friendly enough. But even more likely, church was interfering with their recreation, probably Sunday boating, which has been called the No. 1 cause for sheep straying. In 1960, there were 7,785,000 recreational boats on the roster of the National Association of Engine and Boat Manufacturers. With an average of about three persons using each boat, that meant nearly 23.5 million persons had found their pleasure—probably weekend pleasure—on the water.

"Boats have done more damage to church statistics than anything else," Musselman said. "In the last 20 years, the purchase of boats has been enormous. When do you use them? On weekends. Are you in church? No!"

In a detailed study of churches in various Washington State communities that even went into such matters as placement of signs pointing the way to churches, the American Baptists found boating, along with the location of a church, could be a factor in encouraging attendance. In a report on a specific church, the First Baptist Church of Edmonds, Wash., the researchers found:

"It has been discovered that denomination is not a significant factor in suburban communities as people choose churches. Many persons who may be strong Baptists and who may wish to continue their affiliation with an American Baptist Church, may return to the city. . . . The only reasons why persons from new subdivisions would be oriented toward Edmonds is the railroad station or as they commute to their boats which may be moored on the sound at Edmonds. Also, a great deal of traffic moves through the city from a ferry. But the church, since it cannot be seen easily from the major traffic artery, may not be obvious to many of these persons."

Next in rising order of importance in the general picture comes sheep jumping.

Fickle churchgoers—jumping sheep—are possibly the worst disturbers of the minister's peace of mind. Countless persons—no one could keep track of just how many—have gone from denomination to denomination according to the geographical, economic, social or spiritual needs of the moment.

A major stimulant to sheep jumping is the mobility of Americans. They are in almost constant motion. An estimated 40 million persons in the civilian population move every year. Most go to different abodes in the same county, but about 6.5 million go to different states and slightly more than that to a different county, according to the U.S. Census Bureau. In some years, as many as 25 per cent of Chicago's population alone pick up and move.

If they are churchgoers, the Americans in motion change churches with each move. Home is where the hat is. Americans have roots, but they take them along and set them down wherever they light. They can transplant their religious affiliation as easily as they can move from one house to another. The church becomes a spiritual motel.

A good example of what this does to individual local churches is given by the Brookwood Presbyterian Church in Columbus, Ohio. During the first 10 years of its existence, it had to take in nearly 3,000 members to wind up with a net of 1,275.

This figure could be matched or exceeded by churches across the nation. The Congregational churches in Chappaqua and Scarsdale, N.Y., both suburbs of New York City, have been in constant ferment because of population turnovers. Membership ins and outs in one Chicago area Congregational church were at such a rate that the head minister confessed he had not met half of his flock.

The Rev. Dr. Gerson S. Engelmann, minister of Faith United Protestant Church in the post-war community of Park Forest, near Chicago, reported that in nine years his church had taken in some 5,600 persons who had moved into the community and yet in 1960 had a total of only 1,660 members.

A similar story was told by the Rev. Dr. Lawrence L. Durgin while he was minister of the Central Congregational Church of Providence, R.I., founded in 1852. In his eight years at the church, he said, 692 persons were received into membership and yet he ended his tenure there with 45 fewer members than when he began. He attributed the turnover almost entirely to the fact that people are constantly on the move.

Panorama Baptist Church of Pacoima, Calif., a member of the American Baptist Convention, in its first nine years took in over 1,000 members, of which it could account for only 600 in 1960.

"California is rapidly expanding and the population increase and turnover are tremendous," explained the Rev. Fred A. Fels Jr., pastor of the church. "Because of this, we feel that we truly minister to a passing procession.

"The homes in our area are worth between $10,000 and $13,000, which makes us a true middle-class area. Many of our members are employed at the surrounding aircraft factories or in Civil Service work. As soon as a small equity is realized from their home, it seems that many move farther out in the Valley to more expensive homes, which accounts for this turnover."

The nomadic life of the armed forces presents still another facet of shepherding. So radically has this life changed since World War II that sometimes the 3,000 chaplains feel as though they had never left home. Traditionally, in the past, a chaplain had only his service contingent to worry about. Now he has entire families seeking his spiritual leadership.

The new Army is traveling around the world with wives, children, dogs, schoolteachers and all the troubles of a civilian community heaped on top of military problems. As a result, the chaplain has become a parish priest or a leader of an entire Protestant or Jewish congregation similar to any he might serve as a civilian in suburbia. In one year alone, the more than 800 Roman Catholic chaplains serving in the various service branches officiated at 34,198 baptisms, 13,484 first communions, 7,236 marriages and 11,782 confirmations.

Many Protestant chaplains take their families along on service assignments, which means ministers' wives often participate extensively in parish work among military families. There are men's and women's groups, Sunday schools, Christian Endeavors and even church suppers.

Hundreds of chapels overseas serving the military look like suburban churches at home, and they conduct their programs with an even more rapid turnover of Sunday school teachers, choir singers and scoutmasters.

A key factor in the migrations of churchgoers in civilian life is sheep shopping. Status is a vital part of this phenomenon. Many persons shop for a church the way they would select a country club. Single women are on husband hunts that take them to one church after another, more for social than spiritual succor. Newcomers to a community may hope to make social and business contacts through a church or synagogue. Quite a few parents switch allegiance when their children find that mounting social pressures of the soda pop set call for a classier Sunday school with more up-to-date audiovisual equipment (i.e., television and movies) and a larger swimming pool.

The American Baptist study of Washington State churches brought in the conclusion, in connection with the Clyde Hill Church in Bellevue, that "many parents when choosing a church home consider Christian education facilities as primary. Since denomination is not a crucial factor to many individuals, the type of facilities that a church has will often determine its opportunities for growth."

There are different status criteria in different kinds of communities. In suburbia, it may be a question of who goes to the church. In the cities, it may be the prestige of the pulpit—who is the best preacher, who draws the biggest crowds, whose sermon wins the biggest headlines on Monday newspaper church pages.

A study of churches in New Haven, Conn., turned up among the members one family in the most fashionable upper-class church in town, Congregational in this case, who were miserable in their membership but happy with their status outside the church. The husband was a machine tool worker in a factory. Neither he nor his wife had gone beyond high school. His wife was ambitious and wanted to go to The Best Church in Town, so they joined this one. Their children were accepted in Sunday school, but the parents were ignored when they went to Sunday services. No one said "hello" and the couple stayed away from social functions. They were getting next to nothing from belonging to this congregation, but away from the church, among their own friends, they had prestige because they worshipped on the right side of the tracks.

When Richard Nixon was vice-president, he and his family became sheep jumpers. Nixon had always identified himself as a Quaker, the religion of his youth. But after the Nixons went to Washington, they attended Westmoreland Congregational Church, one of the most fashionable churches in the Capital. Later, when they moved into Washington's Spring Valley section, they jumped again, this time to Metropolitan Methodist Church. They explained that it was more convenient. After Nixon's nomination for the Presidency, he indicated that another move might be in sight, to an Episcopalian church near the White House.

Among the migrating sheep have been many clergymen, but most often they made their moves before entering theological school. The Right Rev. James A. Pike, Protestant Episcopal Bishop of California, was one of these. He has been both a strayer and a jumper. Pike was reared a Roman Catholic, became an agnostic, practiced law successfully for several years and then, to find a new meaning for his life, joined the Episcopal Church, studied for the ministry and was ordained.

Norman Vincent Peale, at his Marble Collegiate Church in New York City, often reads a tabulation of new members at Sunday services, listing the religious bodies the newcomers have left to become members of his Dutch Reformed Congregation. Peale could very well be one of his own statistics, for he started out as a Methodist minister.

He illustrates a kind of denominational change that comes only after long contemplation and prayer and with a deep conviction that this is the right thing to do. It was in 1932 that Peale received almost simultaneous invitations to fill two pulpits—in the First Methodist Church in Los Angeles and in Marble Collegiate

Church. He was at that time preaching in the University Methodist Church in Syracuse, N.Y., a post he was reluctant to leave.

What followed the two invitations was a long period of indecision. Peale sought advice from friends in the church and on the faculty of Syracuse University and listened to their arguments for one or the other of the churches.

"Norman," his wife, Ruth, finally told him, "you're driving yourself crazy and making life miserable for me and everybody else. This can't go on. We're not leaving this room until you've come to a decision. I don't care how long it takes you to reach one. We're not going to open the door until you do."

With that, the Peales knelt together, held hands and prayed for several hours. Finally Peale said, "I think God wants us in New York."

"I think so, too," Mrs. Peale said.

Peale felt regret at leaving the Methodist Church, but he also felt the pull of the Reformed Church in America, which is evangelical in spirit, and he joined it in the conviction that it would not require him to change his theological views.

In a letter explaining his decision, Peale disclosed that he would have preferred living in California.

"If I had followed my desires, they would have taken me to Los Angeles," he wrote, "but, after all, to decide a question of this kind on the basis of the pleasantest place to live would not be the highest motive."

Another minister has provided an unusual variation on the jumping and shopping theme. The Rev. Dr. Robert W. Spike, general secretary for the program of the Board of Home Missions of the Congregational Christian Churches, found himself, his wife and their two children living in suburbia without a Congregational Church steeple in sight.

The Spikes, residents of Teaneck, N.J., a New York City suburb, liked the idea of staying in their own community to worship on Sunday, just as millions of other churchgoers do, so they searched for a church they could attend without threatening their Congregational ties.

"We looked for something that was the closest thing to a church," he said, "a corporate community of God. We ended up being cordially welcomed by an Episcopalian church. They understood our situation."

President Eisenhower has been both strayer and jumper. He was descended from German Mennonites and reared in a Mennonite sect. His parents met at a United Brethren College. During his Army years, when he was moving about the world, Eisenhower did not win any gold stars for church attendance, but when he became President in 1953, he joined a fashionable Presbyterian church in Washington.

Eisenhower's choice may have involved, even unconsciously, what clergymen call upgrading. As a person rises up the ladder to wealth and fame, moving to a larger house, buying another car and owning more gadgets, he may find the church of his youth does not measure up to his new station in life, so he switches denominations. Unless a Protestant is a Lutheran or an Episcopalian, he is likely to shop around if he feels no very strong ties.

Those at the top of the economic and social scale tend generally to seek out the Protestant Episcopal Church, which they find has attracted the kind of people with whom they now wish to worship and engage in fellowship. It gives them a feeling of achievement to belong to the denomination mentioned most frequently in newspaper accounts of weddings.

The next highest echelon on the social and economic scale appears to go to the Congregational Church in New England and the Presbyterian Church in much of the rest of the country. In some places, the Congregationalists or Presbyterians will rank over the Episcopalians.

Eggheads lean toward Congregationalism, Unitarianism or Quakerism. Methodism has become largely well-educated, solid middle class in membership, with the greatest strength in small towns and middle-size cities. The Baptists and Disciples of Christ are on the same general socio-economic level as the Methodists.

The trend is reflected somewhat in the religious affiliations of the Presidents. Nine have been Episcopalian, six Presbyterian, four each Methodist and Unitarian; two each Baptist and Dutch Reformed. Abraham Lincoln attended Presbyterian services in Washington but belonged to no church. Thomas Jefferson never joined a church, either, but leaned toward Unitarianism. Rutherford B.

Hayes was a non-belonging regular visitor to a Methodist church. The other presidents were Congregationalist, Disciples of Christ and Quaker. Now, for the first time, there is a Roman Catholic in the White House.

In the United States Congress at the start of the Kennedy administration in 1961, there was a Senate composed of 87 Protestants, 11 Roman Catholics and 2 Jews. The lineup included 19 Methodists, 15 Baptists, 14 Episcopalians, 11 Catholics, 11 Presbyterians, 7 Congregational-Christians, 4 Lutherans, 4 Unitarians, 4 Mormons, 3 Disciples of Christ, 2 Jews, 1 Quaker and 1 Reformed. Four Senators listed themselves as Protestant, but claimed no denominational ties. A partial breakdown of leading faiths in the House of Representatives gave 97 Catholics, 95 Methodists, 72 Presbyterians, 67 Baptists and 67 Episcopalians.

The Rev. Dr. Jitsuo Morikawa, secretary for evangelism of the American Baptist Home Mission Society, says the idea of gaining status through church is based on false standards. He urges an evangelism based on Christianity rather than culture. The "thing to do" concept of worship must be discouraged, he feels.

"The fact that people are in church is a sign of real hope," he said. "We must make sure that the basis remains Christian rather than material."

The American Baptists take no small amount of pleasure, therefore, in the light of the whole national panorama of migrating sheep, in pointing out that the Rockefellers, possibly the richest family in America, started out as Baptists and Baptists they have remained.

Some church organizations like to boast about the numbers of persons they have drawn from other churches. The United Lutherans reported in 1958 that they had received four times as many members from Roman Catholicism as had been lost to the Catholic Church. The exact figure was 3,566 from Catholicism and 868 to it. Many of the "gains" to Lutheranism were through mixed marriages.

The denomination that lost most heavily to the United Lutheran Church was the Methodist Church. A total of 4,195 Methodists jumped. Other United Lutheran additions included 2,768 from Presbyterianism and 24,570 "from the world." The Lutherans lost 2,617 to the Methodists, 2,352 to the Presbyterians and 16,400 "to the world."

In an announcement that Martin A. McGrory of Washington, D.C., had been re-elected president of the Federation of Lutheran Clubs and had been named "Lutheran Man of 1960," the National Lutheran Council also pointed out that he had been converted from Catholicism—30 years before.

Sheep migrations, for whatever reason, have knocked down many barriers. Probably the most significant development in this connection has occurred within the Baptist movement. The Mason-Dixon Line is a thing of the past as far as the Baptists are concerned. The Southern Baptist Convention, some seven million members strong, has reached into the North on a large scale, even establishing churches and missions in the New York City area. The American Baptist denomination, with more than a million members, is active in the South, mainly in education.

Both would like to heal the 100-year-old breach over the slavery issue that split the Baptist movement. No merger is in sight but a few "feelers" have been sent out, mainly by the Southern Baptists, indicating that a reunion should at least be discussed.

Meanwhile, each of the two major Baptist groups professes to avoid interfering with the other's expanded missionary activities —but neither eschews public announcements when a local church bolts from one convention to the other.

By 1955, there were 192 Southern Baptist churches in Utah, Idaho, Nevada, Montana, North Dakota, South Dakota and Colorado. Between 1940 and 1955, 1,035 churches in the North with a total membership of 140,832 were added to the southern body. The Southern Baptists credit the population shift for their expansion. In the last 15 years, possibly 1,250,000 Southern Baptists have left the South, and their religion has moved with them.

In Elizabethtown, Pa., a town of 7,500 persons 19 miles from Harrisburg, for example, a Southern Baptist mission was started on the second floor of an Oddfellows Hall. Its charter membership was eight adults and nine children. There were no other Baptist places of worship in town. The Sunday school superintendent was Dr. Robert W. Saunderson, medical director of the State Hospital for Crippled Children. Both he and his wife were natives of New York State who had become Southern Baptists while living in Maryland. The other members of the group included a couple from Texas, a native of Elizabethtown who had married a Southern Baptist from South Carolina and a pair of Pennsylvanians who had switched from another faith.

The transfer of a bomber wing from Roswell, N.M., to Pease Air Force Base in Portsmouth, N.H., took a number of Southern Baptists to New England. It resulted in the establishment of the denomination's northernmost church in the continental United States, Screvan Memorial Baptist Church.

Another Southern Baptist church, this one with 48 charter members, was organized in Elyria, Ohio, by Pastor Harry Powell, who with his wife and two daughters had moved from Panama City, Fla. Powell had worked his way through theological school in a Post Office job. Until his denomination could put him on the payroll, he worked as a mailman, earning more than he would receive later from the church.

The Southern Baptists, along with many other groups, are trying to convert Jews to Christianity—an overture that is regretted by some Protestant clergymen and resented deeply by many Jews. While the Southern Baptists have the most active program in this field of evangelism, the Lutherans also are working extensively among Jews.

Speaking for the Lutherans, Dr. Conrad Hoyer, then head of the National Lutheran Council's division of home missions, declared in 1960 that "the time is right for more intensive effort at the evangelization of the Jews." That was the year a Lutheran-sponsored art edition of a Yiddish New Testament, the first of its kind, was published. It was the work of Dr. Henry Einspruch, a convert from Judaism who became a Lutheran clergyman and pastor of the Salem Hebrew Lutheran Mission in Baltimore.

Fifteen thousand copies of the art edition, based on the first Yiddish New Testament of 1941, were distributed in the United States and foreign countries. It took Einspruch five years to revise the text and prepare the art work. The type was set on a machine in the mission by Einspruch and his wife.

The Los Angeles City Mission society has a special ministry to

Jews, forums for Jews and quarterly fellowship dinners for Christians with Jewish backgrounds. The Southern Baptists have "clinics" for the conversion of Jews. They maintain evangelism committees in every city in Texas where they have a mission program. Alaska is regarded as a fertile field for evangelism among Jews. Other "pioneer" areas set forth by the Southern Baptists include New York City, with an estimated two million Jews, and Los Angeles, with about 400,000.

Southern Baptist leaders hope for a Jewish evangelism committee in every area where there are Jews. The denomination conducts special Jewish nights in its revivals. Holiday cards are mailed to Jewish friends. More than 500,000 tracts were distributed to Jews in one year. One week of April, 1960, was devoted to closer fellowship with Jews. The period was timed to coincide with an overlapping of Passover and Easter week.

Of particular annoyance to the Jews is the type of convert-seeking engaged in by the noisy evangelist Oral Roberts, who maintains that the world will not be saved until Judaism has been replaced by Christianity. Roberts maintains that the conversion of the Jews would mean a "blessing for the whole world." He likes to tell about the occasions on which he has preached to Jews in Israel, and in an expensively produced brochure on "13 years of achievement" (by Oral Roberts), he included a photograph of himself shaking hands with the Israeli Prime Minister, David Ben-Gurion.

The report says that "the Bible gives the pattern for spreading the gospel 'to the Jew first' and then to the uttermost part of the earth." To speed this effort along, the Oral Roberts Evangelistic Association set a goal of placing 100,000 Protestant Bibles in Jewish homes at no charge to the recipients.

Christianity often is introduced to Jews through a special edition of the gospel of St. Matthew, because he was supposed to have been a Jewish tax collector and his account of the life of Jesus was written from a Jewish point of view.

These efforts at evangelizing have been received by Jews more in sorrow than anger. They feel that Christian attempts to convert them have been born in ignorance of what Judaism is and what it means.

"You can count on the fingers of one hand the number of Christians who really know anything about the vitality and true character of the Jewish religion as lived and practiced by many of its people," says Rabbi Marc Tannenbaum, executive director of the Synagogue Council of America, representing all three major branches of Judaism.

"They view the Jewish religion, the history and people through attitudes shaped several thousands of years ago. Judaism is as much a factor in the life of its people as Christianity is in the life of its people. The thing the Jews feel most strongly about is that America has so much field work to be done within the Christian faith. There are so many Christians who need attention from their clergy."

Jews fear, according to Tannenbaum, that the Christian effort to convert them will only make mischief, will achieve very little other than to open old wounds, cause unnecessary tensions and create a divisive force in society. There is a deep-seated dread that conversion efforts might rekindle old flames of anti-Semitism.

"It is a disservice to the whole of the American people," Tannenbaum said.

Some Protestants, particularly of a liberal bent, take the stand that while any Jew is welcome to become a Christian if he wants to, it is not the apostolic task of Christians to seek him out, just because he is Jewish.

Somewhere in the neighborhood of 2,000 Christians become Jews in the United States each year, but with no missionary effort on the part of Judaism. The conversions are prompted by marriages to Jews, as in the case of Elizabeth Taylor, the actress, or by spiritual and intellectual need, as in the case of the Negro singer Sammy Davis Jr.

"It is not so much sheep stealing as sheep jumping—fence hopping," in Tannenbaum's estimation.

The churches can thank Madison Avenue for the sheep shopping that sometimes accompanies the leap from one religion to another. Instead of seeking, the church is actively sought. Americans have been taught by Madison Avenue persuaders, hidden and public, that they enjoy the freedom of preference and the right of choice. Millions of dollars have been spent on ads telling people what to look for in baked beans, bread, coffee, cigarettes and beer. Now many people are shopping around for religion, often in cafeteria style, looking over the whole selection before making a final choice. What the shoppers are after, thanks to Madison Avenue, is the church with The Most Mileage or the Longest-Lasting Full-Bodied Flavor.

How do people choose churches? In many ways. Perhaps it is the church closest to the freeway interchange between home and the boat marina. Perhaps it has the biggest sign pointing out "church, three blocks this way." Perhaps it has a steeple standing out above the surrounding skyline.

One popular way to choose a church involves the arrival of Mr. and Mrs. Joe Doakes in a new neighborhood. She was reared a Methodist, he a Presbyterian. In the last community in which they lived, they were Methodists. The time before that, they were Presbyterian. Now they decide to become Congregationalists. They have found the ideal Congregational church, a type known today by the call letters C.N.B. It is the fastest-growing, most-alive church in America. It is the Church in the Next Block.

The quality of the Sunday school also is a leading factor in church choice. The Joneses have three children of Sunday school age. They send the youngsters to the one best equipped to teach them and offering the most compatible playmates of the same social and economic level. The parents are likely to go to the church of their children's choice, too, although suburbia on a Sunday morning still is haunted by spectres of unshaven fathers in T-shirts or rougeless mothers in curlers and slacks driving spruced-up Junior to Sunday school and then returning to pick him up.

When the American Institute of Men's and Boys' Wear, Inc., surveyed hundreds of ministers on what they thought of the way people dressed for church, the Rev. Dr. Knut Halle, pastor of the Church of the Good Samaritan, on New York's Staten Island, responded by advocating a special "come as you are" family service at every church on Sunday to fight the adult absentee rate. By "come as you are," he did not mean slacks, curlers, T-shirts and blue jeans or sloppy garb such as has prompted ministers and members of some churches to take visitors aside and suggest they might tidy up a bit before attending services. Halle and other ministers are encouraging the acceptance of more informal attire to stimulate attendance and combat the many lures of leisure time.

"Suburbanites work in their gardens," he reasoned, "and cannot afford to get dressed three times on Sunday; so they run the kids to Sunday school and go back to their digging! Mothers who expect company cannot easily leave the stove, change, make up, run to the kirk and then come back, change again and finish the cooking, only to change again for the company. Thus, parents do not attend church!"

There are other criteria in the choice of churches besides proximity and educational attractions. A brand-new, modernistic building with all the latest conveniences sometimes provides an attractive package for what still is the heart of the church, the pulpit. In Stamford, Conn., for instance, some persons have left older and drabber churches to attend the new First Presbyterian Church, a spectacular modernistic structure in the shape of a large fish. Even Eugene Carson Blake, who worships there, calls it "the fish church."

Ruoss, in studies for the National Council of Churches, has found that when he asks people around the country to tell him the first word they associate with the church, at least half of them mention a building or something associated with a building.

But the old massive stone churches with beautiful stained glass windows are not the lure any more. Modern architecture not only gives the impression of being less costly; it *is* less costly. The residents of Mortgage-on-the-Mississippi like the idea of attending a ranch-style church that can foot its own bills, even if its split-level members live on a credit card, charge account, fly-now-pay-later economy.

It is possible also that the ministerial leadership may have more to do with the choice of a church than does the denomination or the architecture. If a man is a Good Organizer, a Good Sport with the Kids, and a preacher who delivers short, snappy sermons dealing with practical problems and prayers that get to the point, he is the man for the Joneses.

Many persons find they can move from one church to another without being aware of any ritualistic changes. Most Protestant denominations are undifferentiated in doctrine, belief and form of worship, and often they require no special instruction before membership is achieved. It might be possible to hear the opening prayer in a church of one denomination, a sermon in another, and the closing hymn in a third without being aware that they were not of the identical faith.

Churches often vary more by community than by denomination. The degree of contrast between a Congregational church in Schenectady and one in Sacramento is likely to be greater than that between a Congregational church in Schenectady and the Presbyterian church a few blocks away.

There is a definite sheep-straying pattern during the average life span of the average Protestant, often referred to by Ruoss as a W.A.S.P. (a White Anglo-Saxon Protestant). Small children are regular Sunday school participants, although they may switch from church to church as their parents move about the country. Teen-agers are a little less loyal. In the late teens and early 20's, there is a sharp dropping off. After young adults become parents, they send their children to church and sometimes attend themselves. Then, as their children grow older and drop out, the parents backslide again, not returning at least until they are well past middle age.

Young people leave church because they develop a degree of independence. This leads them to give up habits they kept at home with parental encouragement, but find it easy to abandon once they have gone away to college or entered military service. They also may be going through periods of doubt and questioning during which they feel the church does not have the right answers for them.

One Episcopalian study showed that half the young people left that denomination and never returned. A lack of communication between young people and the parishes was blamed.

Methodist officials are deeply concerned over the rate at which high school graduates have been dropping out of church activities. The program involving older youth is regarded as the weakest link in the church's ministry. There is a feeling that after high school there is not much of a place for young people in church.

One reason Methodists are particularly concerned about this is that they still regard Sunday school as "the growing edge of the church." More than 2,800,000 children up to 11 years old attended Methodist Sunday school in 1957. The youth division, composed of young people from 12 to 23, counted nearly 1,300,000. The attendance rate of the younger children also was far greater than the numerical strength. This absentee problem is expected to become increasingly critical because of a constant increase in the number of people in the 18-to-24 age group.

As far as the Lutheran Youth Research Organization is concerned, young people are spiritual nomads, without close church ties. The organization found in a special study that rural youth leave small communities after graduation from high school to go to college or seek work. Urban churches are unprepared to absorb these young people, so they stray.

Father Fichter said, in his report on "Social Relations in the Urban Parish," that surveys have shown the Roman Catholic loss between baptism and first communion is a little less than 30 per cent, with the loss after confirmation considerably greater. The highest degree of religious observance among Catholics was found in children 10 to 19. The sharpest drop came between 30 and 39. A general upswing in later life was recorded, but a much smaller proportion of dormant Catholics were known to have asked for priests at the ends of their lives than were baptized or married in the church.

Sunday school simply is not the seedbed of church membership any more. It has been found that children will be members of at least three different churches by the time they are adults and six by the time they are 50. Each could well be a different denomination. In 1957, a National Council of Churches study of 15,000 local congregations showed that an average of 35 to 50 per cent of the members came from other denominations. Some local churches reported as many as 93 per cent of their members had come from other denominations.

This is the climate in which sometimes keen competition between churches is developed. Often the competition does not really mean anything, except that the church is American—and the spirit of competition is a keystone of life in America. It is a tribute to the churches that they remain as stable as they do in the midst of all the sheep's meanderings. The church has indeed become a spiritual way station for the moving masses. There are those who stay put, forming the nucleus of a permanent organization, to be sure. But the church today, bigger and more prosperous than ever before, may owe this very vitality to its active circulatory system, in which new blood is constantly replacing old.

4

Mission to America:

The Quiet Evangelists

A NEW KIND of missionary is evangelizing America. From Main Street to Endsville, by way of suburbia, crew-cut, gray-flanneled clergymen are spreading the gospel of the new-time religion.

The need for evangelizing has been found as acute in Beverly Hills, Scarsdale and Evanston as in Harlem, Florida retirement havens and down on the sharecropping farm. The major difference between these locales is that in some the inhabitants know all too well that they need help, while in others they simply wonder what in the world could be wrong with their lives.

In the social and economic upheaval that has swept America since World War II, one-room churches in New England have had to be shut for a lack of ministers. Houses of worship in the Great Plains states have been converted to grain storage houses or meeting halls. Big city churches have had to change their whole approach to the ministry. Suburbia has become a beehive of activity that has made some churches seem more like social clubs than places of worship.

Into this picture steps the new missionary, the new evangelist, the new minister. He makes no secret of his mission, but he shuns the old stereotype of the clergyman out to seek converts. His evangelism is quiet, not the kind that makes people want to shout "hallelujah" or "amen." The sawdust trail has been swept away and replaced by the broadloom carpet.

Billy Graham's voice is heard throughout America, but the words people really listen to are spoken quietly by an army of evangelists, lay and clerical, in a grass-roots missionary effort featuring the "soft sell."

At home as well as abroad, missionaries have taken on a new role. Churches find their task vastly different and vastly expanded. Every church has become a mission and every minister a missionary. Laymen are being drawn more and more into evangelistic service, both to recruit new members and to keep current ones happy. In some denominations, most notably the Methodist and Baptist, every member is an evangelist. The old concept of the home missionary limited to carrying Christ to the American Indian, the Kentucky mountaineer or the illiterate immigrant has faded away. Today's mission field lies in the whole culture of America and the layman has become the hidden asset of the church.

No longer does the Methodist preacher ride the frontier circuit with his Bible in a saddlebag. Today's home missionary flies an airplane, drives an automobile or station wagon, careens along on a motor scooter, lives in a trailer or rides on subways, streetcars or buses to reach his territory. He may even be a Protestant counterpart of the Roman Catholic worker-priest, serving the church while working in overalls in a factory or practicing medicine or law.

This clergyman calls himself a minister with a mission, not a missionary, and the mission is just as likely to be among the ghettoized housewives of swimming pool, two-car, three-TV-set suburbia as hungry tenement dwellers "back of the stockyards" in Chicago. The mission may be the 12,000-member First Baptist Church of Dallas or St. Mary's Roman Catholic Chapel, which occupies a storefront in a Miami, Fla., shopping center. This chapel, which boasts parking facilities only a few feet from its door, is believed to be the first church to provide regularly scheduled devotions in a shopping center. In addition to Sunday services, it offers a mass every weekday at noon for the convenience of shoppers and grocery clerks.

Everyone, rich or poor, is regarded by the churches as in need of evangelistic help today. The specific needs may be different but evangelists are convinced they have something for everyone. Even the evangelized are being re-evangelized to retain and stimulate their interest. This is done through home visits by teams of lay church members, by ministerial calls and in informal meetings in homes.

One of the most unorthodox missionary efforts is being conducted by the Congregationalists in San Francisco's North Beach area. This is a mission to the beatniks, not in a church but in their own milieu, or in their "pads," as they call their homes. A young minister meets the "beats" on their own terms, in coffee houses mainly, and joins in discussions of "beat" literature and music with the bearded and unbathed. He carefully avoids any mention of religion until the "beats" themselves have brought it up. While he does not hide the fact that he is a minister, he does not advertise it either, working to gain the confidence of the beatniks before trying to interest them in attending religious services, which he conducts in a store-front chapel that looks more like a lounge than a church.

A similar program is conducted at Judson Memorial Church in New York City, which is a joint effort of the Congregationalists and Methodists in the heart of Greenwich Village. This ministry is to lower, middle and upper Bohemia as well as to the "beats" and to what is called the solid Village middle class.

Baptists are carrying the gospel to college campuses, where professors, scholars and married student couples discuss theology at evening meetings. The Southern Presbyterians are conducting special laymen's courses in Bible study, the most notable ones, perhaps, being a series of classes for barbers and beauticians to enable them to discuss religion while cropping hair or filing fingernails.

The Methodists have been sponsoring a missionary-in-reverse program, and with considerable success. This huge denomination, which for generations had carried religion to peoples of all races and colors abroad, decided it was time to turn the tables. It brought men and women missionaries to the United States from India, the Philippines, Africa, Japan, Argentina, Peru, Korea and Burma to preach to their fellow Methodists. These missionaries, all natives of the countries they represented, reached a total of 100,000 persons and won 11,704 commitments of new Methodists or recommitments of backsliders who decided to return to the church. Methodist officials were pleased with this reversal of the age-old trend toward white supremacy in Christianity.

The United Presbyterian Church in the U.S.A. also has a missionary-in-reverse in the person of the Rev. Sunny Oey, of Indonesia, who was hired as minister of the First Presbyterian Church in Princetown, N.Y., because of the national shortage of clergymen. Before becoming a missionary to Americans, the 27-year-old minister had sought converts among Chinese residents of the island of Amboina.

The Rev. Paul S. Nishida, moderator of the Hokkaido Conference of the United Church of Christ in Japan, was brought to the United States to participate in the denomination's "Mission to America" program. He was assigned to work mainly through young people's groups in the United Church.

The arrival of missionaries on American shores and ministries to the beat generation are more spectacular evangelistic efforts. While this dramatic work gets considerable public attention, hundreds of missionary-ministers are quietly working away in suburbia, which is regarded by church organizations as possibly one of the most fertile mission fields in the entire world outside Africa.

It would be difficult, indeed, to imagine a young missionary knocking on a suburban door and declaring to a young housewife that he was there to convert her without the thought at least crossing her mind that she would like to pop him in the stew pot for dinner. So the missionary must work through more traditional channels—the local church, civic and service clubs and Boy and Girl Scout troops—in reaching the spiritually needy suburbanites.

Most of them are young people on the way up. Clergymen find that these families never have enjoyed such plenty, and yet it has not brought them the satisfactions they had hoped for. They even worry about how long television will divert them from their worries over what life really is all about. They have discovered that walking on grass instead of concrete has not satisfied the hungers of the human spirit, and they are asking questions. "Why are we here?" they say. "Does life have a purpose?" "What is the meaning of existence?" "What may we hope for?" There is a tremendous longing for some kind of identification. Perhaps the question asked most often of all is "Who am I?" It is to try to answer this wistful query that the missionary has gone into suburbia. He wants to show people there is a great difference between "church work," which involves serving as an usher or cooking church suppers, and "the work of the church," which involves carrying religion into daily life.

"Terrified," is the word some ministers use for suburbia. Another term often used is "wistful." Either conjures images of young couples burdened with doubts and fears at a time when a chicken-in-every-pot and two-cars-in-every-garage are realities instead of political promises.

Suburbia has been called the most terrified segment of America. It is insecure, and it has too much to lose. The Organization Man is under severe strains. He lives in the last really American free enterprise community, but he is afraid he is going to lose what he has. It is out of such a fear that he goes to church. He wants to be reassured that everything is going to be all right.

"Wistful" is the word used by Norman Vincent Peale.

"The individual human beings all over this country have a feeling that Christianity has the answer to their problems," he said. "They want answers; if not answers, at least direction. There is a wistful reaching out. That is why they are going to church in increasing numbers and reading religious books.

"This wistful reaching out is the big characterization of the religious upsurge. There is not a revival of religion but a revival of religious interest. People are in wistful confusion, disorganized.

"Suburbia has a lot to answer for as to the moral decline in America. People get the idea the moral decline is in the cities. I don't believe that affects the moral state as much as the cynical, sophisticated, fast-car, heavy-drinking suburbia, which is where the leaders are."

The Roman Catholic Church also has its suburban problems. Priests traditionally have been trained to serve parishes in metropolitan areas, often crowded ones. They have been shepherds to whole neighborhoods, dealing with economic problems as well as spiritual needs. Now that the Catholics have joined the rush to the suburbs, the priests who have gone with them have found new problems and new demands to fill. The suburban Catholic Church is deeply in debt, and so are its parishioners. Laymen perform many church tasks such as keeping the books, which formerly was done only by priests. The parish is in danger of becoming too concerned with its own internal problems to have time for the rest of the world.

For the Jews also suburbia poses problems. Rabbi Tannenbaum believes suburbia is a valueless void, a vacuum. It is a child-oriented society dedicated to tomorrow's generation. It is a quest for a better life for the children than the parents had when they were growing up. This is laudable as far as it goes, Tannenbaum feels, but it lacks quality.

Suburbia is everything to the women and children living segregated lives in it. But it is only a fragment in the lives of the wage earners who sleep there week nights and tend the lawns on Saturdays and Sundays. New York City suburbs alone send three million workers every day to the southern half of Manhattan Island. These people live such splintered lives that they do not know where they belong, or even if they belong.

The suburbanites may be new versions of T. S. Eliot's Hollow Man, in the opinion of Robert Spike. He believes that part of the mission of the church to suburbia should be to transform anxiety into genuine anguish. If anxiety becomes a penetrating ethical agony, it will require decisions rather than continued brooding, he says.

"A guy being crushed in a corporation situation where the pressure is more than a human being can bear but that pays well makes a choice whether to take a cut in salary and get more basic satisfaction or learns to have more guts in the corporate structure," Spike said. "He takes a stand. That sort of process is what the church has to encourage. The essence of theology is to make moral decisions in the light of confidence about God's purpose in the world."

As a man who has carried the Congregational ministry to

miners, suburbanites, rural residents and city dwellers, Spike has found Greenwich Village an easier evangelistic field than suburbia.

"I've seen hundreds of churches," he said. "All of them look alike—ranch houses with steeples. If you've seen one, you've seen them all. They are sort of religious clubs. But here and there you walk in and see something different. It is a *church*."

In these churches, there are well-organized hard cores of members. They have begun to orient their lives around the church. They read serious books. They ask about the meaning of life and their jobs. They are concerned about others. They give liberally of time and money. The missionary-ministers guiding them are to a large degree responsible; the pastors show the way and then let the congregations do the work.

The First Community Church of Garden City, N.Y., a well-to-do Long Island suburb of New York City, is a prize exhibit of a church that really is a church. Some people say its beautiful new neo-Gothic church building looks like a Howard Johnson roadside restaurant, but that does not worry the enthusiastic members.

This church has study groups that dig into theological and sociological questions. The members think of others as well as themselves. They support a minister in an East Harlem slum parish in New York City along with their own pastor. When pickets marched in front of the New York City Hall to protest the way narcotics addicts were being treated, the demonstrators included seedy Harlemites and Garden City commuters in Brooks Brothers suits.

Big city churches increasingly have come to rely on help, either from national denominations or from sister churches in more affluent areas. The urban church has been shrinking in numerical strength in the last 10 to 15 years. It has declined almost in proportion to the rate the city has shot ahead. The bigger the city, the harder its churches have fallen. The drain to the suburbs and exurbs, accompanied by the arrival of new urbanites from depressed farm areas, Puerto Rico and abroad, has created a situation something like that of trying to fill a bathtub with the plug out.

The problem in most cities is worse than generally acknowledged. One National Council of Churches study concluded, in fact, that church statistics in general were romantically over-optimistic. Big city church figures are particularly so.

There is a need for an intensified missionary effort in the big city jungles, where general urban-renewal programs call for accompanying church-renewal plans. The United Presbyterian Church in the U.S.A. is pouring a million dollars into bigger and better buildings in cities. The United Church of Christ is experimenting with store-front youth centers. The Protestant Episcopal Church has special parish programs aimed at reaching all the people in an area, not just parishioners.

In Chicago, the West Side Christian Parish operates from three store-front churches, a counseling center and a youth center. It helped establish a Home Ownership Association to renovate old buildings and enable poor families to buy homes in their neighborhood.

Brotherhood Service, Inc., in Baltimore, sponsored by church groups, bought a decaying slum house, renovated it and then went to work helping to improve the entire neighborhood. The First Church of the Brethren launched this program, under which block and neighborhood organizations have been formed and day camps and pre-school nurseries have been organized. Churches in the area work together in the program.

Another successful fight against urban blight was waged by the Clinton Hill Neighborhood Council, in Newark, N.J., with help from the churches. Trinity Methodist Church developed a well-financed inter-racial program, with a special minister assigned to neighborhood work. Other Protestant churches, as well as Roman Catholic churches and synagogues, sponsored block meetings and round-table conferences to plan clean-up and renovation programs for the area. They arranged for street rerouting to ease congestion and even explored ways to stop horn-blowing at 3 A.M. What developed was a "theology of community," infusing a religious spirit into an entire neighborhood, with the result that attendance at church and synagogue was stimulated.

Islands of church decline have cropped up not only in old cities but in just about every section of rural America, beginning in

Maine and ending in California. In North and South Dakota, Nebraska, Kansas, Colorado, Wyoming and Montana, the trend has been counter to the so-called religious tide. The farm population dropped by about two million persons in 15 years, and the churches suffered correspondingly.

It is just as difficult to keep ministers as young people down on the farm. Most young ministers regard the country as a place to start their careers. This discourages membership. The potential churchgoers feel that if the minister does not care enough about them to stay, there is no reason why they should stay either. The result has been the closing of church after church.

Part of the rural problem has been that some communities had too many churches. There are towns of only 200 population with six struggling churches. Federated or community churches might thrive, and this has been the remedy in many places.

Another solution for the rural problem would be for prosperous churches elsewhere to adopt small country congregations, assuming some of the financial responsibility and providing the ministers.

The nation's most extensive rural church problem was created in 1959, when Alaska became a state. The churches immediately began to take stock of where they stood in an area once treated as if it were a foreign mission field. They found that most religious activity in Alaska still was performed by missionaries working among Eskimos. Alaska still was referred to as "the land that God forgot."

Some missionaries make their rounds in Alaska in small airplanes equipped with skis. Some travel by dog sled. The Presbyterians have a two-boat "navy," and the American Baptists operate a gospel boat, "The Evangel," which plies between villages and canneries clustered on the edge of the Kodiak Islands. The Lutherans have an active radio ministry, reaching persons in remote, unchurched areas.

There was neither a synagogue nor a civilian rabbi in Alaska when it became the 49th state. But a National Jewish Welfare Board worker and Army chaplains carried forth "Operation Judaism" to the several small clusters of Jews living and working in Alaska.

Specialized ministries long have been accepted in Alaska and among the Indians on reservations in the Western United States. Only recently have special efforts been made to reach other members of the American population. One of the unique programs is that of the Rev. Kirkland West, pastor of the First Presbyterian Church in Medford, Ore. He decided that if he could not lick the country club as a foe of the church, he would join it. So he moved his pulpit to the Rogue Valley Country Club for a 7:30 A.M. informal service every Sunday, after which his parishioners have only a few steps to take to reach the first tee.

The Rev. H. Carl Roessler tried a long shot for his first sanctuary—a race track clubhouse. His United Lutheran congregation set up temporary headquarters at the Los Alamitos track, near Los Angeles, taking care to cover the clubhouse bar during services. Officials of the denomination pointed out that Lutheran mission churches have been started in other unorthodox places, including saloons, dance halls, firehouses, schools, barns, hotels and railroad cars.

A Stamford, Conn., pastor drives 60 miles to Wall Street from time to time to have lunch with parishioners he otherwise would see only at church on Sunday. They gather in a financial district restaurant to discuss world affairs and church and theological matters.

The Rev. James Burnside is a real 20th century missionary. He is the United Presbyterian Church in the U.S.A. minister of visitation for the San Francisco Mission District, traveling through his sprawling parish by car, bus and cable car and on foot. His assignment is to try to help newcomers from rural areas feel at home in the big city.

Mobile ministries, in the air and on the ground, are replacing the old-fashioned itinerant preacher, who covered his rounds on foot. Among the pastors who drive station wagons on widespread circuits is the Rev. Irvin McArthur, who follows a 300-mile evangelistic trail in Florida every week. The Rev. and Mrs. Theodore Allison have made a trailer into a Presbyterian manse, from which they minister to trailer camp dwellers in the West.

Miss Mary Murray is a missionary assigned to a trailer camp near Detroit. She has conducted as many as a dozen programs and services on a single Christmas day in her trailer chapel. After

10 years of work among the Crow Indians of Montana, she went to Detroit in 1942, to serve the wartime residents of trailer courts.

"These 18 years have been challenging ones," she says. "Thousands have come to the trailer chapel which I pull around to the various courts, and several hundreds have become Christians. Alcoholics and drunkards have been redeemed and the spiritually blind have been made to see."

A Presbyterian minister, the Rev. Raymond Nott, makes his church where he finds it. Nott actually is a churchless pastor. He covers a 15,000-square mile parish in Wyoming, conducting services for seven individual groups in homes, schools and community halls. In calling on his parishioners he eats more than 300 meals a year away from his wife and family, who remain in Greybull, Wyo.

An even more specialized ministry is the Unitarian mail-order mission to "lonely liberals," organized in 1944. It is the largest congregation within Unitarianism, reaching 2,159 persons, 695 of them children, across America. These are persons with liberal religious beliefs who do not live within attendance range of any Unitarian Society. The Rev. Richard B. Gibbs, pastor of this farflung flock, sends his congregation newsletters, sermons, educational materials, newspapers and other aids to their solitary worship.

The vocational ministry is a special field still in the development stage. A leader in this effort is the Presbyterian Institute of Industrial Relations at McCormick Theological Seminary in Chicago, in which ministers take special training and then actually work in industry, often incognito. The aim of the program is to make better ministers for industrial areas, rather than to make labor-relations experts out of clergymen.

Dr. Marshall L. Scott, dean of the institute, founded the Ministers-in-Industry program because of a conviction that Protestant churches were out of touch with industrial workers.

One of his most successful former pupils is the Rev. Donald Mathews, who served as full-time pastor of North Presbyterian Church in Kalamazoo, Mich., for six years while working full-time as a lathe operator in a truck transmission plant. He found time to serve as a union shop steward and learned to deal with the problems of working people in his congregation and among his co-workers with equal understanding and skill.

Robert Walker, a former revival-tent evangelist preacher in Texas, has made a pulpit of the driver's seat on a Fifth Avenue bus in New York. He says "thank you" for every coin dropped in the fare box and calls out principal stores and landmarks in a loud voice. In his spare time, he serves as director of the Metropolitan Pacers, a hot rod club dedicated to taking teen-agers out of street gangs and giving them something constructive to do. His first duty, however, is to his daily passengers.

"I can spread more religion driving a bus than standing in a pulpit," he explains.

There is a need for lay theologians to work also among professional people. These would be men and women schooled in theology but not necessarily ordained. They would work in the professions but with a religious point of view. A doctor practicing medicine might mix a dash of scriptures with his prescriptions. Or, as in the case of William Stringfellow, a Harvard graduate practicing law in East Harlem, one might quote the Bible along with Blackstone.

Robert Spike, as an evangelist with modern ideas, would like to see a minister assigned as a missionary to the Hollywood film colony, following the example of the San Francisco beatnik pastorate.

This minister would be an itinerant evangelist with a deep interest in the theater. He would mingle with the struggling actors, directors and producers in Hollywood, talking shop with them and listening to their problems.

"The denominations should divide the responsibility for the professions," Spike recommended, "not have professional people just serve as ushers on Sunday, but use them to bridge the gap between ethical pronouncements and the world. You must have the right guy for the job. He must talk the language of the people with whom he is working. He must not be suspect and nothing must be hidden."

Laymen have been drawn upon to participate in grass-roots evangelistic campaigns of local churches, mainly to recruit new members. Their search for people to evangelize has been put on a fairly scientific basis, beginning with the parents of church school pupils and relatives of members and then branching out through entire neighborhoods. The roll is taken in each church every week for a month and then studied for the names of non-members. Visits are made to the homes of non-member families served by pastors at funerals and weddings. Memberships of church organizations are sifted for those who turn up for week-day fellowship but not on Sundays. In some churches, each member is asked to submit the names of two persons he would like to see in the church.

There are other techniques, such as getting the names of new residents of a community from the Chamber of Commerce, credit bureaus or utility companies. Membership lists of luncheon clubs and fraternal organizations are gleaned for prospects. A "spotter" committee may be organized to look for new residents. And if a community is not too large, the committee might manage to telephone everyone in town to find out who is—or is not—affiliated with a church.

This sort of evangelism is a long way from Billy Graham and Oral Roberts. The people involved in it believe they will be so successful that the day of the big revival meeting may soon be over. The accent is on teaching, rather than preaching; personal satisfaction, rather than emotional ecstasy.

Examples of the quiet evangelist at work are many and varied.

St. James' Church, in Houston, Tex., commissioned laymen as "Crusaders of St. James'" for a Lutheran visitation evangelism campaign. They conducted three crusades each month, one by teams of women, one by husband-and-wife teams, and one by two-man teams. This was personalized evangelism, in which the teams called on prospects in their homes and talked about the church.

"Rainy day" evangelism is recommended by Dr. Harry Denman, general secretary of the Methodist Board of Evangelism. He suggested that visitation campaigns should be scheduled only in bad weather. Not only are the prospects more likely to be home, he reasoned, but they will be more impressed with the earnestness of their visitors if they bother to call in unpleasant weather.

The Evangelical Lutheran Church has been trying to carry

religion to the unchurched through a Church-of-the-Month Club. The denomination's Board of Home Missions organized the club in 1958, to raise funds to establish churches where there were no Evangelical Lutheran parishes and money was short. Money contributed by club members has paid for hiring pastors and buying Sunday school books, hymnals, chairs, typewriters, mimeograph machines and other equipment.

Here is how the program worked: When a person enrolled in the club, he agreed to pray regularly that the United States would become a "truly Christian nation"; to give at least $1 a year to each of at least six new churches, for a minimum total of $6 a year, and to encourage others to enroll. Every month, the member received a request for aid for a specific church, along with a pamphlet describing its situation.

The first appeal was made in behalf of Florida's first Evangelical Lutheran congregation, Bethel Church, in St. Petersburg. The first 16 churches of the month were supported by more than 4,000 club members, who gave nearly $50,000 in sums ranging from $1 to $300.

A Willmar, Minn., banker conceived the idea for the club. He, in turn, got his inspiration from an employee who had been contributing every month to "Frontier Friends," a similar organization in the Mission Covenant Church. "Frontier Friends" was the main source of funds for the Mission Covenanters; the Evangelical Lutherans used their Church-of-the-Month Club for supplementary funds.

In the first months, the Lutheran club helped found churches in Helena, Mont.; Honolulu; Wheaton, Ill.; Fargo, N.D.; Phoenix, Ariz.; Woodcliff Lake, N.J.; Tacoma, Wash.; Denver; Houston; Nisswa, Minn.; San Jose, Calif.; Clearwater, Fla.; Regina, Sask., and Minneapolis.

Twenty million members of eight Baptist bodies have joined in the Baptist Jubilee Advance. Twelve years in the planning, it began in 1959 and will end in 1964, when the 150th anniversary of the organization of Baptists in North America will be celebrated for an entire year. The advance is reaching all 70,000 Baptist churches in the United States and Canada and has extended into colleges, universities and homes. The primary target is un-churched America, but Baptist leaders also hope for the religious rededication of those already on church rolls.

Each Baptist denomination planned its own program. The American Baptists, in the first year, conducted a Mission to the Academic Community in which professors sat down together to discuss religion. Special efforts were made to meet the spiritual needs of students. One college helped start a new church—a reversal of the historic practice of churches founding colleges.

The second year, 1960, featured the Mission to the Local Church. This involved stepped-up local evangelism, visitation, carrying the church to the community and a full-scale church census and in-depth study of exactly how much members were involved in the congregational life.

The year 1961 was the time set aside for the Mission to the Unchurched. Later year-long campaigns called for a Mission to the Social Frontier, featuring studies of slums, wealthy areas, community resources and neighborhood problems, and a Mission to the World, a full-scale study of the foreign mission field.

Most evangelistic efforts are on a much more modest scale, however. They may involve simply offering a "mother's morning out program" under which children may be left at the church for a few hours once a week while their mothers shop or go to the hair dresser. Or they may involve something so mundane as counting water meters in the area around a church. That is what the pastor of a church, in Spokane, Wash., did. He learned from the water company that there were 650 meters in the surrounding area. That meant an approximate population of 1,800 persons. The church had only 60 or 65 members, but its potential was high because it was the only church in the vicinity. Teams were sent out to call on prospective members and the work of the church was publicized in the neighborhood, stimulating member-ship growth.

St. Mark's Lutheran Church in Clarksburg, W. Va., gave itself an "x-ray treatment" developed by the United Lutheran Church in America's Board of Social Missions. The program, called the New Life Mission, involved a three-month examination of the church's situation in the community, an interpretation of this situation, the development of a program of immediate action and planning for a long-range program. To arrive at its conclusions, the congregation used the New Life Mission self-study guide containing 30 pages of questions and charts. This was the x-ray.

What the church members learned was that they were falling short of their evangelistic task. Only 36 of the 181 men over 20 in the congregation were active in the United Lutheran Church Men. Of 243 women 20 or over, only 86 were active in the United Lutheran Church Women. Neither group had any plan for winning new members.

The study found almost no activity to attract young unmarried adults, who were too old for the Luther League and not qualified for the couples' club. It also found that a remarkable number of persons in the community went to no church.

As a result of its study, the church organized a New Life Mission worship group to discuss ways to remedy the situation. Its members decided that "inreach" was as important as "outreach," and launched a do-it-yourself evangelism program of daily Bible reading, family devotions, prayers and a generally fuller spiritual life for all the church's members.

The Methodists are engaged in what is perhaps the quietest quiet evangelistic effort on record with its "Decade of Prayer," which started on New Year's Day, 1960, as part of a "decade of dynamic discipleship" sponsored by the denomination's Board of Evangelism. The theme of the observance is World Peace and World Revival through Bible reading, Christian belief, starting a new church every 22 hours, recruiting preachers and missionaries and conducting prayer vigils.

A feature of the "Decade of Prayer" is the "Prayer Partner Movement." An estimated 235,000 persons paired off to pray for one another daily by name. Each person who signed up for the program received a card with the name of his prayer partner. Both were asked to pray for other persons, but mainly for each other.

The "Decade of Prayer" was touched off with a special New Year's Eve observance at the stroke of midnight Dec. 31, 1959, in Knoxville, Tenn. At that moment, the Methodists unveiled a

10-year prayer calendar measuring 10 by 12 feet. It was made by the Rev. Elton F. Jones, pastor of the Central Methodist Church of Knoxville, and his wife, in more than 400 hours of labor. They fashioned the calendar out of white felt with a rubberized backing and a gold cross in the center. The task consumed 33,400 yards of thread, which was used to embroider the names of different countries in each of 120 monthly calendars.

This epitomized the quiet evangelism that may yet drown out Billy Graham.

5

The View from the Pulpit

T HE MAN in the gray tweed suit slumped suddenly in his chair. His friendly face grew solemn. He removed his rimless glasses with one hand and rubbed the area around his blue eyes with the other. Obviously he was tired, and he sat silently for a moment before he spoke.

"You know," he said, "sometimes you see so much sorrow in the world, you wonder how you can go on—but you do."

This was a minister speaking. It could have been any one of the nation's 373,500 clergymen, but as it happened it was possibly the most famous of them all: Norman Vincent Peale.

This was the Norman Vincent Peale whose reassuring smile and words, whose reputation for optimism, whose cheerfully given advice, have reached millions—and judging from the letters he receives, with considerable impact.

No success, not even this kind, comes easily. No minister, not even Norman Vincent Peale with his "Power of Positive Thinking," is invulnerable to the troubles that beset men and women in an era of mounting anxieties. He, like most other clergymen, is on call 24 hours a day, and most of the calls come from people with troubles. He, like most other clergymen, spends more time in personal counseling of wistful, worried and bereaved people than in any other activity, despite the fact that he has a staff of 30 persons at his church to perform such duties, while most churches have only one man on whom to rely—the minister.

From his pulpit in the Marble Collegiate Church in New

York City, in his books and through his magazine and newspaper writings, Peale has been telling a running success story for years. The plot seldom changes. It concerns people who have found success of one kind or another, and how they found it, largely through prayer.

Peale is the first to admit he could have written more millions of words about the power of negative thinking, but he says that he always is "carried away" by stories with happy endings. He is convinced it helps others to know that things turn out all right sometimes.

"I think I've laid it on the line about the rugged toughness of life," he said. "Life is very tough. I've come out of many a place so broken up I could hardly carry on. But you never show people that. No day passes that you don't have to bring comfort in tragedy. I think people are wonderful. Some people say people are sinners. I'm criticized for showing that there is good in man. Man is both bad and good."

This is only one man's view from the pulpit, but it also represents what many clergymen see from their vantage points in churches large and small. The clergyman's main job is to minister, to practice churchmanship, and today that means he spends more time counseling people who need help, reassurance or comfort than in preparing sermons. The church study has become a confessional, where people who are unable or unwilling to solve their own problems are heaping them on the pastor, who may have some insurmountable worries of his own.

Peale is well remunerated for his efforts. So are a handful of the other prominent big-city ministers and rabbis. What many persons do not realize is that most of these men share their good fortune with others. Peale, for example, tithes. He also contributes generously to the American Foundation for Religion and Psychiatry and other institutional causes.

Most clergymen receive only modest compensation, however. A minister usually ranks as possibly the most overworked, underpaid and loneliest man in town. Just about everyone except the minister has a person to whom to take his troubles. The man of the cloth suffers alone, in silence. He develops ulcers and neuroses, according to psychologists, at the same rate as any other man and faces just as much danger of becoming a mental patient as any member of his congregation.

There have been suggestions that each denomination appoint special ministers-to-ministers to do nothing but tour the churches and listen to the problems of those who find the conflicts of being clergymen in a materialistic world becoming too much for them to endure.

A minister toils 65, 70 or even 80 hours a week in a profession that requires not only dedication but years of expensive training for which he is likely to go deep in debt. It costs money to become a minister, just as it does to become a doctor or a lawyer. In return for his effort, a man may receive considerable personal satisfaction in knowing that his life is dedicated to helping others, but he cannot live on love for his fellow man. His spirit may be satisfied, but his earthly reward is likely to be somewhat less than that of the man who delivers milk to the manse every morning, despite the fact that the church in America is one of the richest, most heavily endowed corporate structures in the world.

Whether people like it or not, the church has become big business in the era of the social climber, the status seeker and the struggle for SUCCESS, with the corporation reigning supreme. A businessman is judged by the tangible results he obtains. So is a minister. A clergyman's effectiveness often is gauged by the size and location of his house of worship, by the number of persons in church on Sunday and by the amount of cash dropped in the collection plate, with a crunch, not a tinkle, every Sunday. If he remains in a small town or country church, he is regarded as lazy or a failure. If he goes to a big church at a big salary, he is too materialistic for some. Should he become famous, he may be regarded as an opportunist. This is the heart of one of the dilemmas of the minister of the new-time religion: how to be successful without being too much of a Success.

There are ministers, such as Dr. Ralph W. Sockman, pastor of Christ Church Methodist, on Park Avenue in New York City, who sits with the clock-watching poise of a corporation executive in a well-furnished office with a beehive of aides buzzing around him. And there is the pastor of a one-room church on the Kansas plains who scrubs the sanctuary floor himself.

Quite a few churches in the larger cities have two, three or four ministers, each with a separate assignment in the life of the congregation. Some have staffs of secretaries, social workers, typists, custodians and even business managers. But each of the largest number of the 310,000 U.S. churches relies on one man, who serves as a minister with many portfolios.

There was a time when, simply by being a clergyman, a man was about the best-informed person in town. His was a quiet, contemplative life in which he preached on Sunday; puttered in his garden on Monday; studied, prayed, prepared sermons and called on church members during the rest of the week, and took an annual summer vacation. He and his family were frequent dinner guests in the homes of members of their congregation. People looked up to him as one of the most important persons in town. It was a good life, secure and uncomplicated.

Just as the rest of the world has changed, so has the life of the minister been altered. No longer is it true that he automatically becomes the community intellectual. He faces a congregation that is becoming better educated every day, a congregation of television fans, sitting there on the rows of church pews every Sunday and silently defying him to be as knowledgeable about world affairs as an Edward R. Murrow, to speak in the golden tones of a Lowell Thomas or to be as persuasive as a Bishop Fulton J. Sheen.

The clergyman today has to struggle to keep abreast, or perhaps a step ahead of, his well-informed congregation on matters literary, scientific, political and economic. He has no trouble becoming better informed about the Bible, for most clergymen are in agreement that churchgoers today are Biblical illiterates; they may own the Good Book, but they do not read it.

To prepare students to become the virtual supermen expected in the pulpit today, theological seminaries have had to expand their courses so drastically that the time devoted to theology, preaching and Bible history has shrunk to make way for practical courses in how to run a church, and even in psychology.

A study of seven typical theological school catalogues showed 923 courses listed, 407 of them related to practical matters. Formerly, Biblical, theological and historical courses made up almost the entire curriculum. Now as much as half the time is devoted to such subjects as legal problems, how to run a Sunday school or the conduct of public relations in the pulpit.

If a student at Yale Divinity School were to take every course offered, he would be a seminarian for 16 years. Yale has added courses in church administration and a new full-year omnibus course called "Care of the Parish," which deals with the administrative, legal and business problems of the church and the minister.

Union Theological Seminary in New York, which receives students from all over the world, also has expanded its curriculum in the last 15 years. During the 1945-46 academic year, the school offered 140 courses. In the 1960-61 year, there were 188 listed in the catalogue, most of the new ones being in the fields of religious drama, psychiatry and advanced theology.

No matter how much theological training is offered a man and no matter how much of it he absorbs, he still cannot be prepared for the avalanche of demands he must face when he goes out to his first pulpit. He suddenly finds that he is required to serve as a no-fee psychoanalyst, a group therapist, marriage counselor, scoutmaster, civic leader, fund raiser, Rotary luncheon speaker, bookkeeper, administrator, mimeograph machine technician, public-relations expert, typist and even gardener, janitor and plumber. When he has the time, he prepares his sermons and the order of his Sunday services.

There should be time each day for study, personal prayer and reading. There must be time to call on the sick, aged, newcomers to the community, backsliders and church members who make demands on the minister's time for superficial personal reasons, often selfish ones, such as sampling a fresh batch of brownies.

When the day is over, the minister hopes to have a little while to spend with his family, to relax and to perform the do-it-yourself tasks around the parsonage that any husband does in his home, before returning to the church for a board meeting, a men's social, a Cub-pack session or counseling—or just to think without interruption.

A minister can have friends, but that is difficult to arrange within a congregation. If he socializes with one churchgoer, he must socialize with all, so he remains aloof. In many cases if he likes a cocktail before dinner or an occasional cigarette—as many ministers do—he must have them alone. When people need him, they want him around; but when they seek a good time, they hope he stays away.

The one sad fact that emerges unanimously from surveys of ministers and individual comments made in conversation is that they are essentially lonely men. They feel set off from the rest of society despite their efforts to be one of the fellows. Because they are clergymen, laymen think they are different. A clergyman is likely to be left out of parties, dinners and other functions just because he is a minister.

Many a clergyman will say that it is at just these social events, even cocktail parties, where he is likely to meet the people who need him most. But he is excluded on the theory that his presence is not appropriate at such a gathering.

The new-time clergyman, in short, is a spiritual handyman, a salesman and a servant, a religious organization man—and yet he does not really belong anywhere except in the church, and this in a society that demands churchmen to be more worldly than ever before.

As is the case with other professions, only a few men get to the top in the clerical field. There can be but a limited number of Norman Vincent Peales, Eugene Carson Blakes, Franklin Clark Frys, Bishop Sheens, Abba Hillel Silvers, Daniel Polings and Judah Finkelsteins. A minister works no less because he is Norman Vincent Peale, but Peale can devote his full time to his ministry of sermons, speeches and writings. He does not have to take time out to repair the church plumbing.

So many and varied are the demands on a clergyman that the Methodist church magazine *Together*, with one of the largest circulations of any religious publication, printed an appeal from a minister's wife entitled "Let's Not Waste Our Pastors" (Used by permission from *Together,* August, 1960. Copyright 1960 by Lovick Pierce, Publisher).

Mrs. "Rev. Bob." Holmes of Rapid City, S.D., said church-goers must realize that times have changed. The modern minister cares as much about his parishioners as did his pastor grandfather, but friendly calling today is only one of many important things he has to do.

"He is expected to team with doctor and lawyer to promote the total health and welfare of anyone in—or outside of—his congregation," Mrs. Holmes wrote. "A vast radio and TV audience may lay on his heart as part of his mission, or he may have responsibilities for such groups as Alcoholics Anonymous, city and state councils of churches, the U.S.O., labor-relations boards, or a myriad of other community enterprises that today request the guidance of the professional servant of God.

"Moreover, in any fast-growing parish, when the minister calls to pass the time of day with a loyal member who is getting along just fine, he may do so at the expense of somebody who needs him badly.

"Every time he rings a doorbell his conscience asks, 'Is this where I'm needed most?'"

Mrs. Holmes said that her husband, early in his career, consulted his Pastoral Relations Committee on what was expected of him. The answers showed that several persons expected him to devote a total of 100 hours a week to his calling. One listed a 135-hour schedule for each week, leaving fewer than five hours a day for sleep.

"I suggest that it is reasonable to give your minister the same consideration you extend to your doctor," Mrs. Holmes said. "When you need him, you call him, even if it's only for a cold. But meeting him on the street, you don't say, 'Drop in for coffee sometime, Doctor,' expecting him to read your mind and divine that you have a pain, nor do you expect him to see all of his patients—plus every new family in the neighborhood—every six months, sick or well."

Contrary to the wishes of some church members, Mrs. Holmes said, much of a pastor's time is spent with people who never will give anything back to the church. That is to be expected, she said. There is no bill of accounts, so far as a minister is concerned.

"He would not trade his profession for any other job in the world," she wrote. "There is no work that pays so well in the real value of life."

To this sentiment, many a minister says "Amen." But it still does not solve the dilemma of a clergyman who is in the world without really being part of it, much as he would like to step in.

"A minister is the loneliest person you can find," said a man who learned first hand that this was true. He is a deeply dedicated Protestant clergyman who formerly had a pulpit but now is a key officer in a major denomination.

"He doesn't dare become socially intimate with anyone in the congregation for fear of favoritism. He accepts invitations out, but he can't return them. He can't invite anyone to dinner. His only contacts are outside the congregation, which means other ministers. It is a deadly life.

"A minister in a small town must go outside for his friends. He can go to Rotary or Kiwanis or lunch with various men, but when it comes to entertaining in his home or going to the homes of others, he has to look out.

"A minister is looked upon as not quite human. Isolation is part of a priest's life, but not of a minister's. He must fight in the area of public opinion but personally he is isolated. He knows what is going on in the community, but he knows so many personal problems that everyone is cagey with him in public. He is always set aside. This is not true of a doctor, though. I guess it is because people think the minister is always judging."

Although many church leaders hold that a man is not a good minister unless he is lonely and set apart, socializing has become a matter of concern to those who worry about keeping the clergy contented and maintaining liaison between the church and the people who need it most—the members of the anxious generation.

The social life—or lack of it—of the minister was considered important enough to be included in a survey of pastors of the United Lutheran Church in America. The results showed that the time-honored custom of inviting the minister and his family to dinner was on the wane. Only a little more than half the pastors said they received one invitation to dinner about once every two weeks. The rest said they were asked less than once every three months—or never. That is a long way from a generation ago, when ministers were likely to receive so many invitations to dinner that they could not possibly accept them all.

To the minister who likes people, this is a severe blow. One of these men is young Dr. Spike, who is active intellectually and quite a sociable fellow. He feels deeply about being set apart from the rest of society because he is a minister.

"In the profession of clergyman, I am happy in my work," he said, "but I think that if I knew then what I know now, I would not choose the ministry. The minister, by profession, is walled off from places of influence. He is a kind of ornament. People like ministers. They say nice things to them. They want them around, but at the same time, they don't want them around."

When an evangelist such as Spike says he would not choose again to be a minister, he does not mean he would not work for the good of the church. He would rather have become a sort of Congregational version of the Roman Catholic worker-priest, serving the church while earning his livelihood in another profession.

Such introspection is typical of the ministry and the church today. The churches are doing what apparently comes most naturally to Americans; they are making surveys, polls and samplings of clergymen—what has come to be known as the In-Depth Study.

Hardly a religious organization has spared its clergy from appraisals of their psychological, physical, emotional and worldly needs. Madison Avenue could learn a lot from the motivational research of the church.

It should come as no surprise that money is the chief topic of church studies of ministers, because money is the chief concern of the ministers themselves. They are just like everyone else on that score.

The National Council of Churches is among the many organizations that have pored over the salary problem. The Council and all the other pollsters have come up with the same conclusion: Ministers are underpaid.

Salaries of Protestant ministers were found to be so low in the National Council study that many of their wives had to go to work to pay the bills. The average cash salaries of Protestant ministers totaled somewhere around $4,500, for a 60-to-80-hour week, about what a well-paid college instructor receives. For an 80-hour week, that would be in the neighborhood of a dollar an hour—less than the Federal minimum wage per hour for a 40-hour week for millions of Americans.

The study found that New England ministers were the lowest paid of the Protestant clergy—an average of $4,018 a year. The Southwestern states paid the most—an average of nearly $5,000 a year.

Many persons erroneously believe that the minister's salary is only a fraction of what he really receives, that there are fringe benefits adding enormously to his livelihood. This is not so, said the National Council. Allowances for housing and auto travel, and for the fees and gratuities paid for presiding at weddings, baptisms and funerals, averaged a total of nearly $1,500 per minister. But professional expenses cut heavily into this. The average travel allowance was less than $300 a year, and most ministers received no travel allowances at all, paying for their own gasoline to drive on their rounds.

More than 90 per cent of the pastors reported that they received housing or rental allowances but that many of the free manses were old and too large, with enormous heating bills.

The Council found that two-thirds of the ministers had gone into debt, mainly in order to send their children to school and to meet automobile and medical expenses and the inflationary pressures of everyday life.

"Most people want the preacher to live on earth and board in heaven," an Indiana preacher noted on his questionnaire.

The fiscal pulse of the ministry has been taken also by the Ministers Life and Casualty Union of Minneapolis, an insurance organization. This examination brought statements indicating 48 per cent of the ministers had found their earnings adequate to meet living expenses and 44 per cent had found them inadequate. The rest did not indicate the status of their domestic budgets.

The American Baptist Convention reported that ministers of 2,396 of its smaller churches—with fewer than 150 members each—received "bare minimal salaries, hardly enough to buy a suit of clothes and pay a maternity bill much less buy a book."

Denominations paying the highest total average salaries are the Episcopalian, Presbyterian and Congregational Christian—all over

$6,000 a year. The highest median salaries are paid by the Episcopalian, Congregationalist, Presbyterian, Lutheran and Disciples of Christ Churches.

Ministerial surveys have gone far beyond money matters. The National Lutheran Council, representing most of the larger Lutheran bodies, found that time consumed in church administration was the cause of almost universal complaint among Lutheran pastors. It was suggested that theological seminaries train laymen to serve as church business managers so ministers could get on with their spiritual tasks.

Many of the clergymen said it would be helpful if their congregations could provide them with secretaries, parish workers, directors of religious education and associate pastors. But such luxuries obviously are only for churches with large and generous memberships. They are not for the rural church that may not even have a lavatory or furnace and seldom attracts more than a handful of persons to services.

The Lutherans reported that they spent an average of 2 hours and 20 minutes preparing sermons and slightly less than that on civic matters each week. An average of 18 hours and 34 minutes were devoted to calling on the sick, various members and prospective members, and tending to funerals, weddings, christenings and counseling. An additional 4 hours and 31 minutes a week—less than an hour a day—were reserved for personal recreation such as sports, exercise, reading, radio, TV, gardening, house jobs, socializing, travel and hobbies.

By the time he finished his computations, including the time spent in travel and sleep each week, the average minister found he had 15 hours and 31 minutes a week for his family—just a little more than 2 hours a day.

In the Ministers Life and Casualty Study, most clergymen indicated they liked the job security of their profession; few, if any, had any fears of being out of work. But there were other complaints. Some felt they did not have enough leisure time in which to earn additional money through lecturing or writing. Others thought their parishioners were failing to serve the church adequately. There was a general feeling that there was a lack of interest in religion and the Bible among churchgoers. Also expressed was worry over friction among church factions and concern about shortages of youth leaders.

A Methodist Church survey of ministers disclosed that more than half felt they were underpaid, but 90 per cent still would choose the ministry as an occupation if they had it to do all over again—this despite the fact that not one thought the ministry was a good way to earn a living or gave a man any special standing in the community.

The survey also showed that 2 out of 5 Methodist ministers performed janitorial tasks in their churches. One-third complained that laymen in their congregations tried to "boss the preacher around."

The Methodist analysis, covering a scientifically selected cross-section of all 24,000 of the denomination's pastors, representing every age and type, found that Methodist clergymen do not like to wear clerical collars away from the pulpit. More than half said they sometimes used prayers written by others. The average man drove 12,062 miles a year in his work.

A total of 73.4 per cent of the Methodist ministers surveyed said they were in debt. This was 11 per cent over the figure for all Protestant ministers. The Methodists owed for their college and seminary educations, medical bills, household goods, clothing, children's educations and retirement real estate purchases. It was a debt picture that could have been reproduced in the homes of many laymen in their congregations.

One out of two in the red owed more than $1,200. The average was $1,871. Seven per cent owed more than $5,000. One in six owed $3,000 or more. Mortgages were not their problem, as in the case of many laymen. It was day-to-day living that was putting them in debt.

Of his income dollar, the typical Methodist reported that 77.4 cents was in cash salary, 10.6 cents in parsonage, 5 cents in auto allowance, 3.6 cents in funeral and wedding earnings, and 3.4 cents in free utilities. But many of the ministers received no auto allowance or free utilities and some had to provide their own homes.

What such figures often add up to is a shortage of ministers. The only denomination reporting a surplus was the Southern Baptist

Convention, in which it is possible to be ordained without a theological education. All the others, Roman Catholic, Protestant and Jewish, reported they did not have enough clergymen to fill the vacancies open for teachers, preachers, missionaries and administrators. They did not say exactly how many clergymen they needed but were unanimous in saying there was a need.

To help fill the gap, many denominations have accepted women as ordained members of the clergy—usually in secondary jobs or posts men spurn. There also are training programs for lay workers to serve with youth groups, choirs and visitation committees or to perform other non-preaching tasks.

Women gradually are breaking down the various traditional professional barriers, and the ministry is included. Every year, more and more women are ordained and assigned to churches of their own. One covers a circuit of Maine islands in a rowboat. Another tours the nation in a station wagon. Still another makes her calls on horseback among Western Indians.

There are more than 7,000 clergywomen, with about 3,000 of them pastors of their own churches. The rest are assistants, teachers or missionaries, or perform other church-related tasks. Approximately 65 religious bodies ordain women. About 15 others give them some sort of status beyond singing in the choir or cooking church suppers.

Women have gone a long way in church work since Anne Hutchinson was banished from Boston and later excommunicated in the 17th Century for her liberal preachments. She claimed she was a minister, which would have made her America's first clergywoman, but historians have not been able to establish this as a fact.

The Rev. Ellen B. Shaw of Mazomanie, Wis., president of the American Association of Women Ministers, says there still is a prejudice against women in the pulpit, but it is abating. What she did not say was that women are being welcomed, for the most part, to pulpits men turn down—principally small rural churches that pay very little.

"There is a need for more ministers," she said. "I feel that women can fill this need very well, so why should they not be used more than they are?"

Among the most recent gains by women in their struggle for equal rights in the pulpit have been those scored in the Methodist and United Presbyterian, U.S.A., churches. Sweden's Lutherans have accepted women pastors, but Lutherans elsewhere are resisting.

"There is no moral right to oppose women ministers," a Methodist official said.

Fewer than 10 women were ordained by the Presbyterians between 1956, when they were accepted, and 1960. One of them was Mrs. Lilias Dulles Hinshaw, daughter of the late Secretary of State John Foster Dulles.

The American Baptist Convention has between 30 and 40 women ministers, one of them a Negro. Their salaries range from $520 to $3,500 a year—much less than the national average for all Protestant ministers. A large proportion are either the wives or widows of ministers.

The Unitarian and Congregational Christian Churches have long histories of acceptance of women ministers. One of the first American women to be ordained was the Rev. Antoinette Brown Blackwell, who started as a Congregational minister in 1853 and later was listed as a Unitarian. In 1959, Dr. Sophia Lyon Fahs of New York was ordained at the age of 82, bringing the grand total of women Unitarian preachers as of then to two. The other was the wife of the Rev. Donald Harrington, of the New York Community Church. Mrs. Harrington is one of her husband's assistant ministers.

Most seminaries open to women admit them on an equal footing. Few women students prepare for preaching careers, however. At Union Theological Seminary, for example, there were 600 women enrolled in one year, but only about 30 sought Bachelor of Divinity Degrees. A few planned to become preachers. The rest were interested in becoming missionaries or serving churches in staff capacities.

The first woman ordained as a Presbyterian minister was Miss Margaret E. Towner, minister of Christian education at the First Presbyterian Church in Allentown, Pa. She was a medical photographer at the Mayo Clinic when she decided to study theology.

By the time she was graduated, the ordination of women had been approved by her denomination.

Another of the early Presbyterian acceptances was Miss Priscilla Alden Chaplin, daughter of a former missionary to China, where she was born. She set out to become a concert singer, but when she developed throat trouble she turned to the church. Miss Chaplin financed a large part of her theological education with $6,000 she won on the "Name That Tune" television quiz show. Her first pastorate was at the Union Presbyterian Church in Sauquoit, N.Y., where her feminine touch almost doubled the attendance in her first months there.

Because the number of women who want to enter the clergy is small, even with full acceptance, churches are having to turn increasingly to laymen for help in the face of the ministerial shortage. Rabbis, priests and ministers all are accepting lay help. In synagogues and Protestant churches, laymen and laywomen are taking up greater roles in non-preaching jobs. In the Roman Catholic sphere, the churches still remain almost entirely in clerical hands, of course, but more and more lay teachers are being recruited by parochial schools because of shortages of both nuns and priests.

The Protestant Episcopal Church is especially concerned about the failure of laymen to give their rectors the help they need. The basic difficulty is that members tend to sit back and let the minister do most of the worrying and just about all the work. It is the conviction of church officials that the minister needs a lot of help that he is not getting. It also is their conviction that the more active a person is in his church, the more vital the church. The Mormons provide a good example of this. They have no ordained clergy, taking turns as preachers, and they become deeply involved financially in church work in addition to devoting much of their spare time to church matters. Every child is taught public speaking so thoroughly that any Mormon adult is a potential preacher for the church.

Bishop Arthur C. Lichtenberger, Presiding Bishop of the Protestant Episcopal Church, believes there is a great need for a better understanding of the relationship of the clergy to the laity.

"On the whole," he says, "many churches are suffering from

clericalism. Lay people think they have no place in the life of the church other than going to church and doing what the rector asks them to do. They don't realize their responsibility for evangelism. It is taken for granted that the responsibility for the church is the minister's. Actually, the minister should say to his members, 'I am here to help you do the work that is primarily yours.' "

Lichtenberger sees the minister as an overseer, a coordinator or an adviser, with the church members actually doing the bulk of the work. This would leave a clergyman more time to minister to the spiritual needs of his congregation and at the same time intensify the full participation of members in the life of the church.

Dr. Eli Ginzberg, professor of economics at Columbia University, told the Rabbinical Assembly of America that Conservative Judaism, like all major religious groups, was having a difficult time recruiting leaders and training scholars largely because of a failure to use properly the leadership already available.

"A career which demands the wide variety of skills which the average congregation demands of its rabbi is not likely to attract the most able of our young men, who correctly foresee little chance for personal growth, for spiritual development, or even for true service, in a life which is a frenetic round of weddings and funerals, sermons and sisterhood meetings, luncheon speeches and book reviews."

Ginzberg said the rabbi who allows himself to become entangled in such a web does a disservice to his congregation, because he has no time left for the quiet contemplation that alone can produce the insights and understanding necessary for spiritual leadership. But the pressures put on the rabbi to serve in all these capacities are almost intolerable, Ginzberg said.

He called for a redefinition of the rabbi's role in which he would become a specialist, not a Jack-of-all-trades. The rabbi would serve as the head of a team of experts who perform the tasks ranging from leading youth groups to visiting the sick.

There is another ministerial field, in addition to missionary work, that is shared by clergymen and laymen—church administration. The usual image of the minister is that of a pastor preaching from the pulpit or tending his flock, but hundreds of clergymen have no church assignments and no congregations. They are the administrators. Many are ministers approaching or beyond retirement age but still able to contribute to the life of the church. Most are younger men who for many reasons find they preferred desks to pulpits. More than half the 400-member administrative staff of the National Council of Churches is composed of clergymen; the offices of every denomination are manned at least partly by ministers; priests tend to most of the administrative tasks in the Roman Catholic Church, and rabbis run the affairs of various Jewish organizations.

In the course of pastoral work, some men become interested in committee work. They grow more and more expert at it, and move up in the ranks of their denominations, eventually taking a denominational position or a post in a national religious body.

Administrative assignments do not always pay better than the best of parish pulpits. Some men take desk jobs at financial sacrifices, although with greater satisfaction in their work.

The biggest drawback to administrative church work is the travel involved. Some men are away from home more than they are with their families. Ministers with churches are busy men. They may not get home for dinner every night, but they usually can manage to spare a little time for their families each day. The man in an administrative post may not be at home for weeks at a time.

Even those clergymen who hold administrative positions try not to get too far from local church activities, no matter where their jobs take them. Nearly all of them preach on Sundays whenever they can, as vacation substitutes, in churches without regular ministers or as guest preachers.

To these ministers and most others, the sermon still is the heart of the matter. While it is true that what the preacher once said in a few thousand well-chosen words in 90 minutes or so now must be boiled down to accommodate the 20- or 30-minute attention span of the modern churchgoer, the weekly potion still is supposed to sustain the congregation from one Sunday to the next. It takes all the talent a minister can muster to provide the right prescription for the large majority of his parishioners addicted to predigested news and information.

Among the clergy there is considerable comment on the style and content of today's sermons. Professor Sittler complained that too many sermons were delivered in poor grammar and with faulty pronunciation and were peppered with clichés, repetitious prayers and foggy thinking. Quite a few sermons, he said, gave evidence of a lack of preparation and rehearsal. He suggested a tape recorder as an ideal instrument for a preacher to use in judging and improving his delivery.

Peale, one of the masters of pulpit oratory, gives the identical sermon twice on Sunday morning, without the use of notes, after careful preparation with his wife as audience and critic. He says seminaries do not teach ministers to make a public speech, which is what a sermon is.

"They are trying to put a premium on dullness," he said. "We have got to have great men who can sway people and communicate. In the seminaries, they tell them how to outline sermons and all that. They are concerned with structure rather than delivery.

"They don't let these boys be themselves. They are rolled in a package pattern. They talk and act alike, roll their eyes around and spout platitudes. What we need is greater individuality."

Peale said his point was proved—and at his own expense—by a student at the New Brunswick Theological Seminary in New Jersey, who wrote a paper on Peale as a sermonizer.

"He said I'd fail in a preaching course at that school because my sermons weren't organized according to *their* techniques," Peale said.

Sockman, another famous preacher, said he put in 18 to 20 hours preparing a sermon it took him less than 30 minutes to deliver. It is doubtful, he said, whether any minister preaches the old-fashioned hour-long sermon any more.

"People are too impatient," he said. "They won't sit through them. I usually preach 28 minutes in church and 13 to 14 minutes on radio. You can't hold a congregation today with the same sort of sermon as 40 years ago. Radio, television and the movies compel preachers to preach more colorfully, dramatically and briefly."

While preaching still is the key to many a ministry, particularly in large cities where personal meetings between the pastor and his flock are rare, it takes up a relatively minor amount of time. The parish minister still must be a general practitioner, with about 85 per cent of his work residing in pastoral care.

As is often the case with the general medical practitioner, the ministerial practitioner is an overworked man. The supply of ministers is spread so thin that there are not enough in any field. But it is important to note that while complaints are universal about shortages of ministers, there are no real recruitment programs to fill the many vacancies. Vocational guidance advisers seldom if ever mention the ministry to young men in search of careers. There is a popular notion that men turn to the ministry only if they are "called," but there are different kinds of calls. If the possibilities of the clergy were outlined, if the profession were accorded the status it once rated, more young men might become interested in it.

Many clergymen are recognized to be misfits, persons who found they did not belong anywhere else but were accepted by the church out of brotherly love. They have not been satisfactory ministers, and churches often are at a loss to find something constructive for them to do. Vocational guidance and higher standards might help solve this problem. The very fact that many men today are turning to the ministry after starting out in other professions may be the sharpest indication of all that vocational guidance is needed at the college level. Perhaps that is where the inclinations and talents of these career changers leaned all the time, but there was no one who could or would advise them; they had to find out the hard way.

There is the further possibility that ministers are not being properly used by some denominations. A large number of clergymen are filling office jobs that require no theological training. When you find a minister working as a statistician or public relations director in the office of a major church body, you wonder why he is there. Why not hire a statistician to handle statistics and a newspaperman to deal with the press? Are music ministers and recreational ministers really necessary? Could not laymen perform these tasks as well?

The principal problem here is that although the churches like to talk about how affluent they have become, the wages they pay are low. A minister who is a dedicated man will work for small financial reward, content in the knowledge that he is serving The Cause, even though a layman could do many of the same chores with equal skill. A way needs to be found to interest lay experts in working in denominational offices so more ministers can be members of their profession in more than name only, viewing the world from a pulpit instead of a desk.

6

Meanwhile, Back at the Manse . . .

THE SCENE *is a drafty, three-story Victorian frame house in Somewhere, U.S.A., population 5,523 and not growing.*

The time is 6 P.M., just about any day of the week.

Our heroine sits in the center of the stage at a dinner table with two small children. She gets up every few minutes to answer the telephone and make a note on a memo pad. The doorbell rings twice. Once it is a child delivering a freshly baked batch of cupcakes sent by his mother. The other caller is a woman who wants to borrow a vase.

The lights dim, denoting the passage of three hours.

The young woman now is sitting alone in the living room, the children having gone to bed. She is darning socks between telephone calls. One call is from someone asking her to send her husband "right over—it's an emergency." Another is from a Rotary Club official, wanting her husband to make a speech next Wednesday. A third seeks his sponsorship of a youth rally.

The list of names and numbers still is on the telephone table when, three hours later, just at the stroke of midnight, a weary young man enters. He is ending a day that began at 6 A.M., when he got out of bed to tend the furnace and shovel snow from the front walk. He has not seen his wife since morning. After kissing her and glancing at the memo pad, he stumbles off to bed, too tired for a late supper. (Curtain.)

This is not the home of a rising young doctor or lawyer. It is the manse of the town's youngest minister, four years, three months and two days out of theological seminary and already on call day and night as a consoler of the bereaved, comforter of the ill and aged, supporter of worthy causes, marriage counselor and psychiatric social worker. He and his wife met at a church-related college, became engaged while he was in seminary and were married the day he was called to his first pastorate—the Community Church of Somewhere (congregation 185), salary $2,500 a year, manse provided free, utilities included, no car allowance and working hours up to 80 a week, with a two-week annual vacation, to be spent at a ministerial summer school.

Mrs. Young Minister may be one of several types of mansekeepers. She may be so dedicated to the church that she is 100 per cent behind her husband and does not resent the loss of his companionship in the periods when she herself is not involved in her many activities at the church. She may be a wife who, regarding her husband's career as a doctor's wife regards the medical profession, acts strictly as a homemaker, with her church participation limited to being another member of the congregation. Or she may be one of the tortured women who has awakened to the fact that this is not the sort of life she had in mind when she became a minister's wife.

Most wives of clergymen seem to fall in the first or third category. Few have been found who either wanted to be just homebodies or whose husbands' congregations would allow them to lead the normal, appliance-adorned life of any young wife and mother. A large proportion of the manse wives look upon themselves as having gained a vocation simply by saying "I do."

In any case, the young minister's wife is likely to have been one of the girls who have been flocking to church-related colleges and theological schools. One reason they have given for wanting religion-oriented educations is a desire to play Real Roles in the religious upsurge. But, in the same manner that many thousands of girls hope to find husbands at state universities and other secular schools, so these girls are searching in classroom and corridor for their Mr. Right—the REVEREND Mr. Right.

That the search is on there is no doubt. Clergymen like to say that the girls who turn up on seminary campuses are prettier than run-of-the-mill husband hunters. One self-confessed seeker after a clergyman appeared in a beauty contest, and in a low-cut bathing suit, at that. She was Christine McSwain of York, S.C., "Miss Tennessee" in the 1960 Miss Universe Contest at Miami Beach. Miss McSwain made it clear that, more than being acclaimed the world's most beautiful beauty, "I'd really like to be a pastor's wife." She was trying to achieve this ambition at a Southern Baptist school, Carson-Newman College, in Jefferson City, Tenn. The reason she gave for entering the beauty pageant was that she wanted to prove that one could be beautiful in both body and soul.

Girls who want to burn their first biscuits in a parsonage oven often appear to have a preconceived notion that a clergyman makes a more loving, ethical, moral, reliable, loyal and understanding husband and father than the average man; that he remains aloof from the toil and sweat of everyday life; that he will be home for dinner every night, and sometimes for lunch; that he will never look at another woman, and that he will have real job security, with a pension at the end of the line. Not least, there is status simply in being a clergyman's wife.

Wide-eyed and idealistic, a bride with such notions moves into the manse only to realize, often to her dismay, that she is playing second fiddle to a formidable rival, the church. If the wife is as dedicated to the religious life as her husband, the church is a partner rather than a competitor, and theirs may be a happy match. Otherwise, trouble may lie ahead in the busy fishbowl existence of the parsonage and rectory, in which the wife finds herself catalogued, segregated and denied many feminine freedoms, including the freedom to wear slacks and hair curlers to the supermarket.

There are no statistics setting clergymen apart from the rest of society on the question of marital success, but it is the conviction of some ministers in a position to know about these things that the clerical divorce rate is rising and that the main causes for the broken manse listed in court records are those two old stand-bys, incompatibility and mental cruelty.

One factor in the increase of clerical divorces has been a relaxation of old social taboos against broken marriage, even among churchmen. Some ministers still cling precariously to unhappy marriages lest their careers be tarnished by divorce, but there are many cases in which they not only have been divorced but

have married again without any objections from either denominational officials or congregations. It has been conceded in these
cases that ministers can make the same mistakes as other folk.

A prominent churchman said some women made a great mistake
by marrying preachers just because they were preachers, placing
the fact that they are men second. Such wives, he said, fail to
realize that the minister's home is his refuge, his safety valve,
the one place where, if he wishes, he can be free to vent his
frustrations and irritations, possibly even to the point of losing
his temper once in a while—in short, behaving more like a man
than a minister.

Because a wife is likely to be shocked at such a sight, some
clergymen are beginning to advocate celibacy for their young
colleagues during the early years of their pastoral careers, or at
least until they have had a chance to find out what the life of a
minister is like and whether they want to include wives in it.

This is a matter of controversy among church leaders, however.
Many ministers believe that the companionship of a wife and
children adds so much to the effectiveness of a clergyman that the
resulting problems are a low long-range price to pay.

Those who draw the most somber picture of the domestic life
of a young parson and his wife acknowledge that many ministerial
marriages are made in heaven. There is distress, however, over
the number that are not, and congregations are blamed for this
as much as the couples who find unhappiness in the fact that the
parsonage may be more of a community center than a home.

One solution to this difficult aspect of the life of a minister's
wife might lie in moving the manse. There is no good reason why
the home of a minister must be next door to his church. Few
if any other men have their homes so close to their places of
employment. Congregations that have provided manses or rectories
a reasonable distance away have found the ministers' families
much happier. The wife has neighbors from whom to borrow
eggs and sugar just as any other homemaker has and the children
have a chance to grow up out of the shadow of the church. The
wife also has the opportunity to serve the church on a more equal
footing with other members.

Ministers' wives tend to be less religious clubwomen than their prototypes of 50 to 100 years ago. More and more of them lean toward giving background support by training others while refraining from actually running things themselves. But there still are many who feel they must supervise the church office, direct the choir, teach Sunday school, oversee the ladies' aid, head a Brownie pack or hold weekly open-house for teen-agers. It may be that a wife engaged in such a range of activities did not set out to become so deeply involved, but one thing has led to another, and there she is, a sort of ex-officio co-minister, working full time for nothing and not really being a wife.

Regardless of the degree of participation, the wife's life is not her own. She is always being studied by women in the congregation to determine whether she is dressed properly, has her hair combed right or is not wearing too much make-up. So important is the question of dress that when a group of ministers' wives sat down for a discussion at the Methodist Church's 175th anniversary meeting in Baltimore in 1959, one of the topics they considered was: "Is it proper for a minister's wife to wear slacks and shorts at home if living in an area where other young wives dress this way and weather permits?"

The wife worries also about what other people think of her, lest a poor opinion harm her husband's relations with his flock. She lacks the freedom of other wives to run next door to gossip with a neighbor or play hooky from the weekly wash occasionally for a frivolous afternoon at the bridge table or the movies. She often feels confined and frustrated by the conflict of *wishing* to be a normal woman and at the same time *having* to be the paragon who lives in the parsonage.

In bright light or dim, the minister's wife appears as a lonely figure. She is limited in the friendships she can make within a community and the confidences in which she can indulge. If she is too friendly with one woman, others will resent it. If she goes to one ladies' circle meeting, she must go to all. If she declines to head the Girl Scout troop, she is a shirker. If she attempts to give leadership to a wide variety of activities, she is trying to take over the church. Her home is merely lent to her by the congregation, and may be in a state of perpetual activity, with women bursting in to borrow her treasures for a church social as if they were in their own homes.

While they are helping themselves to the parsonage wife's possessions, the women of the church might pause to look around. They most likely would find the clattering washing machine that used to be in Deacon Jones' laundry room, the unreliable refrigerator passed on to the manse from the home of Vestryman Smith or the aging stove and other white elephants generously donated by parishioners who still have the Neanderthal notion that second best is A-1 for the poor minister's wife.

This sort of attitude is waning but still is prevalent enough to disturb the hard-working manse wife, who feels that if she cannot be paid or her husband cannot be paid adequately, they should at least have the same sort of labor-saving appliances that are in other homes, rather than rejects.

When a "pulpit committee" casts about for a new minister, it often scrutinizes the wife as carefully as a big corporation looks over the wives of potential executives. There is a growing need in the minds of administrators in many fields to make certain a wife will be right for her husband's job. Few women are so intimately associated with a husband's profession without actually being part of it as is the wife of a clergyman. Even so, the wife-screening practice is a controversial one in the ministry. On one side are those who say a wife should have nothing to do with her husband's career, whether it be plumbing or preaching. On the other are those who think it would be better to eye wives more closely, as a favor to them, the church and the minister.

A prominent manse wife who takes a middle-of-the-aisle stand is Mrs. Loulie Latimer Owens of Greenville, S.C., one of the founders of the ministers' wives organization of the Southern Baptist Convention. She observed that some ministers' wives participated "much too much" in the life of the church. Most in her denomination hold three church offices in addition to positions in the national organization.

"As a rule, I believe ministers' wives are expected to do more than they should," she said. "Some wives are not trained at all for their role. More are trained than not. And most preachers

I know out-marry themselves in brains, culture and initiative.

"I believe that in the future the wives can make a bigger contribution by a supporting role rather than trying to wear half the harness. We've overdone this in the past."

Mrs. Owens said that in her own surveys on the most difficult aspects of being a manse wife she found that the lack of family life has led all other complaints. Next, she said, has come the restricted life imposed on ministers' children, especially socially.

"The benefits of the life of a minister's wife are a position in the community, the opportunity to lead—for those who like that sort of thing—and satisfaction of a desire to be of service," she said.

So important has the clergyman's wife become that the Boston University School of Theology has undertaken the first broad survey ever attempted of life as seen from the manse. A three-year study of the minister's wife was launched in 1959, aimed principally at helping wives to learn their individual ways of supporting the ministerial vocation and finding personal fulfillment. It began with the gathering of statements by denominational officials on what they expected of a minister's wife. These presented an "ideal" that would set most brides to trembling.

Study findings reported here are preliminary. Final results will not be available until after the conclusion of the study in 1962. It was agreed in the early results that, among other things, a wife must accept her husband and his career on an equal basis. She must grow increasingly useful to him in his ministry and the community. She must share her husband and her home, serving as a gracious hostess, often on the spur of the moment, and as an efficient and resourceful home executive with a slim budget. On the other hand, she must learn that sometimes her responsibilities lie at home, with a sick child, a sewing project or the Monday wash, and she must not feel guilty about staying away from church because of such obligations.

To achieve this condition, a minister's wife needs, according to denominational officials quoted in a survey progress report:

"1. A vital Christian experience and dedication akin to her husband's;

"2. A social, intellectual and religious background which enables her to understand and support her husband's ministry;

"3. Alertness of mind, awareness of the needs of others and willingness to submerge personal interest for the common good;

"4. A sense of humor and the poise and graciousness of a good hostess;

"5. The desire to participate in parish affairs and yet not dominate any of them, and

"6. The ability to maintain 'respectability' without ostentation, and often on a very limited budget.

"*But above all else,* she is a good and loyal wife and mother, with the understanding of when to be encouraging and when critical of her husband."

Even among the Jews, who traditionally subordinated women, the rabbi's wife has become part of "the team" in the modern society of organized religion.

"Women have emerged in almost an official capacity," said Rabbi Marc Tannenbaum. "Many congregations, when they interview a rabbi, ask whether his wife can teach, speak, conduct recreational activities or provide Sisterhood leadership.

"This is new in Jewish tradition. The rabbi's wife in the past was a retiring figure, a housewife. She kept out of the limelight. But just as the role of the rabbi has changed radically, so has the wife's role changed. She is a personality in her own right. She often plays a commanding role. It depends on the personality of the woman. Many women welcome it, and have made extraordinary contributions."

Nearly everyone with ideas on the subject of ministers' wives has made a list of requirements for their success. The Seventh-Day Adventists put their itemized qualifications in a "Ten Commandments for Ministers' Wives," prescribing:

"1. Thou shalt have no other interests more important to thee than thy husband's.

"2. Thou shalt not make unto thee any church clique or anything resembling it.

"3. Thou shalt not take thy husband's name in vain.

"4. Remember thy intimate family matters, to keep them secret.

"5. Honor thy husband by keeping thy place, that his years of ministry in the cause of God may be long.

"6. Thou shalt not gossip.

"7. Thou shalt not be a burden on others.

"8. Thou shalt not appear untidy.

"9. Thou shalt not covet a taste beyond thy husband's income.

"10. Thou shalt not covet thy lay sister's, or fellow minister's house, furniture, car, or whatsoever thy sister may have."

In other words, if a minister is expected to be something of a superman, his wife must be pretty much of a superwoman.

The "ideal minister's wife," as drawn by the Boston University researchers, is a loyal church woman. She is hostess in church as well as at home. She avoids being bossy at church, exerting leadership indirectly instead, by helping to train and guide others. She may accompany her husband on sick calls or visits to bereaved church members and to newcomers.

"She is expected to be the sort of person the parish can be proud of—attractive, neat, educated and well-informed as well as 'down-to-earth,' mature in judgment, one who loves people and is a wise counselor and trustworthy friend," the progress bulletin said.

Denominations reporting in the Boston survey complained that a minister's effectiveness often is hampered by a wife who strays too far from being the ideal. Replies to survey questions indicated that the wives too often are immature or emotionally disturbed. These failings were attributed to church and community situations as well as personal stresses.

Also considered handicaps by some church officials were a wife's inability to keep confidences, physical illness, a secular outlook or apathy toward the husband's work, poor background and lack of proper preparation to be a minister's wife, a desire for a career of her own, or such personality traits as extreme shyness or an aggressive, officious or demanding attitude.

Dr. William Douglas, assistant professor of psychology at the Boston University School of Theology and director of the survey, reported, however, that these "handicap wives" were definitely in the minority. An overwhelming majority of those reached in the study said their lives had been enriched and they felt supportive of their husband's work in such a way that the ministries were theirs, too.

In the more than 40 denominations covered in the study, widely divergent views are held regarding the wife's proper relation to her husband's vocation. At one extreme is the Salvation Army, where a husband and wife both must be officers subject to the same discipline and devotion; at the other is the Protestant Episcopal Church, where the wife usually may be "just a member of the congregation" if she chooses.

Taking an over-all view, Douglas commented that "at the same time as life is expanded in terms of people and interests and opportunities for service, it is often contracted. A number feel 'squeezed in' by limited finances and family time. They appreciate the values of their husbands' work, but often feel that it dominates too much of home and personal life, that too much of the responsibility for home and children is placed on them."

Other problems were encountered. Some wives resented having to sacrifice their individuality to "play a part" or conform to a pattern determined by the congregation. There was a sense of artificiality and superficiality about personal and family devotional practices.

One important difficulty uncovered—beyond a feeling of loneliness—was the jealousy of some wives over their husbands' attentions to other women in the parish. Quite a few were upset over the interest that women in the parish took in the minister.

There were women, also, who appeared to be driven by their own expectations of what a minister's wife should be rather than by the wishes of the congregation. Sometimes, according to Douglas, the wives are pulled apart by competing demands and pressures because they have not worked out systems of priorities enabling them to say "no" to some requests without feeling insecure or guilty.

Such manse misery has been known to cause emotional breakdowns. Some women simply cannot take the church life. The Rev. Bill West, minister of the First Baptist Church in Okmulgee, Okla., reported in *The Baptist Standard*, a Texas religious weekly, that every meeting of preachers brought word of another minister's wife about to break down.

West said the preacher's wife must combat the stresses pulling her in every direction by learning to be herself and educating the congregation to accept her as she is.

A minister's wife who has seen others go through this misery is Mrs. W. Arthur Milne, a veteran of 30 years in a Methodist manse and a leader of retreats for ministers' wives. She has observed that other wives sometimes have "given themselves away until they have not anything left to give."

Mrs. Milne, a graduate of Vassar and Boston University and the wife of the president of the Bethesda Hospital and Deaconess Association in Cincinnati, Ohio, has time now to help direct retreats at which women can gain new perspectives of their roles in their husbands' ministries.

"We feel the need for greater spiritual resources in order to be more adequate in our homes, our churches and communities," she said. "Also, we sometimes want to share our experiences and problems, perhaps get a new idea in solving them—or living with them—and also we find we feel better about the whole deal when we learn that others have the same problems."

After one retreat, the women who attended were asked to list their reasons for being there.

"I appreciated the opportunity to read and think without being under pressure from phone, home or other duties," one woman said.

"I really needed this time to be alone," another responded.

"It was helpful to see that our problems in any church are similar and most can be overcome through spiritual growth," commented a third.

It is the opinion of women who have been married to ministers for many years that there should be some preparation. Mrs. Ruth Youngdahl Nelson, wife of the Rev. Clarence T. Nelson, pastor of Augustana Lutheran Church in Washington, D.C., and "Church Woman of the Year" in 1960 of the Religious Heritage of America, has definite views on the matter.

"I think it might be helpful for ministers' wives if early they were alerted to their peculiar opportunities for service," she said; "if they were faced with the necessity of being willing to lose their lives in order to know the life abundant which comes with Christian sharing."

Mrs. Nelson, a prominent lecturer and writer, said she had always felt she was in partnership with her husband, but "not solely because I am a clergyman's wife."

"Love him, pray for him, make home as happy a place as possible and join him in loving others," she advised. "We have found Christian hospitality to be a fine witness and a great opportunity."

There can be occasions when a wife also will preach for her husband. Mrs. Walter C. Eyster, wife of a pastor who for many years filled the pulpit at the Epworth Methodist Church in Marion, Ohio, preached once for her husband when he had laryngitis. She also served as his secretary and gathered material for his funeral sermons, but she still felt that it would have helped her as a bride if she could at least have read a book on parsonage life. A few seminary courses would have suited her even better.

Such opportunities now are afforded young wives, largely because of the radical change that has come over theological schools. Before World War II, seminaries were almost monastic, with the sight of a woman on campus a rarity. Since the war, the campuses have become little communities of married students with children romping on the lawns of near-by housing projects. One result of this has been the inclusion of some wives in teaching programs—to a limited degree.

Baptist and Methodist seminaries have active student wife groups, which engage in social, educational and spiritual programs. Some schools sponsor lectures on the tasks and responsibilities of the minister's wife. Others give courses in how to conduct a Bible study class, counseling, home decoration and "how to help your husband." There are even a few courses for prospective brides of ministers.

A number of seminaries have allowed wives to audit courses at half-tuition or for nothing. In some, special lectures outline various courses to familiarize the wives with their general content. The Berkeley Baptist Divinity School urges wives to take courses as preparation for their husbands' careers. The Candler School of Theology at Emory University gives a credit course on "the parsonage family," covering such subjects as "achieving a Christian family life and facing the peculiar responsibilities and opportunities afforded a parsonage family."

The value of such courses is questioned by a well-known clergyman who observes the lives of other ministers from a vantage point in a responsible administrative post. He feels that "a little learning is a dangerous thing" in this regard, that it is as undesirable for a minister's wife to get a smattering of theology as it would be for a doctor's wife to attend a few medical school lectures and then stand at her husband's elbow in the operating room.

"The husband and wife become a committee of two people running the church," he said. "In what other business does the wife help run her husband's career? One reason for this is that ministers are guiltier than most other men of being easy-going. That is one of the first roads to disaster."

Wives are inclined to take issue with such a strong view as this. One of the most outspoken supporters of the practice of pastoral partnership is Mrs. Warner R. Cole, president of the Ministers' Wives Fellowship of the American Baptist Convention. She worked with her husband to build the Covenant Baptist Church of Detroit from 250 members in 1933 to 2,000 twenty-five years later.

"I think a minister's wife is more than just a member of the congregation," she says. "She is more or less an under-leader of the flock.

"I suppose there are some drawbacks to being a minister's wife. I have never felt too frustrated by them. I think we all miss many of the cultural things of life, for lack of time to attend lectures, concerts, etc. I have never been a social climber so I have never felt too left out of social affairs.

"The advantages of being a minister's wife are many. Just the position itself is very satisfying. People come to you for help and advice. It is a privilege to serve them. There is a great joy in being a friend, a very special sort of friend.

". . . There are times when a minister's wife's life is lonely. I have often said I would like to talk over my problems with a friend in the church. I have tried it at various times, but it really doesn't work."

Mrs. Cole said that more and more ministers' wives have been taking jobs outside the church, possibly because of financial need, but "I do not think that is the only reason. I have suspicion some are not too happy in their job as a minister's wife."

Regardless of the degree of success or of personal satisfaction, a manse marriage is unique. The minister's wife must learn to accept the fact that she often must tend the lawn and perform other household chores, give the children extra companionship to make up for the absence of their father and spend Sunday afternoons at home alone while her husband makes pastoral calls.

She has greater responsibilities than many other wives. Her shoulder must be available at all times for her husband to lean on, for there is no one else for him to turn to for support. And she has to accept the fact that she must share her husband with his calling.

For these reasons—and many others—a girl who is setting her cap for a minister would be well advised to take a long pause to think about it. She should ask herself: "Do you know what you are doing?" "Are you aware of the implications for the future?"

If her answers are yes, and if she really loves the minister of her choice, then she has a good chance for success in the manse.

7

Fundamentalists and Fundamentals

THE EAST-WEST ideological struggle has spared no one, not even ministers. Clergymen have been caught in the cold war crossfire, much to their sorrow and embarrassment.

As a result, the decade of the 1950's was a troubled one for the church, and a real crisis came in 1960, when the pulpit was shaken by charges of Communist infiltration and complaints that it was too worldly.

The Communist cry was raised by conservative clergymen whose fundamentalist creed was so outraged by the appearance of a new version of the Bible that they charged many of the illustrious scholars who prepared it and their sponsors with being under the Kremlin's influence.

This in turn engendered a renewal of the periodic debate over whether it is proper for a clergyman to discuss politics, economics and international affairs in his sermons. Should a minister try to relate his religion to what is going on in the world, or should he stick to the once traditional last—dissemination of the Gospel?

Few events have troubled the clergy in recent years quite so much as the publication of a United States Air Force Reserve training manual on subversive activities that included a charge of Communist infiltration of the National Council of Churches. As the largest cooperative church body in the United States, the Council represents 38 major Protestant and Orthodox groups, with a total membership of around 40 million, and lays claim to the limited participation of 40 other denominations, including two of the largest, the Missouri Lutheran Synod and the Southern Baptist Convention. Full members include the main branches of the Methodist and Presbyterian churches, three large Lutheran bodies, the Protestant Episcopal Church, four large Baptist bodies, the Greek Orthodox Church, two Quaker groups and the United Church of Christ (composed of the Congregational Christian and Evangelical and Reformed Churches).

The Council was not prepared when the Air Force manual was issued by the headquarters of the Continental Air Command at Mitchel Air Force Base, New York, on Jan. 4, 1960, carrying a declaration that "Communists and Communist fellow-travelers and sympathizers have successfully infiltrated our churches. . . . It is known that even the pastors of certain of our churches are card-carrying Communists!"

As supporting "evidence," the manual offered the following:

1. It said the National Council had sponsored the new Revised Standard Version of the Bible, with 30 of 95 persons who worked on the translation having been affiliated with Communist fronts and pro-Red projects and publications. No sources were given for most of this information.

2. It implied a link between the National Council and communism through two highly respected clergymen with long service to liberal causes—E. Stanley Jones, a noted missionary, author and "Methodist of the Year" in 1959, and Harry F. Ward, a militant anti-Fascist and veteran faculty member of Union Theological Seminary. No proof was given of any association between these two men and the Reds.

3. It reported that Herbert A. Philbrick, former undercover agent of the Federal Bureau of Investigation, said in a speech to the Daughters of the American Revolution in 1956 that ". . . there are more names of ministers than any other profession on the list of Communist supporters in this country. . . ."

The National Council did not learn of the manual until Feb. 10, more than a month after it was issued. James W. Wine, then the Council's associate general secretary for interpretation, immediately tried to reach the general who had authorized the manual. He was not available. Copies were obtained and the following day the Council sent letters of protest to Defense Secretary Thomas S. Gates Jr. and other officials.

That was on Feb. 11. Four days later no reply had been received, so the Council sent a personal emissary to Washington, but to no avail. Wine himself then went to Washington, only to learn that his letter was in the hands of subordinates; it had not reached Gates. On Feb. 17, Wine was invited to meet with Gates and the Air Force Secretary. At this meeting, Wine was told the manual had been ordered withdrawn. The public apologies came later.

In the meantime, denials of the manual's charge were issued by the score. One of the most forceful was that of J. Carter Swaim, executive director of the Department of the English Bible of the National Council. He found that the charges linking the Bible revisers with communism were based in part on faulty mathematics and a failure to read obituary notices.

By the time the Bible appeared in 1952, thirty-two scholars had worked on it. The total number of persons associated with the project, including administrators and advisory board members, one from each of 52 major denominations, was 91, not 95, Swaim pointed out. Of the 30 named by the "source" quoted in the manual, only 13 had been involved in the actual translating. Eleven of the 32, including five of the translators, were dead when the manual appeared.

Swaim said a pamphlet cited in the manual listed 90 subversive organizations receiving support or cooperation from Bible scholars. Of these, 72 were not on the Attorney General's list of such organizations. The persons said to belong to the remaining 18 either never had heard of them or had cooperated with them briefly "during that era in American life when Dwight David Eisenhower was writing to the Committee on Soviet-American Friendship that 'American-Soviet friendship is one of the cornerstones on which the edifice of peace should be built,'" Swaim said.

A person identified as "Dan Gilbert, Evangelist," published a pamphlet entitled "Debate Over the New Bible," charging that the Revised Standard Version was inspired by communism. His "opponent" in the supposedly transcribed debate was one "George R. Stevenson," who claimed to be associated closely with the Standard Bible Committee and to be familiar with its procedures.

"Stevenson" was quoted as saying the Bible translating committee had to include pro-Communists in order to "find favor with those of Communist convictions."

"In this new Bible we have a splendid blending of the Red viewpoint, the pink viewpoint and what I suppose should be called the 'white' or Christian viewpoint," the "Stevenson" argument went on. ". . . Of course, we must make some concessions to the Communists in order that they will make some concessions to us."

Swaim said the Bible committee never had a George R. Stevenson in its membership and knew of no such person. Ecclesiastical yearbooks and lists of scholars failed to disclose any individual with that name. Gilbert insisted many persons heard the debate as it later was published but Swaim said Gilbert could not recall where the debate was held, where Stevenson lived or the name of the institution where Stevenson was supposed to have been a professor.

Thomas Nelson & Sons, the publisher of the new Bible, offered a standing $500 reward to anyone who could identify "Professor Stevenson." No one stepped forward to claim the money, but the story of the debate continued to circulate and the Air Force manual of 1960 contained the charges of communism.

While some accusers may not have been willing to stand up and be counted, the defenders of the Council and its Bible were numerous. Among them was Dr. Truman B. Douglass, executive vice-president of the Board of Home Missions of the Congregational Christian Churches. He said his first reaction was "one of sheer terror at the stupidity of the performance." The adverse information used in the manual, he said, was drawn largely from the writings of "disgruntled and discredited persons" who attacked responsible church groups and leaders for having opinions on questions of national policy and social problems.

"What they really want is to silence the witness of the church on all social problems and issues . . . for the first action of every totalitarianism is to silence the churches and to prevent them from expressing any judgment on national and social affairs. In the assault upon liberty, religious liberty is always the first freedom to be lost."

Douglass characterized one of the instigators of the attack on the council as "an unfrocked Presbyterian minister, who has made a career out of attacking the National Council and the World Council of Churches."

The reference was to the Rev. Carl McIntire, dropped as a clergyman by the then Presbyterian Church in the U.S.A. in 1936 for defiance of church discipline and "disturbing the peace" of the church. He formed his own fundamentalist Bible Presbyterian Church in Collingswood, N.J., and in 1960 still was engaged in his 30-year-old fight against "modernistic heresies" of Protestantism. McIntire heads two organizations he founded, the American Council of Christian Churches and the International Council of Christian Churches. The American Council claims about 15 fundamentalist denominations with a total of about 1,500,000 members. Other estimates give these groups a total of as few as 225,000 members.

From his headquarters, McIntire has denounced the National Council and the World Council of Churches in statements, brochures and letters.

In its booklet of reply to the Air Force manual, the National Council charged that McIntire was one of a handful of hate-mongering "church destroyers" playing into the hands of the Communists by trying to link leading Protestants with the Reds. The Council named as its other principal attackers the following:

Myers G. Lowman of Cincinnati, Ohio, executive secretary of the Circuit Riders, Inc., and a public-relations agent. The Circuit Riders was formed to oppose "socialism and communism" in the Methodist Church. Lowman is a foe of the Revised Standard Version, which is used widely in Methodist churches, and he has published pamphlets aimed at proving that Protestant clergymen are Communist sympathizers. One of the pamphlets was used as basic source material for the Air Force manual's charges against the Bible translators.

Verne P. Kaub of Madison, Wis., organizer of the American

Council of Christian Laymen to fight Communism in churches and councils of churches and author of the pamphlet, "How Red Is the Federal Council of Churches?" He has had high praise for McIntire.

Edgar C. Bundy of Wheaton, Ill., general chairman of the Church League of America and a major in the Air Force Reserve, who lectures on the menace of communism "for pay, before women's clubs, American Legion posts, Rotary, Kiwanis, the Daughters of the American Revolution and other community organizations." He was a leading supporter of an American Legion statement condemning as "un-American" the omission of the Declaration of Independence from a Girl Scout Handbook. (The Girl Scouts explained that the omission was decided upon because their copy of the declaration was so small it was almost impossible to read without a magnifying glass.)

Billy James Hargis of Tulsa, Okla., president and publisher of Christian Echoes National Ministry, Inc., and Christian Crusade, both in Tulsa. As an outspoken supporter of charges that the National Council and Protestant clergymen were Communists or were soft on Communism, he wrote two pamphlets cited as source material for the Air Force manual. He has promoted the writings of Joseph P. Kamp, who once charged that "notorious un-American elements" were behind President Eisenhower before he went to the White House.

Publication of the National Council rebuttal brought an immediate demand from McIntire that the Council be dismantled and its leadership repudiated.

"We welcome this [attack]," he said. "They cannot meet the evidence of the Communist mischief in their own camp so they forget their 'brotherhood' and defame. Diversionary tactics never satisfy.

"At last the country can find out what the National Council of Churches has been doing to compromise and destroy the historic Christian faith and to soften us for Communist peaceful coexistence."

McIntire called for a "genuine reformation in the churches if we are to preserve historic Christianity. We are through with its [the Council's] propaganda for a one-world church and fraternization with the Communists who run the Iron Curtain churches," he said.

His reference here was to what he called "the greatest daylight robbery the Communists have staged in the churches"—their control of the Russian Orthodox Church. He said that Metropolitan Nikolai of the Russian Church, whom he called an "agent of the Soviet secret police," was an honored guest of the National Council in 1956.

Hargis charged that he had been the victim of a smear by the National Council. He said "the fantastically unbelievable smear attack . . . is typical of Communist technique. Rather than answer the charges they smear the accusers.

"Somewhere in this controversy the N.C.C. [National Council of Churches] is going to have to get around to either denying or explaining my authenticated charge of subversion in their ranks— smearing me is not enough. The American people are going to demand an answer to the charge."

This was Hargis' statement despite the fact the charges had been denied repeatedly by the church groups under attack.

Bundy added his cry of "smear." He said the National Council had been smearing him personally for years.

"Every statement which the National Council of Churches has made on these smear sheets is absolutely false," he said. "The National Council of Churches has not even been able to get my birthplace correct."

He complained that the Council refused to acknowledge that he had been made a major in the Air Force Reserve in 1956, but Council documents listing his background have included this fact.

Bundy said the Red charges he presented were based on "documentation which is available from the original sources, such as J. Edgar Hoover, Herbert A. Philbrick and . . . witnesses who have appeared before the Government committees."

Hoover, as director of the F.B.I., remained silent throughout the debate.

How a small coterie of fundamentalists representing only a fraction of all churchgoers was able to get its charges aired in an official Government publication never has been officially discussed. The manual attributed the accusations to a handful of men and gave no indication that the accused had been asked to present their side.

It received widespread publicity, and for a number of days the question of whether some of the most potent causes for religious good in the nation were getting their guidance from the Kremlin was front-page news. Immediate denials were voiced by the National Council and by individual denominations and leaders. Roman Catholics and Jews jumped to the defense of the Protestant groups.

The charges were nothing new. The Council has been subjected to periodic barrages since its founding in 1950. Its predecessor, the Federal Council of Churches, was attacked before that. What was new was the fact that the attack came in a Government publication. Also new was the decision by the Council to reply to its accusers instead of treating them as if they were not there, as had been the practice in the past. Wine said that the moment the first encroachment is threatened is the moment to put your foot down. There might not be a chance to do so later, as in the cases of Franco Spain and Nazi Germany, he said.

"This was the first instance in the history of the United States where the Government has encroached on churches and violated the First Amendment," Wine said.

After the manual appeared, he said, "pastors across the nation were scared to death. They did not dare to speak up in their pulpits for fear they might be tagged Communists."

Many of these clergymen looked to the National Council for guidance and support, and they got both. The organization mustered all the forces at its command. It launched a public-relations campaign in the press and on radio and television. It issued a manual of its own and sent it to churches and other groups as "ammunition" to fire back at the accusers. It demanded and received not only a formal apology from the Secretary of Defense but the withdrawal of the manual and assurances that such a thing never would happen again.

A Congressional hearing on the manual failed to turn up a single Red cell among the clergy or to silence the critics who saw a Communist behind every liberal pulpit in America, but Wine felt it reasonable to forecast that the beginning of the end had come for the sharpshooters.

"The Air Force manual incident was the last step in boldness of attack," he said. "There was no other place to go after it was fed into an agency of government. But now we have come to the end of an era and are on the threshold of a new era."

What he called the "old era" dawned at almost the moment the National Council was created out of the old Federal Council. The sniping began with the pamphlet entitled "How Red Is the Federal Council?" The word "Federal" was crossed out and "National" printed above it.

In 1953, several witnesses professing to have great knowledge of United States religious institutions testified before the House Un-American Activities Committee, triggering a new onslaught against the National Council. Bishop G. Bromley Oxnam, one of Methodism's foremost apostles of liberal causes, was a target. His name was cleared only after he had appeared before the committee to dispute charges that he had Red ties.

Then, in 1958, the National Council really got into hot water when its Department of International Affairs sponsored the Fifth World Order Study Conference in Cleveland, Ohio. The outcome of the conference was a long document addressed to the churches summarizing world conditions. One paragraph caused all the trouble. It recommended that steps be taken toward including Communist China in the United Nations and granting it official United States recognition, but carefully stipulated that "such recognition does not imply approval."

"We have strong hope that the resumption of relationships between the peoples of China and of the United States may make possible also a restoration of relationships between their churches and ours," the document added.

This brought a shower of criticism on the National Council, only part of it from its old foes, the fundamentalists. Others spoke up. One of the loudest protests came from J. Howard Pew, multi-millionaire Philadelphia oil man and president of the United Presbyterian Foundation, a church endowment organization, who immediately stepped up his campaign against clerical participation in world affairs. By 1960, Pew was claiming that many business-men had reduced their financial support of the Protestant churches because of the Red China action and other stands.

Pew and other conservatives felt the church was here to save souls, not society. The moderates and liberals retorted that the church was concerned with society because it was part of society and that, therefore, ministers had a duty to apply the Gospel to every phase of life.

There was dissension within the ranks of Protestantism about this to such a degree that the First Baptist Church of Wichita, Kans., the largest local church in the American Baptist Convention, withdrew from the denomination to protest against its continued affiliation with and support of the National Council. The Wichita Baptists regarded the Council as a breeding ground for modernists who viewed the Bible as a "myth" and denied the Virgin Birth.

Clergymen reported increasing economic pressures by Pew and others to try to convince them to stick to spiritual topics.

Eugene Carson Blake said a concerted effort had been made to silence the churches through economic pressures. Blake, in a speech at Colgate-Rochester Divinity School in 1960, said the church had a moral responsibility both to individuals and society.

"We live at a time when the big contests for power are among the state, business management and trade unions," he said. "The churches stand at the side, some silent and some under pressure to be silent, while statesmen, entrepreneurs and union officials all want the churches silent and irrelevant except when they may be exploited by one side or another of the contest for power."

He told of attempts to "tame and silence" churches from within by putting pressures, chiefly economic, on ministers and official boards.

"Some denominations in some cases are finding unofficial organized lay forces attempting to drive a wedge between ministers and people," Blake said. "Other denominations are facing attempts within official organizations to make it appear that the corporate church is incompetent to take moral positions in real issues in our social and international life."

The form the pressure takes is to refuse to discuss the issues themselves and then to attack the ecclesiastical leadership, he said.

"The threats are seldom explicit, but implied are threats to withhold financial support or to substitute more amenable leadership," he said. "The effect is to confuse the church as a whole and to weaken the church by the spread of mistrust."

Joining Blake in his complaint was the Rev. Dr. James E. Wagner, president of the Evangelical and Reformed Church and co-president of the United Church of Christ. In a letter to pastors he reported evidence of a "deliberate, calculated, organized and well-financed campaign to drive a wedge between lay men and women and their ministers." The Air Force manual was just one more example as far as he was concerned.

Ministers are far from being in agreement on the question of how far one should go in the pulpit in dealing with worldly affairs. Norman Vincent Peale discussed this very question in a sermon, saying that Protestantism had become "so broad that it is shallow."

"The vigorous old Gospel has become diluted with a curious blend of humanitarianism, socialism and every other nicey-nicey-ism to the end that it has lost its appeal to the people," he said.

"Leadership got the notion that the function of the ministers was to make a perfect world, with everything sweetness and light, everybody happy, everybody getting fine wages—everything just beautiful.

"The men who lead Protestantism are the finest men God ever made, but the movement has become so highly intellectualized that the assumption is that the salvation of mankind is through some political mechanism. Get a law through Congress and the Kingdom of God is on the way.

"The old, strong, narrow Protestantism that made the United States is a crying necessity today."

In an interview, Peale said that when he was a young man, many ministers decided to preach the social gospel—the idea was to "get everyone in a labor union and everything would be hunky-dory."

"They worked on that 25 to 30 years," he said. "Now there is more world, less Kingdom of God in evidence. Labor improved its status. That was good. But this wasn't the real essence of religion. It was a by-product. The real essence is that you believe and accept and live by Jesus Christ, Son of God, Saviour of mankind. You have to find identification. That is the old-time religion stated in modern terminology."

A course closer to the middle was taken by Lichtenberger as presiding officer of the Protestant Episcopal Church.

"The minister should relate the issues of the day to basic Christian convictions," he said. "The pulpit is not a forum for discussion of any sort of issues in themselves. But if related to the Christian Gospel, it is necessary to speak out on social, political and economic issues, always as illustrative materials. Sometimes this is difficult to do. Very few clergymen are competent to speak about technical details. It is not their job. They must be required to speak about broad moral issues."

This is an old debate. It did not begin with the publication of the Air Force manual and it did not end with the Government's apology for some of the material in it. Wherever ministers speak or gather, it is a topic for discussion, sometimes on bitter and sometimes on friendly terms. It is doubtful that it will ever be resolved, especially with such opposing viewpoints as those of Blake, who says the greatest problems in the world today are race prejudice and materialism, and McIntire, who replies that by accentuating such social issues Blake and his partisans are highballing along the high road to communism.

In the middle years of the 20th Century, the socially oriented clergymen appear to be in a majority. But in other times this has not been so and perhaps it will not be so again.

8

Facing the Issues

THE MODERN PULPIT is not limited to the church. It is wherever the minister is, and a minister is likely to turn up almost anywhere —walking in a picket line to protest slum housing, sitting on a lunch counter in a Southern ten-cent store to protest racial segregation or testifying before a Congressional investigating committee about pornographic literature in the mails.

Many church organizations maintain offices in Washington staffed with knowledgeable clergymen who serve as "spiritual lobbyists" in presenting religion's case to Congress and other government bodies. When the Republican and Democratic parties draw up platforms for Presidential campaigns, they include distinguished clergymen among those whose advice they seek on such matters as foreign aid and labor legislation, as well as on separation of church and state.

Religious organizations and their leaders have been taking stands on a wide variety of issues—segregation, gambling, reckless driving, drinking, sex and violence in movies and television, divorce, Federal aid to schools, foreign aid and birth control, to mention only a few.

POLITICS

The chorus of clerical comment was tuned to a high pitch during the 1960 Presidential campaign, when religion became a national political issue for the first time since 1928. It was the same issue—whether a Roman Catholic should be President. Brotherly love fell by the wayside when clergymen exchanged views, sometimes in bitter language, on the question of whether the White House might become a branch of the Vatican if a Catholic was in residence. Some clergymen strongly feared a Roman Catholic President would set back the Protestant cause. Others ruled out this view as unfounded. Still others simply took the stand that a man's religion had nothing to do with whether he should be President. An opinion was even expressed that the compromises required of the President precluded the presence of a deeply religious man in the White House.

Long before John F. Kennedy had won his fight for the Democratic nomination, the churches were beginning to take sides on the issue. One of the earliest participants in the debate was the Southern Baptist Convention, which made public the anti-Catholic views of a number of its members and leaders. Some pleaded separation of church and state. One said a Catholic in the White House would abolish the public school system.

Also, before Kennedy was nominated, two of the most liberal Protestant leaders in the country stated their views in a jointly prepared article for a national magazine. Eugene Carson Blake, as a Presbyterian, and G. Bromley Oxnam, as a Methodist, agreed that they were "uneasy" at the prospect that a Catholic might be President. They did not rule out voting for Kennedy; they simply said they were "uneasy" about him, solely on religious grounds.

After Kennedy's nomination, the bruhaha intensified. The most virulent anti-Catholic propaganda was disseminated in the names of laymen or non-religious organizations. Some church groups kept their mimeograph machines whirling away with tamer materials. Clergymen refrained generally from issuing hate literature, however, and softened their statements perceptibly after the interdenominational Fair Campaign Practices Committee headed by Charles P. Taft, brother of the late Senator Robert A. Taft, warned them their organizations might lose their special tax-exempt status if they persisted in disseminating political materials.

The clergy's role in the debate over a Catholic in the White House reached a climax with the issuance in Washington of a statement signed by 150 churchmen questioning whether Kennedy would be able to conduct the nation's foreign affairs independently of the Vatican if he were elected. One of the 150 signers was Norman Vincent Peale. He presided at one session of the meeting at which the statement was approved. And when it was over, he was the chief spokesman at a news conference at which the statement was made public and he commented on its contents to reporters.

That ended Peale's association with the group. He went off to a religious retreat in Washington, which was the main reason he was in the capital at that time; he said later that attending the conference was incidental. But that did not mean Peale had heard the last of the matter. Clergymen of less conservative political persuasion launched a broadside attack on the statement and its signers. They called the 150 signers "the Peale group" because of the prominent role the author of "The Power of Positive Thinking" had played in making the statement public.

The two sides in the religious debate were lined up generally according to their political persuasions, but there were some who planned to vote for Nixon and at the same time deplored the injection of religion into the political campaign. Nixon himself asked for a halt in the discussion.

Peale, disturbed by the criticism directed at him, disavowed any further association with the 150 or their statement. The day after the *Philadelphia Inquirer* canceled his weekly column as a protest against his role in the Washington meeting, he issued a statement of his own through the Hall Syndicate, which distributes his column, saying he had had nothing to do with the drafting of the Washington statement and would have nothing further to do with the organization that grew out of the original meeting. In a sermon at Marble Collegiate Church, where he had been minister for 29 years, Peale said he had acted unwisely and asked for the prayers of his 4,000-member congregation. This was after church officials had refused his offer to resign from his pulpit, and after he had sent letters to all the members of the church explaining what had happened and expressing regret over his participation in the conference.

Those around Peale were convinced he had been wronged, by the press and his critics, despite the fact that his public pronouncements had expressed his own feeling that he had acted unwisely and was sorry. There was an indication that the good name of Norman Vincent Peale may have been put to priceless publicity use by some of the leaders of the 150, but Peale gave no indication whether he was aware of that possibility.

The debate between Peale and such an eminent clergyman as Dr. Reinhold Niebuhr, the voice of liberal Protestantism, lasted only a few days, but its effects may have been enduring. One factor that should be considered in any judgment of the controversy is that those who criticized Peale in this connection have criticized him through the years for much of what he has said and done. It would be interesting to know what proportion of the unfavorable response to Peale's participation in the meeting of the 150 was associated directly with the Presidential campaign and what part with the perennial attacks on him.

How much the raising of the Catholic issue had to do with the closeness of the election may be difficult to determine. But it did bring the pulpit actively into politics as never before. It also intensified long-time personal and political frictions between a number of men of the cloth. One of the final barbs was delivered by the Rev. Dr. Daniel A. Poling, editor of the *Christian Herald*, a signer of the Washington statement and a close friend of Peale's. He said that on some matters, principally on the subject of whether Communist China should be in the United Nations, he felt closer to the Catholics than he did to his fellow Protestants, Niebuhr and the Rev. Dr. John C. Bennett, dean of the faculty of Union Theological Seminary.

BIRTH CONTROL

Catholics and Protestants are divided sharply on the issue of birth control. To the Protestants, the population explosion is one of the world's biggest problems, with the solution lying mainly in a reduction in births. The Catholics acknowledge the problem, but say there are other ways to cope with it; science, they say, will find a way to feed the increasing number of mouths in the world.

Aside from the Orthodox Jews, who favor contraception only

for reasons of health, the Jews are lined up almost solidly with the Protestants on "family planning."

Without a persistent and outspoken campaign of the Protestant Council of the City of New York and the American Jewish Congress, a ban on the provision of contraceptive information in New York City municipal hospitals probably would have remained in force. The controversy began when a tax-supported hospital denied a contraceptive to an impoverished diabetic mother whose life would have been imperiled by another pregnancy. Word of the refusal was made public, stirring a barrage of statements, letters to editors, meetings and speeches by rabbis and ministers, all demanding that the woman receive the medical aid she needed.

The campaign ended in a victory for the Protestants and Jews, but without jeopardizing the stand of the Catholics, who vigorously opposed the final verdict. Non-Catholics who seek contraceptive advice and devices now may receive them in hospitals supported by tax money, so long as their health would be jeopardized by pregnancy and if they *ask* for help. The city assured Catholics they need not be affected one way or another by the decision.

A sharper dispute arose after the Roman Catholic Bishops of the United States issued a statement opposing the use of public funds to stem the world population explosion. President Eisenhower, asked at a news conference to comment on the statement, said he did not think the provision of funds for birth control advice or equipment was a proper area for foreign aid.

This set off a cross-country debate. Vice-President Nixon said he favored provision of knowledge about birth control to nations desiring to limit their population growth. The Unitarians praised Nixon's stand, and Bishop Pike proposed a "crash" program to perfect the rhythm method, approved by the Catholic Church, to limit the population. Pike, a former Roman Catholic, later was named head of a clergymen's national advisory committee to the Planned Parenthood Federation of America. It was made up of major Protestant and Jewish denominations and was asked to devote its energies to encouraging a better working relationship between the birth control movement and religious organizations.

Mrs. Ernest T. Hoeldtke, president of the United Presbyterian

Women, sent a letter to Senator J. W. Fulbright, chairman of the Senate Foreign Relations Committee, and Representative Thomas E. Morgan, chairman of the House Foreign Affairs Committee, stating the Presbyterian view that women have a right to determine how many children they will bear and rear. She said it was unethical to refuse birth control assistance to mothers who ask for it.

"To preclude the use of welfare funds by others for planned parenthood purposes is an unwarranted meddling in the personal lives and the societies of others," she said.

The Rev. Edwin T. Dahlberg, speaking as a Baptist as well as head of the National Council of Churches, took the Eisenhower viewpoint. He said birth control was a religious question and was not properly a concern of politics or government. Archbishop Iakovos, head of the Greek Orthodox Church of North and South America, sided with Dahlberg and the Roman Catholics and charged that the issue had been handled "like a football," even by clergymen.

Msgr. Irving A. deBlanc, director of the National Catholic Family Life Bureau, confused the issue somewhat by injecting into the debate the disclosure that Roman Catholic married couples seemed to be using contraceptives in about the same measure as Protestants and Jews. He said some Catholics are influenced more by their neighbors than by the Church.

While the debate raged over whether Indians, Africans and other national groups were to be given birth control information along with more conventional foreign aid, some Protestant denominations quietly went on with what they had been doing all along—providing medical missionaries with whatever birth control supplies and leaflets they could afford for distribution to persons who wanted them.

The Congregational Christian Churches have participated for several years in a Planned Parenthood experimental program in Puerto Rico, for example. In their Ryder Hospital on the island, the Congregationalists administered a new contraceptive pill to enough Puerto Rican women for the Planned Parenthood organization to decide it was an effective weapon against the population explosion.

SEGREGATION

Segregation is an often embarrassing as well as explosive issue in the churches. The effectiveness of the Christian Gospel may stand or fall on this issue, in fact. The Protestants, Catholics and Jews have come closer to unanimity on this question than they have on other issues. Nationally, there is scarcely a denomination that has not declared itself against racial discrimination. On the local level, the story is different, however. The individual churches follow local customs and prejudices in the main, regardless of what their denominational officials advise.

Denominations that split in the Civil War still have not healed their wounds. The Methodists got back together, but continue to have many segregated churches. The Northern and Southern Baptists remain on opposite sides of the Mason-Dixon Line on this matter.

The Right Rev. Charles C. J. Carpenter, Bishop of the Protestant Episcopal Diocese of Alabama, asked the National Council of Churches to repudiate a statement by two Council units expressing sympathy for sit-in demonstrations at lunch counters in segregated Southern chain stores, despite the fact that the National Episcopal Council stood fully for desegregation and employed many Negroes in its offices.

During the Little Rock, Ark., controversy over school integration, the Rev. Wesley Pruden of Broadmoor Baptist Church, an affiliate of the Southern Baptist Convention, called integration "a Communist conspiracy to destroy our segregated society and mongrelize the white race." Moderates in his church left and started a new congregation, the University Baptist Church, next door, to offer "a Southern Baptist church with a Southern Baptist program." The Pulaski County Baptist Association ousted Broadmoor from membership and voted in the University Church. Broadmoor still had a right to belong to the State and National Conventions, however.

The Southern Baptist racial policy appears to be "separate-but-equal." The denomination's Home Missions Board and the Department of Research and Statistics of the Sunday School Board found that one out of every four Southern Baptist churches was "co-operating" with a Negro Baptist church in some activity—vacation Bible school aid, scholarships, pulpit exchanges, construction of Negro churches, simultaneous revivals or sending Negro boys and girls to summer camp.

This was not exactly integration, but the Southern Baptists said they were spending $3,500,000 a year and employing nearly 400 full-time workers to help Negro churches.

When Billy Graham, a Southern Baptist, arrived in New York from his "Crusade to Africa," he said he was convinced that segregation would not work there, but he declined to comment on racial problems in the United States beyond telling Yankee news-men, "I don't think Southerners appreciate people sitting in New York and pointing the finger at them."

The Congregational Christian Churches, an avowedly liberal integrationist denomination at the national level, found to its chagrin that only 12 per cent of a cross-section of big-city members reached in a survey accepted Negro members freely on an equal basis and only 49 per cent were willing to do so. This prompted an intensification of a campaign to win acceptance of Negroes.

One of the most distressing findings, as far as the Congrega-tionalist officials were concerned, was an indication that members were more willing to accept desegregation in other activities than in church.

"Surely there is cause for disquietude in the very indication that church people are more willing to accept a desegregated society than a desegregated church," Truman Douglass declared.

The survey also indicated that the Southern pattern of racial discrimination may exist in the Midwest and the West as well.

National offices of a number of denominations employ white and colored staff members on an equal basis. In addition to the Epis-copalians, these include the American Baptist Convention, The Methodist Church, the United Church of Christ and the United Presbyterians, U.S.A. The National Council of Churches also adheres to a policy of strict racial equality.

At the 1960 General Conference of The Methodist Church—a meeting held once every four years—delegates approved a special report acknowledging the denomination's failure to live up to its own racial principles. The conference voted to retain the all-Negro Central Jurisdiction, formed in 1939 when the Northern and Southern branches of Methodism were reunited, but approved machinery for its eventual abolition. This was a compromise reached after the Southern delegates indicated they might secede, as they did before the Civil War.

"The failure of our church to live up to its own pronouncements is a fault that must be shared by every section of the church," the report approved by the conference said. "Our failure to achieve the aims of Christian brotherhood is grievous since Methodism is a world church."

Nationally, The Methodist Church is desegregated. It supports 12 theological schools, one all-Negro, nine integrated and two segregated—the Duke University Divinity School and the Candler School of Theology at Emory University, Atlanta.

Divinity school students formed the nucleus around which the successful sit-in demonstrations were organized to end segregation at stores operated by F. W. Woolworth and other chains in the South. The dean of the Vanderbilt University Divinity School and 11 faculty members resigned when a Negro seminarian was expelled for participating in the sit-ins. Their withdrawal brought a statement by the University's Chancellor, Harvie Branscomb, that racial progress must be based on obedience to the law.

"Not so," responded the United Presbyterian Church in the U.S.A. It stated that "some laws and customs requiring racial discrimination" are "such serious violations of the law of God as to justify peaceable and orderly disobedience."

The National Catholic Conference for Interracial Justice also endorsed the lunch counter sit-ins and other peaceful protests against segregation. The National Conference of the Methodist Student Movement offered its support and the United Church of Christ volunteered financial aid to any student expelled from a school for participating in the demonstrations.

The sit-ins were followed by other demonstrations along the same lines. Small groups of Negro college students launched "kneel-in" protests in white Protestant churches in Atlanta by attending Sunday services usually restricted to white persons. A "swim-in" attempted by 10 white and Negro college students was thwarted, however, when they were turned away from the Southeastern Methodist Assembly Swimming Pool in Lake Junaluska, N.C.

The Presbyterian Church in the U.S. (South) was the first denomination to go on record in support of the Supreme Court desegregation ruling in 1954, but most of its churches still are segregated. All of the denomination's seminaries are integrated, however, and the national organization of the church draws no color lines. There are separate Negro congregations in nearly all the presbyteries except in the five "Deep South" states, but the synods in those states are integrated.

"The Assembly cannot coerce in this area of life," a denominational spokesman said. "It simply recommends and waits for the pressure of conscientious conviction to make its effect."

Positive action has been taken in some places, one of them New Orleans, where Archbishop Joseph Rummell of the Roman Catholic Church set a day of prayer for integration of public schools. The American Baptist Home Mission Societies took the stand that wherever segregation appears, "there is a denial of Christian love and justice and of the democratic rights of citizens." The Roman Catholic Bishops of the U.S. have called for the ending of all segregation. The Council of Bishops of the Methodist Church has unanimously supported the Supreme Court order.

In Raleigh, N.C., an Episcopal society for cultural and racial unity was formed by an interracial group of 100 clergymen from North and South. In Atlanta, clergymen issued a "manifesto" urging the use of reason and obedience to law in race relations. It was signed by 311 clergymen of 16 denominations, including both rabbis and ministers. Catholic priests and some Jewish leaders had taken a similar stand previously. All rejected any suggestion that churches be used for schools as a means of getting around the integration order, but they doubted the wisdom of massive integration, calling instead for gradual steps in that direction.

E. Stanley Jones paid high tribute to the Atlanta Manifesto, saying: "The diehards will die hard, and they will die expensively, but they will die. I believe that when history is written it will be recorded that the turning of the tide began in Atlanta, when 300 ministers signed a manifesto saying that Negroes should have equal rights."

The Rev. Dr. Herman L. Turner, "father" of the Atlanta Manifesto and champion of interracial brotherhood, was elected moderator of the United Presbyterian Church in the U.S.A. The Rev. Dr. Edler Hawkins, a New York Negro minister, was named vice-moderator after narrowly losing the top post to Turner.

The Rev. Dr. James J. Thomas, also of New York, became the first Negro to be elected president of the governing body of the Dutch Reformed Church in America. He also was the first member of his race to be ordained in the denomination, which dates from 1628.

The churches point with pride at such a development, but they have reason much of the time to hang their heads in shame. No denomination could stand more strongly for integration than the American Baptists, and yet only a third of their churches are integrated. The parishioners of a once-fashionable Lutheran church in New York engaged in a controversy when Puerto Ricans began attending Sunday services. Traditionally, the entire congregation had shared the same large cup at communion. Many of the old-line members balked at drinking from the same vessel as a Puerto Rican. The solution to the problem came with great difficulty— the purchase of tiny individual communion cups.

A willingness to share the same religion but not the same pew has put Christianity in an anomalous position around the world. Millions of dollars a year are spent by the major denominations to convert persons of other races to Christianity in foreign lands, but many of the contributors of these funds would balk at accepting these new Christians as fellow church members. Officials of the denominations are distressed over the fact that so many professed Christians do not practice what their religion preaches.

DIVORCE

Another church concern in which the division is largely Catholic vs. Protestant and Jew is divorce. Just as vexing as divorce itself are the problems of what steps to take to try to prevent it and what course to take when a divorced person seeks to marry again.

The Methodist Church voted in 1960 to relax a policy dating back to 1884 under which remarriage was allowed only for "innocent persons" in cases of "adultery" and was amended later to include "other vicious conditions." The new policy leaves the decision largely to individual ministers.

The Southern Presbyterians have relaxed their former rule that adultery and willful desertion can be the only allowable grounds for divorce. Under the new policy, individual churches are asked to do all in their power to prevent separation and divorce through counseling. But both physical and spiritual unfaithfulness are accepted as grounds for divorce. Remarriage is sanctioned by the church if the minister approves. He may call on a committee of advisers for guidance or refer complicated cases to a presbytery committee. He is required, however, to counsel couples and accept separation or divorce only when he is convinced it is a last resort.

The United Lutheran and American Lutheran Churches also have relaxed former policies of approving remarriage of a divorced person only if he is the victim of adultery or desertion. Now either party may remarry after giving evidence of repentance.

The American Baptist Convention has no rules against remarriage after divorce, but ministers have been asked to conduct regular courses on marriage preparation and to become acquainted with marriage counseling agencies to which they can refer couples.

Divorce and remarriage have the approval of the United Presbyterian Church in the U.S.A. when "sufficient penitence for sin and failure is evident, and a firm purpose and endeavor after Christian marriage is manifest." It is the denomination's policy for its ministers to shoulder the responsibility of determining whether there is penitence. It also believes that a minister should require one year to pass before remarrying a divorced person, except with the approval of a presbytery or authorized representative. Each presbytery may elect a committee on Christian marriage to advise ministers.

Unitarians hold that everyone should be free to follow the dictates of his conscience in matters of marriage and divorce. The Southern Baptist Convention allows each minister to decide for himself how to handle marital problems of his flock. Officials of the Congregational Christian Churches say that divorce is deplorable but often necessary. Counseling is their only remedy.

The Protestant Episcopal Church is opposed to remarriage after divorce, but Bishops are allowed to grant ecclesiastical annulments. The House of Bishops is working on new marriage canons and may act on them in a few years.

Churches generally are taking a more lenient view toward divorce and remarriage. They have accepted the fact that opposition to divorce and bans on remarriage of divorced persons did not cut the divorce rate and have turned their attention to preventive measures. Many clergymen hope to obviate wrong marriages through the counseling of engaged couples. Others work with miserable married couples in an effort to help them solve their problems. But there is a general willingness in the new-time religion to accept the fact that people do make mistakes sometimes and that there is no reason to read them out of the church for their errors.

ALCOHOL

Demon rum is a traditional subject for church concern, with the Baptists and Methodists the most outspoken foes of drink. The Methodists, who spearheaded the fight for passage of the Eighteenth Amendment, have changed their approach, however, from one of outright and indignant opposition to one of trying to deal with alcohol as a psychological and physical problem as well as a social issue.

A new Methodist department called the Division of Temperance and General Welfare was formed to replace the old Boards of Temperance, World Peace and Social and Economic Relations. This single department now copes with drinking, smoking, narcotics, gambling, pornography, juvenile delinquency and crime, the penal system, rehabilitation of criminals, mental health, planned parenthood, traffic safety, problems of the aged and other social issues. The lumping of alcohol with this hodgepodge of problems is a reflection of what is called "The New Concern" of Methodism over social matters on a broad spectrum.

All member churches have been called upon to attack alcoholism on a wide front, through pastoral care, education, clinics and co-operation with other groups dealing with the problem. Many Methodist churches now have chapters of Alcoholics Anonymous, an organization they frowned on a generation ago.

The entire approach is sharply different from that of 15 or 25 years ago, when the town drunk was ousted from the church as a pariah. Now the Methodists invite the alcoholic in and offer to help him solve his personal problems as a first step toward discouraging the consumption of liquor.

The "new look at alcoholism" program was adopted as the result of a study showing that the old Temperance Board's approach was out of step with the times. Until recently, the Temperance Board, founded in 1810, had concentrated on legislation outlawing liquor. Whole sermons were devoted to John Barleycorn. The drunkard was viewed as a man seized with demons.

Now, legislation banning liquor is last on the list in the Methodist temperance campaign, ranking after education, vows of total abstinence and rehabilitation. The Methodist Church spent a fortune winning Prohibition only to see it go down the drain along with bathtub gin. Now it spends more money every year on the rehabilitation of drunks than on any other phase of its anti-liquor campaign. The church has come to believe that if Prohibition returned tomorrow, it would not halt drinking any more effectively than it did in the 1920's. The view now is that until education can bring about a universal desire for Prohibition, there should not be a return to it.

GAMBLING

The handmaiden of drinking, in the minds of many Protestants, is gambling. One leader of the fight against games of chance is the Protestant Council of New York, which has waged a tireless campaign against a proposal for legalizing off-track betting and taxing its proceeds in order to eliminate bookmakers and increase city revenues. The Protestants say such an arrangement would be a social and moral evil, through which a "virulent parasite" would aid government prosperity.

The Council was successful in this area but lost a battle against legalized bingo. The Catholics, who conduct bingo in many of their churches, remained silent while the game was made legal. In the two years after the favorite indoor sport of many a housewife was approved in New York State, the institutions sponsoring the game made a $5,000,000 profit, the prizes totaled $15,000,000 and the taxes came to $336,820.

Among those opposing the use of games of chance in church is the Luther League of America, which has criticized raffles and similar money-making methods often used at church socials.

The Rev. C. B. Studstill preached against gambling and "clip joints" in his Darien, Ga., pulpit too effectively to suit the gamblers. Five rifle bullets were fired into his parsonage bedroom and the occupants of a speeding auto shot at him and his wife. No one was hurt and Studstill was not deterred.

"I'll keep on preaching along the same lines," he declared.

Sunday Laws

When is the Sabbath? Can it be Saturday for Jews and others and Sunday for Christians? These are the questions that arise in the blue law controversy.

Robert E. Huldschiner, assistant editor of *The Lutheran,* a magazine published by The United Lutheran Church in America, has said the controversy is being fought mainly by business rivals who are more concerned about economic than religious factors. The issue, he said, is how to keep out-of-town chain stores from moving in and being so competitive that local merchants must work seven days a week to stay in business.

Most Sunday closing laws are archaic, he said, calling for a modern law providing for one day of rest for all. Since Christians are in a majority and Sunday is their traditional day off, he reasoned, it should be the universal day of rest.

The Seventh Day Adventists, Seventh Day Baptists and Jews observe Saturday as the Sabbath. Leaders among them regard Protestant demands for a universal Sunday Sabbath as Puritanical. In the days of the Puritans, those who failed to observe Sunday as a day of rest were punished. Opponents of the universal Sunday Sabbath say it is a violation of religious freedom.

The Catholics want Sunday closings and have conducted a nationwide campaign for the signing of pledges by individuals promising not to do any unnecessary buying, selling or shopping on Sunday. Thirty-five states have laws curtailing work and business on Sunday. Suits brought in five of them are pending before the United States Supreme Court.

These are just a few of the issues in which individuals, churches, denominations and entire religious communities are concerned. Some have involved sharp divisions and ill-feeling; others mark steps toward greater understanding. There are many other issues involving clerical opinions—foreign aid, swearing on television, sex in movies, capital punishment, just to name a few. Some clergymen are worried more about the role of space exploration in religion than about any of the many earthly problems. The question has even been raised by a Vatican scholar of whether men who may live on the moon might be without Original Sin.

Name the issue and there will be a clergyman to voice an opinion on it. He may use Biblical references in what he has to say, but they will be pertinent. And he will speak up, no matter where he may be, on any day of the week, not just on Sunday. Something else new has been added: the minister's words are not always accepted as gospel. Members of his congregation and of other churches or no church at all feel free to debate with him if they think he is wrong. This can be a stimulant to a clergyman's thinking—if he listens.

9

The Church in the Marketplace

JESUS ROUTED the money changers from religious temples 2,000 years ago. Now the churches are active in the temples of finance. Religion has gone to Wall Street—not for converts, however, but for cash.

There is scarcely a religious organization of any size that has not shared handsomely in the nation's post-war prosperity through investments in stocks, bonds, mortgages and real estate or through actively engaging in the insurance business.

Bingo, raffles and bazaars have become just a drop in the collection plate, for vestried interests in blue-chip securities, some bought, some bequeathed, continue to reap tax-free dividend incomes and there are no worries about capital gains. The clerical investors have another advantage over others: they have the voluntary services of some of the best brains in the world of the bulls and the bears. One reason New York City is a national capital of religion is the desire of church money managers to be near Wall Street and the best possible investment advice.

Nearly every major Protestant denomination has at least one affiliated insurance company or fund that sells annuities or life-insurance policies to ministers and congregations in direct competition with commercial concerns. The income from these activities is used for pensions, church building, education, missionary projects and other denominational work.

Active advertising campaigns are conducted in behalf of the insurance programs. There also is considerable advertising appealing to members to "remember the church in your will" as a "dividend for eternity."

Along with prosperity has come the natural desire to keep it. Some large local churches have hired business managers or professional fund raisers to help fulfill this wish. Increasing wealth also has brought an increasing concern over it. Security measures are receiving more attention from church leaders. Safes and burglar alarms have been installed in some churches and more and more persons who handle money are being bonded.

The American Association of Fund-Raising Counsel reported that religious property and endowment in the United States had reached a total value of $14.6 billion in 1958. That covered all holdings, including commercial real estate, securities and institutional properties ranging from camps to cathedrals. The total figure was $1.2 billion in 1906, when there were about 35 million church members. In 1958, churches and synagogues claimed 109 million members.

It is estimated that 50 per cent of the total philanthropic giving in the United States goes to religion. One per cent of all disposable income is given to churches and synagogues.

In its annual report on stewardship, the National Council of Churches said late in 1960 that contributions had risen slightly in 1959, but hardly enough to keep pace with the expanding economy. A slight slackening in generosity was attributed to a delayed reaction to the 1957-58 recession; it usually takes at least a year for a general economic trend to be reflected in philanthropy.

Merely to keep pace with both inflation and membership rises, giving to religious organization must increase 5 per cent a year. To manifest a genuine increase in generosity, it therefore must go up more than 5 per cent. The rate dropped to 4.6 per cent in the most recent figures, failing even to meet church expenses, which increased 6.6 per cent.

This result covered only the 35 denominations that National Council of Churches statisticians determined had comparable figures in two consecutive years. The total Council computation covered 49 denominations, but their statistics represented such a wide variety of fiscal years and such a jumble of accounting methods that even electronic brains could not straighten them out. The

Methodist Church, the largest single Protestant body, was not included in the comparison table of the 35, for example, because it had changed accountants and methods of computation. It was the only major Protestant body omitted from this list.

The grand total of donations compiled for 49 groups, including the Methodists, reached a record of $2,407,464,641 in the computations announced in 1960. This surpassed the figure for 49 denominations the previous year by less than $100,000,000. But they were a different 49, so the significance of this figure is doubtful.

Only a partial picture of national religious giving can be presented by the Council because the Catholics and Jews do not participate in the annual study. Neither do they make their own financial figures public.

As usual, the National Council reported that the average weekly contribution of the individual churchgoer in 1959 was less than the price of a first-run movie. And also, as usual, the most generous churchgoers were members of the smaller denominations or sects, while the Methodists were near the bottom of the list of per capita offerings.

The average individual gift among the 10 million Methodists was only a few pennies more than a dollar a week. The average for the 37,213,981 members of the 49 denominations was nearly $65 for the year.

The highest per capita giving in 1959 was reported by the Free Methodist Church, with 55,000 members donating an average of $269.71 each. The Free Methodists were the most generous in the preceding year, too, with an average of $243.95 each. Others at the top of the list included the Wesleyan Methodists, with $228.13; the Evangelical Free Church of America, with $203.54; the Pilgrim Holiness Church, with $200.48, and the Brethren in Christ, with $168.31.

The largest denomination in the top 20 was the Reformed Church in America (Dutch Reformed), with an average of $103.23. All the other main-line bodies, the Southern Presbyterians, Lutherans, Baptists, Episcopalians, Congregationalists, United Presbyterians in the U.S.A. and the rest, were also-rans, falling below the $100 per capita mark.

In its discussion of the 35 churches whose figures it found comparable with those of the preceding year, the National Council said that they represented 24,813,702 persons who gave a total of $1,715,505,635. This was an average of $69.13 per member, a gain over 1958 of $3.03, or 4.6 per cent.

Officials of the Pilgrim Holiness sect, which consistently ranks either at the top of the list or among the first five, credited tithing for their church's full collection plates.

"Perhaps another reason why our church ranks high in the statistics of church giving is because we hold more strictly to our membership requirements," a spokesman said, "and a much larger per cent of our membership is active in the church because of this."

The Mormons—Church of Jesus Christ of Latter-Day Saints— also are prosperous, and have strict membership requirements. A person must undergo rigid training and study before he is accepted. Once a member, he tithes with his whole life—both time and money.

The subject of Mormons and their tithing has been financial-page news. George Romney, president of American Motors, a Mormon and a tither, sold 10,000 shares of his company's stock, after which the market price dropped. This caused such a stir on Wall Street that Romney called a news conference to explain that he had sold the stock for $900,000 to meet several financial obligations, including his tithe. After taxes, the 10 per cent for the church and other considerations, he said, there was $500,000 left.

The economic uncertainties involved in relying on gifts is a principal reason for large and diversified church investment portfolios. Religious bodies could not otherwise guarantee ministers and missionaries pensions after years of hard and often sacrificial work; they could not construct new churches, hospitals, schools or homes for the aged, and they could not support much of the work of the church. Officials of religious organizations therefore feel it would be foolish not to reap the largest possible profit for the greatest possible good by investing funds in reputable fields almost certain to provide greater income than a savings account.

Big church investments on Wall Street began when wealthy parishioners started donating and bequeathing large sums of money, real estate and securities for religious purposes. Such tax-deductible benefactions are responsible in large part for church prosperity today, and the religious recipients enjoy a tax-free status. The possibility has been posed by Eugene Carson Blake that the day may come when the churches, if they operate prudently under present laws, may own most of the property of this country. He suggested that it might be time for churches to consider making voluntary contributions to local, state and federal governments to pay for the services they now receive free.

The past generosities of wealthy parishioners have left some of the most sparsely attended big-city churches among the wealthiest.

One of these once-great churches is Grace Episcopal, which stands majestically at the head of New York City's Bowery. Its membership list formerly read like a high-society Who's Who; now Bowery bums stumble in looking for a place to rest. Yet this is a rich church, financially. In searching for something constructive to do with its wealth, it established a school that now rates as one of the finest private institutions in the country.

The largest proportion of church-associated investments help pay the pensions of retired ministers and other church workers and support missionary work. Thanks to the booming national economy, a retired Protestant Episcopal rector in Dubuque had his pension increased 20 per cent and a Lutheran missionary in Liberia was presented with a new $16,000 airplane to use in his work.

Church investment activities have been so brisk that 24 groups have banded together to hold an annual Church Pensions Conference. The members include most of the major Protestant denominations of the United States and Canada and the YMCA and YWCA. The participants reported at the end of 1960 total assets of more than $867,000,000 and payment of nearly $45,000,000 a year to some 50,000 pensioners. That meant the average pension was about $900 a year.

The largest of the individual pension funds, with assets of nearly $128,000,000, was reported by the United Presbyterian Church in the U.S.A. The Methodist Church was second, with more than $112,000,000.

"We are sharing in the nation's prosperity," said William F. Treiber, a vice-president of the Federal Reserve Bank of New

York and one of the chief investment advisers to the Congregational Christian Churches. "A good common stock is a good investment."

Treiber, president of the annuity fund for Congregational ministers and of the denomination's retirement fund for lay workers, sits on church boards that include bank vice-presidents, a former investment banker, an insurance company executive and a minister. If they charged for their services, the bill would run well into the thousands of dollars a year to oversee the management of more than $80,000,000 in assets.

Investment banking and brokerage houses vie for the privilege of handling church securities business. Church officials attend weekly briefings at which company representatives discuss investment possibilities. The thought in most cases is of long-term investments rather than of making quick speculative profits.

The Morgan Guaranty Trust Company has two big church "clients." It advises the Protestant Episcopal Church on when to buy and sell. It also serves as one of The Methodist Church's chief investment counselors, with the aid of a church investment committee made up of the president of the Prudential Life Insurance Company, several bank vice-presidents and the treasurer of the Ford Motor Company.

The Southern Baptist Home Mission's Board recruited several prominent Southern financial leaders to advise it on church loans. Among them are Wallace O. Duvall, president of the United States Savings and Loan League and of the Atlanta Federal Savings and Loan Association; Ben H. Wooten, chairman of the board of the First National Bank of Dallas, and Frank P. Samford, chairman of the board of the Liberty National Life Insurance Company of Birmingham.

Some church groups have taboos against investing in any company associated with the alcohol or tobacco industries. The Presbyterian Church in the U.S. (South) voted, however, to reject a moral argument for selling its tobacco stocks. The vote to keep the shares was considered by delegates to the denomination's annual convention to be based solely on financial considerations. It was argued by the Rev. A. V. Gibson, pastor of Atlanta Morningside Presbyterian Church, that "if we wanted to dispose of it (the stock) as a moral issue, the only right thing to do would be to burn it."

The Methodists, Baptists and United Presbyterians in the U.S.A. spurn tobacco or alcohol holdings. So concerned over the issue are the Baptists that they shy from the idea of commercial television for religious programs for fear a beer company might buy time just before or after a spiritual offering.

"We probably would not invest in a company that makes dice tables or invests in Hialeah, either," said Ashton A. Almand, Associate Treasurer of the Methodist Division of World Missions. "I'm not sure we would take any Graham-Paige stock now that they own Madison Square Garden."

Churches holding real estate try to avoid acquisition of undesirable or substandard buildings, but quite a few pieces of property have turned out to be slum dwellings. At the other end of the scale, the Episcopalians' Trinity Church at the head of Wall Street owns some of lower Manhattan's most valuable real estate and the Baptists own the Hotel Salisbury, a New York City hotel on 57th Street, in the heart of the shopping district. It is run just as any commercial establishment except that there is no cocktail lounge. The hotel towers over the sanctuary of the Calvary Baptist Church. They have separate entrances but share the same building.

The student sit-in demonstrations against racial segregation at lunch counters in F. W. Woolworth stores in the South caused concern to members of some denominations owning Woolworth stock. A group of New York Presbyterians urged the United Presbyterian Church in the U.S.A. to sell its shares as a protest against the chain's southern practices. The United Lutheran Church in America considered similar action. Before either could make a final decision, the situation was eased considerably, with Woolworth's and other large chains announcing that many of their southern stores had opened lunch counters to Negroes as well as whites.

Methodist investments totaling around $85,000,000 include railway and public utility bonds, stocks in General Motors, General Electric, Shell Oil, Continental Can, Douglas Aircraft, American Airlines and the Scott Paper Company. The Methodists also have established an investment fund to grant loans for church buildings, because existing commercial sources could not meet the demand for a $100,000,000-a-year program.

The Protestant Episcopal Diocese of Michigan drew the attention of the magazine *Business Week* for its use of modern business methods. The Diocese established financial districts, named a layman to serve as the diocesan planning director and streamlined administrative procedures.

Robert Worthington, executive vice-president of the Protestant Episcopal Church pension fund and a long-time J. P. Morgan executive, said annual increases in the fund's investment income have played an important role in raising pensions to their present levels.

Malcolm Carey, assistant treasurer of the American Baptist Convention's Ministers and Missionaries Benefit Board, said economic conditions had made it necessary for churches to rely more heavily on equity investments to preserve, to some extent at least, the purchasing power of their dollars.

The Baptist board got its big impetus on Sept. 24, 1919, when John D. Rockefeller Sr. gave the denomination securities worth more than $2,000,000. His gifts finally formed a base of nearly $7,000,000, which the board has built to around $92,000,000.

The board has had the advice of a finance committee of Wall Street experts that has included a partner in Kuhn, Loeb and Company, a partner in Price, Waterhouse and Company, a former board chairman of one large bank and a vice-president of another.

Lumber also is a source of wealth to the American Baptist Convention, thanks to the generosity of Truman Doud Collins and his son and grandson, who endowed the denomination's missionary retirement fund with a total of about $7,800,000, all from the development of a 100,000-acre California-Oregon pine forest.

The Mormon Church itself was in the banking business for many years. It established a bank in Salt Lake City because, at the time, that was the only way it could have one. The Zions First National Bank was sold to Utah and Midwestern business interests for nearly $10,000,000 in 1960.

Another major Mormon investment born out of necessity is "The Bishops' Storehouse," established during the Depression. It consists of 700 church-owned farms, ranches, food-processing plants and other enterprises across the country worth a total of about $50,000,000. The Storehouse gives work and welfare help to the needy. Church members donate nearly 250,000 man-days to the program every year.

Agencies and institutions affiliated with the United Lutheran Church in America hold shares in the denomination's Common Investing Fund, a church version of a mutual investment fund. It declares regular quarterly dividends—in 1960, 12.5 cents a share on stock then worth $13.92 that sold in 1954 for $10 a share.

Also in 1960, the Lutheran Church-Missouri Synod reported that it had ended its second consecutive year in the black. It retired an $871,000 debt and added $200,000 to its building and loan capital.

The Southern Baptist Home Missions Board said in 1960 that it had more requests for church loan funds than it had money to lend. Arrangements were made to provide a total of $4,000,000 over a four-year period, but that was not expected to be enough. The fact that more churches wanted loans, combined with a tight money market, made it difficult for congregations to borrow from commercial sources. A drive for 30,000 new churches and missions by 1964 intensified the problem.

Another major area of church financial activity lies in the insurance and annuity field. The Presbyterian Ministers Fund, an interdenominational organization formed in 1717, claims to be the oldest life insurance company in America. The Lutheran Brotherhood Life Insurance of Minneapolis is one of 78 of the nation's 1,400 insurance companies in the "billion-dollar club," which means it has a billion dollars' worth of policies in force.

Until the 1830's, the Presbyterian Fund confined its business to Presbyterian ministers. Later it expanded to include all Protestant ministers and their wives and children. As of May 31, 1960, it had more than $226,500,000 in insurance in force and assets of about $75,000,000. It sold more than $22,000,000 worth of life insurance in 1959, with net rates among the lowest for American life insurance companies.

"The longevity of Protestant clergymen—which is better than

any other class of risks—permits us to pay larger dividends than any other company," explained Alexander Mackie, president of the Fund. "We have the cream of the life insurance business."

The Lutheran Brotherhood and The Ministers Life and Casualty Union, a mutual insurance company, agreed that clergymen were good actuarial risks, although they had made no study of the matter.

"We are able to give higher dividends due to our nature as a nonprofit organization and the favorable mortality experience among the members of our church," said Dr. R. H. Gerberding, board member and consultant to the Lutheran fund.

David F. Hobart, treasurer of the Ministers Life and Casualty Union, said that although little data is available to prove it, he is satisfied with the conclusion that clergymen "have more favorable mortality experience than members of other professions.

"Two companies almost entirely insuring clergymen are the Ministers Life and the Presbyterian Ministers Fund," Hobart said. "The mortality experience of the two has been comparable and has been much better than that of other companies. This does not prove anything since a company's experience is affected by its method of sales, quality of underwriting, servicing of policies and other factors. But it is an indication.

"Another bit of evidence comes from the group insurance provided by another company on the lives of all the ministers of a sizable denomination. The deaths were substantially fewer than would have been expected on the basis of other groups.

"There are many reasons for this. Generally speaking, for instance, clergymen are better educated, they live well-ordered lives, they are not prone to accidents, they live in desirable environments, and they avoid excesses of all kinds."

The American Bible Society is the largest and oldest issuer of annuities in the religious field. The society originated the idea of the gift annuity in 1843. Only in the last few years, with high taxes and inflation, have such plans become popular, and a growing number of churches, religious organizations and other institutions are offering them, under the central regulation of the Conference on Gift Annuities.

Most of the church-related groups dealing in retirement income policies call them "gift annuities." These provide for a contract under which an institution receives a gift of a specified sum, in return for which it promises to pay an annuity, with the residue going to the institution on the death of the policyholder. The difference between the purchase price and the final value of the annuity is the gift portion and may be written off on income tax returns. Part of the annual payment also is deductible.

The Methodist Division of World Missions has about $3,500,000 in "gifts" on which annuities are paid, with the total annual payments amounting to about $193,000. The Methodist Division of National Missions has more than that. Both funds have invested much of their capital in stocks, bonds and mortgages.

The Moody Bible Institute of Chicago began its annuity system in 1907 and boasts it never has missed a payment. The program is called "double dividends," for the individual and the institute. The Salvation Army also has such a program.

None of the activities in this area can come up to the Lutheran Brotherhood, which remains the giant in the church insurance field. The Brotherhood invests for maximum earnings as "a living endowment for the church." It grants about $1,000,000 a year to church colleges and seminaries, for research and writing projects advancing church objectives, and to stimulate expansion of the Guild of Lutheran Nurses, the Boy Scouts and other such organizations.

The Brotherhood took 26 years to record its first $100,000,000 of life insurance in force, and four years to attain the second $100,000,000. In 1959 alone, it sold $200,000,000 worth of policies through 800 agents in 40 states.

The organization had to borrow $6,000 to get started in 1917. In 1959, it had outstanding loans to 717 Lutheran congregations totaling more than $23,200,000.

On the local level, individual churches seldom deal in such high finance. To raise money they usually either must borrow from banks or the parent denomination or rely on simple fund-raising measures.

In the case of a California church, a novel technique of financing was tried, and it worked. The Westwood Community Methodist Church, in a Los Angeles suburb, reorganized its entire financial structure and at the same time created a new spirit of participation among its members.

Officials of the church, guided by the Direct Mail Advertising Association, sent a series of letters to its members and others interested in the church beginning with this announcement:

"It may be news to you, but we are going to sell Westwood Community Methodist Church!

"We're going to sell the grounds, buildings, traditions, the services—yes—even the chimes and the spire.

"If that gives you a sharp twinge, it's understandable—but don't let it, because we're going to sell it to you!"

Copies of this letter went out in 1958 to the 1,800 members of the church plus 700 other persons. The first mailing and several subsequent appeals cost $1,966, mainly for stamps. This investment brought in gifts of $180,000, which was the original goal and twice the amount raised by other methods in the previous year. The campaign also won Westwood Community Methodist Church a place in the Direct Mail Advertising Association Hall of Fame. It was rated as one of the six most outstanding direct-mail solicitations in the association's history.

As far as church people were concerned, the drive also pointed up the fact that it often takes a special gimmick to inspire a person to contribute to any cause, whether church or charity. Complaints on the absence of spontaneous stewardship have been many. One was registered by the Rev. Jon L. Regier, executive secretary of the National Council of Churches' division of home missions. He told a conference of missionaries that too many American Christians thought they had fulfilled their obligations to the church "by dropping pennies in the mission piggy or used clothes in the barrel, or perhaps pledging a chocolate sundae each week for a year to campaign for new churches."

Porter Routh, executive secretary of the Southern Baptist Convention, said individuals were giving a smaller percentage of their total income to benevolent and religious causes than they did during the Depression of the 1930's.

The Rev. Dr. Arthur R. McKay, president of McCormick Theological Seminary in Chicago, has said that in recent years the American people have been spending more money on prepared dog food than the ten major Protestant churches have invested in their total missionary effort, both at home and abroad.

But is it not possible that the churches themselves are at fault for any financial negligence on the part of the churchgoers? Is it not possible that they have given a false picture of prosperity that has caused the churchgoers to conclude that their money is not needed as much as it was in leaner years?

The religious organizations themselves, through their at times haphazard fiscal policies, appear to discourage giving in many instances. They should do more than pass collection plates or present members with pledge cards. A statistically and fiscally minded congregation is more likely to respond when presented with the facts.

As is the case with church membership figures, church financial data is in a state of confusion. It would serve the religious organizations well if they were to enlist the aid of some of the successful businessmen and industrialists in their congregations to help them prepare annual reports patterned after those issued by most businesses, large or small.

These financial statements would describe sources of income and how much was received; give detailed descriptions of investments and equally informative accounts of where the money went, and state how much was left at the end of the fiscal year. The churches then would know where they stood. They would be able to pass this information along to church members. The members, in turn, would know exactly what was expected of them, and they might also see areas where more efficient procedures could be introduced.

Religious leaders might protest such a proposal. But if they are going to talk about money, they should know exactly what they are talking about down to the last dollar and cent. If they already know, they should share this information with those whose money they are soliciting.

As is the case in the somewhat helter-skelter membership counts, the churches are guilty of unbusinesslike practices in a businesslike field. A business or industry would go into bankruptcy with such haphazard bookkeeping methods.

Most persons naturally regard statistics as absolutes, so it is no wonder that the figures being produced by organized religion are gazed upon with equanimity, if not downright pleasure. But many of the statistics that come from church groups must unfortunately be taken with a grain of salt. They indicate trends and possibly little more.

10

The Church and the Professional

Persuaders

"Find the strength for your life. . . . Worship together this week."

This catchy "commercial" is Madison Avenue's plug for religion.

More than $8,500,000 worth of time and space, enough to sell tons of soap, are contributed during one month each year for a national advertising campaign to carry this non-controversial message to Protestants, Roman Catholics and Jews. Local campaigns worth millions more are conducted in more than 500 cities.

The sponsor is an organization known as RIAL—short for Religion in American Life.

RIAL is a nonsectarian movement dedicated to emphasizing the importance of religion to the individual and the community. The program, started in 1948, is supervised by a 70-member lay committee headed by Robert T. Stevens, a textile manufacturer best known as the Secretary of the Army who battled the late Senator Joseph R. McCarthy on television.

The aim of RIAL's campaign is as simple as trying to convince people to brush their teeth at least twice a day and see their dentist twice a year. It seeks to persuade as many families as possible to go to church or temple together every week.

This message is splashed before the nation on 7,000 billboards,

8,000 posters and 84,000 advertising cards on buses, streetcars, subways and commuter trains for a month every fall. It pops up on the ends of bread wrappers, on restaurant paper napkins and on cartons of milk. Campaign slogans are stenciled on pedestrian crosswalks and are flashed on movie screens. Tens of thousands of spot announcements on radio and television urge worship. TV programs, ranging from Ed Sullivan to Lassie, promote it.

The vast advertising campaign surpasses in value the usual promotions for bras, cigarettes and detergents. In all of 1959, Seven-Up spent $8.7 million on advertising; Pabst beer, $8.5 million; the Prudential Life Insurance Company, $8.3 million and American Airlines, $6.2 million. RIAL's figure covers only one month.

The campaign is a goodwill project of the Advertising Council, an organization representing most of the major agencies. The Council estimates it places $180 million worth of free advertising every year for such worthy causes as Smokey the Bear and his forest fire safety campaign, better schools, united funds, mental health and traffic safety. The J. Walter Thompson agency, one of the giants of Madison Avenue, donates its efforts to RIAL's cause as a public service. Many highly-paid members of its staff work on this "account" with as much enthusiasm as they show for the latest compact car. Every bit of advertising strategy and space is provided free by the various media.

RIAL's relationship with the Thompson agency is no different than it would be if RIAL were the name of an improved detergent or a crunchy breakfast food.

"We supervise the whole thing," a RIAL official said. "We are the client. We have to approve of everything. We're hard to please. We throw back stuff we don't like."

Getting RIAL's campaign under way often is complicated by the fact that there actually are three sponsors—not the usual one. Every slogan, every poster, every word, every drawing must be acceptable to Protestant, Catholic and Jew. A church cannot be shown without a synagogue, or a cross without a Star of David, and vice versa. Neither Saturday nor Sunday may be used in referring to the day of worship; "this week" or "every week" is preferred. All races and both sexes also must be objects of the appeal. Old and young must have equal time and space.

A container manufacturer had the RIAL message stamped on his cartons—146,444 of them. Advertising analysts who compute that sort of thing calculated that "exposures" totaled 1,100 per carton, an exposure being a glimpse of the slogan on a carton by one person. These figures, based on industry statistics for the average number of persons "exposed" to the average container, meant that a grand maximum of 161,088,400 persons, or only 20,000,000 short of every man, woman, child and babe in arms in the United States, could have seen the cartons advertising RIAL's product.

No other religious advertiser can make that claim—but that does not mean others are not using advertising to get their messages across. There was a time when almost the only church advertisements were the uniformly dignified little squares on Saturday church pages giving little more than data copied from church bulletin boards. Those ads still run, but there are others, too.

The United Lutheran Church in America, on a much smaller scale than RIAL, to be sure, has conducted a continent-wide newspaper advertising program in daily and weekly newspapers. A series of 18 prepared newspaper advertisements, based on the theme "Lutherans Believe," was made available without charge to all the denomination's congregations. The local churches then bought space or arranged for it free.

The Advertising Council reacted to the scandals over fixed television quiz shows and disk jockey payola by announcing a campaign to "reaffirm and reactivate America's moral fortitude." The campaign, headed by Lee H. Bristol, council chairman and also chairman of the board of Bristol Myers, sought to swell the ranks of those "disgusted with deceit, fed up with phoniness and appalled by the apathy towards it."

Before planning the actual campaign, the Council brought together a round-table of prominent men and women to discuss the matter and "point up the issues." Then advertising agency experts set to work charting a multi-million-dollar campaign chock full of slogans aimed at stiffening the national moral fiber.

The United Presbyterian Church in the U.S.A. has experimented with advertising for several years. It conducted a pilot project on "evangelism through newspaper advertising" for 24 weeks in Rochester, N.Y. An advertising concern handled the campaign under the sponsorship of a committee headed by a minister. The ads offered booklets about the church to those who clipped coupons and sent them in. Then arrangements were made for trained laymen to visit within a week every person who had responded to each ad. The results were inconclusive; a further trial was voted by the denomination's national leaders.

The Rev. Dr. Ralph Stoody, Methodist Director of Information, says that religion and Madison Avenue actually have more in common than many persons might think. He went into the matter in some detail in a book entitled "A Handbook of Church Public Relations." It is Stoody's theory that the churches actually led the way for advertising copy writers.

They were centuries ahead, he says, in the use of the singing commercial—the hymn. And where, he asks, could you find a package more distinctive than the church building? It has been much more effective than the billboard. Church spires also are advertisements. So is the placement of a church in a prominent location, and beauty can be a drawing card. The first broadcasters used church bells to summon worshippers. The new aromatic movies are just a modern adaptation of the use of incense to communicate to the sense of smell. Clergymen adopted distinctive garb, so they would be known and recognized. All of these Stoody characterizes as advertising at its best.

It is doubtful that any church actually has organized an advertising agency, but nearly all have public-relations departments. Public relations, the handmaiden of advertising, is a well-developed activity among religious organizations. The church public-relations official has become a key person in nearly every religious group and denomination. Those who fill the posts prefer to be known as "communicators," "community relations experts," or "information officers"; they regard "public relations" as beneath the dignity of religion. What these people may not know is that in many newspaper city rooms they are called "press agents," not derogatorily, but because that is what they are to the editors, and they must vie as hard as the next press agent for space in the news columns.

The little army of church public-relations officials, including priests, nuns, rabbis, ministers, laymen and lay women with varying degrees of newspaper, radio, TV and magazine experience, courts space in 1,800 daily secular newspapers, 9,000 weeklies and the output of 1,000 news agencies and syndicates.

There are more than 400 publicists representing 19 denominations on the rolls of the Religious Publicity Council. The American Roman Catholic Press Association, with more than 500 Catholic editors—laymen, priests and nuns—represents 400 Catholic newspapers and magazines with 25,000,000 subscribers.

Religious newspapers and magazines in the United States total about 1,500. One-third are Roman Catholic, one-tenth Jewish and the rest Protestant. An additional 50,000 parish publications and thousands of small bulletins and leaflets are issued locally or regionally. There also are about 20 church-related book publishers.

Of all the periodicals published by religious groups, only one, *The Upper Room*, a devotional magazine issued by The Methodist Church, claims a circulation of more than a million.

The total output of all these publications and publicists is enormous and much of it is showered on the 400 church writers and editors of daily newspapers and news agencies.

Stoody, speaking as an instructor at a Methodist writers' conference in Lake Junaluska, N.C., said the press had been both unrecognized and unappreciated by many church officials for its service to religion. Newspapers sometimes seem to be better organized for advertising sin than public virtue, he said, but they manage to give quite a bit of space to religious news, too.

"Religion is more and more being recognized as news by editors of newspapers and magazines," he said. "A century ago, churches did not welcome publication of news of their activities. They thought it a sacrilege and protested against it. Today many churchmen are studying and organizing to give newspapers intelligent cooperation."

Dr. Harold E. Fey, editor of *The Christian Century,* a non-denominational weekly, told another seminar that reporting of religious news in the daily press had developed to a point where controversial subjects could be discussed openly.

"The press is no longer starry-eyed and non-discriminatory about everyone who wraps himself in the cloak of religion," he said.

Its function, he added, is not to print whatever the church organization sends it, but to judge each item on merit. If it is news, it should be printed, and it is the burden of the churches to produce news.

Dr. Martin E. Marty, associate editor of *The Christian Century*, speaking during a Religious Emphasis Week at Gettysburg College, said churches were taking a long second look at mass media of communications and their shortcomings. Instead of finding fault with the secular press, radio, TV and other media, he said, churches should find what is good about them. Instead of condemning, he said, the churches should take a positive approach and find a way to work with them.

Despite the criticisms and reservations religious leaders may have about the press and their approach to it, they are, momentarily at least, in a favorable position in the competition for space. They have come a long way, when one considers that 25 years ago almost the only religious news consisted of announcing on Saturday what ministers would say in their Sunday sermons and reporting on Monday what they actually did say.

Just how far religion has come on this score can be seen by examining a single newspaper for a single day. One page of the *New York Times* on a recent May Monday is a good example. This was a day that in times past would have featured a page reporting sermons of a strictly spiritual or inspirational nature.

Here are the headlines for that day:

JAZZ HYMNS FAIL
TO SHOCK CHURCH
Mild Modern Rhythms Tried
at Episcopal Service
by Actor Donald Swann

RECTOR OPENS 'SIDEWALK MINISTRY'
TO DOZEN IN DRIZZLE

GOALS OF BUDDHISM
LINKED TO MATURITY

MARY EXTOLLED
IN MOTHER ROLE
In Reply to Jesuit, Bonnell
Suggests Protestants May
Venerate, Not Adore, Her

MINISTER CITES LAMENT
FOR NEGLECTED CHILD

MORE RELIGION URGED
Release of Spiritual Energy
Asked by Syracuse Dean

PARENTS CRITICIZED
Jewish Leaders Blame Them
For Teen-Age Vandalism

On another day, a Friday, the *New York Herald Tribune* published a selection of articles on page 3 that demonstrated even more clearly how the church had become part of the world of news. Instead of being segregated, as religious news usually has been in newspapers, they were mingled with strictly secular occurrences.

There were articles on a housing bill, a Congressional investigation of the Interior Department, the revolt of Barnard College girls against a ban on shorts in classrooms, accompanied by a five-column picture of co-eds in the banned shorts, and the revocation of an indictment of a Teamsters Union official. Among these were accounts of a Methodist church's plan for gradual racial integration of its membership, of the views of two Southern Presbyterian leaders on birth control and segregation, of the merger of two Lutheran churches, and of an announcement by a former Protestant Episcopal Bishop of West Virginia that he was supporting John F. Kennedy, a Roman Catholic, in the West Virginia Presidential primary.

At the bottom of the page was a tiny item reporting that President Eisenhower had played golf.

The *New York Times*, on another day, demonstrated the desegregation of religious news even further. The regular contract bridge column was nearly surrounded by items about church activities.

Other evidence of the favorable position of religion in the news columns is seen in an annual list of the ten most significant religious news events compiled by Richard T. Sutcliffe, associate director of the Department of Press, Radio and Television of the United Lutheran Church in America. His list for 1959 began with Pope John XXIII's call for an ecumenical council on Christian unity, which Sutcliffe also rated the outstanding news event of the 1950's.

Other news stories on Sutcliffe's 1959 list were:

"U.S. debates issue of birth control."

"American voters contemplate issue of Roman Catholic President."

"Rome-Istanbul-Geneva rhubarb develops over inter-faith talks."

"Billy Graham crusades in Australia."

"Chinese Reds crush Buddhism in Tibet."

"Louisville Baptist Seminary faculty fired."

"Jews break precedent by embracing evangelism techniques."

"Seven Lutheran church bodies blueprint pair of mergers."

"Arguments over ecumenicity upset Korean Presbyterian merger."

At least six of these were front-page items in many newspapers.

Almost all Sutcliffe's choices for a list of the ten best religious news stories of the 1950's were on front pages. They included the United States Supreme Court decision on racial segregation; Protestant church mergers in the U.S.; the deciphering of the Dead Sea scrolls; Communist oppression of Christians behind the Iron and Bamboo Curtains; exchange visits between Soviet and Western church leaders; organization of the National Council of Churches; the death of Pope Pius XII and the coronation of John XXIII; Billy Graham's London and New York crusades, and the reduction of control over foreign mission activities by U.S. denominations.

Religion made big headlines in 1960 with the election of Kennedy. The victory for the first Roman Catholic President was at the top of various lists of the top 10 religious news stories of the year. Runners-up on the annual list of the Religious News-writers Association included, among others, the meeting of Pope John XXIII and the Archbishop of Canterbury at the Vatican, the Air Force manual controversy, church mergers and the church's role in race relations.

Public-relations experts from the religions were not needed to "sell" most of these events to editors, but they made themselves available to explain and interpret the complexities. In several cases, of course, publicists were needed. Billy Graham, who relies heavily on press agentry, sends a team of advance men to a city months beforehand to whip up enthusiasm for his crusades. Even more important, he has people trained to practice another kind of public relations by drumming up the nightly capacity crowds he finds necessary to put his message across. Before Graham made the first appearance of his highly-publicized Madison Square Garden crusade, the audiences already had been recruited. They traveled to New York by train, chartered bus and automobile, and many of the same faces were seen in the auditorium night after night staring raptly at Graham.

Few other churchmen have personal publicity staffs. However, major denominations maintain central public-relations bureaus with budgets of well over $100,000 a year. They do not pay the staffs highly, as a rule, but their total expenditures often are large, particularly for the making of films.

Possibly the largest total publicity effort of any denomination is that of the Southern Baptist Convention. The denomination's headquarters publicity budget is less than $100,000 a year, but that is just a fraction of the total effort. There also are public-relations staffs for 20 boards, commissions, institutes and agencies. Radio and television operations are separate, costing a total of about $500,000 a year. And there are public-relations personnel in all 28 state conventions, 30 senior colleges, 21 junior colleges, 8 academies, 4 Bible schools, 40 hospitals and 30 orphanages. About 325 Southern Baptists have direct public-relations responsibilities.

W. C. Fields, a minister with extensive experience in the field of religious journalism as well as in the pulpit, is the first person to have the title of Public Relations Secretary of the denomination, which sent out its first press release in 1950. Fields said the publicity effort had brought an increase of at least 1,000 per cent in press, radio and TV coverage of Southern Baptist activities.

"Much of this increased publicity and much of the improvement in public relations have come as a result of the intensified interest in recent years in religion generally," he said. "It is my opinion, however, that the greater part of the increase has come because of more intelligent and deliberate use of public-relations tools and techniques, as we Southern Baptists have tried to declare the Gospel in the light of our understanding."

Fields advises Southern Baptist journalists to "write modern," to throw away clichés such as "felt need," "the overall program" and "view with alarm." He also would like to see some ecclesiastical jargon scrapped.

"We live in a very charitable and forgiving environment," he said. "Baptist writers have been getting away with murder—what they murder is journalism. . . . We've heard a lot about why Johnny can't read; we ought to know why Johnny Grown-Up can't write."

Accompanying the "write modern" theme is a new Southern Baptist communications system with a name worthy of Madison Avenue—"Instant News."

The denomination put into service a Teletypewriter network,

believed to be the first leased-wire communications system operated by a religious organization. It began March 1, 1960, linking 25 offices in 19 cities from Washington, D.C., to Wichita, Kan. The network operates eight hours a day, five days a week, with the cost paid by the various agencies, state offices and Baptist newspapers that get the service.

To announce the launching of the "Instant News" program, the executive committee of the convention placed an advertisement in Editor and Publisher magazine saying, "To the Southern Baptist Convention, being 'up to date' in proclaiming God's word means being 'up to the second.' "

Ramsey Pollard, convention president, said the network provided a novel way to spread "the good news."

"Baptists have not heretofore taken full advantage of the tremendous power of public relations," he said. "Other denominations have far surpassed us in many areas of this nature. Some have criticized newspapers, television and radio stations for our lack of coverage of our tremendous Baptist activities. And the fault was our own. We did not give the news to the proper people at the right time.

"Now the picture is changed. Southern Baptists are delighted with this momentous step in the right direction. The world will know what we are doing."

Not even the National Council of Churches, which represents the bulk of Protestantism in America, can boast more extensive publicity activities than the Southern Baptists. The Council has a well-trained headquarters staff in New York City and a Washington office, but the volume of its press releases is far short of that of the Southern group, which draws on the skills of clerical and lay experts alike to tell its story.

One of the largest single news operations in the field of religion is that of the Religious News Service, more usually referred to as RNS, which was founded by the National Conference of Christians and Jews in 1933 to provide interdenominational news about religion. The service, which offers objective news reporting about Christians and Jews alike, still is sponsored by the Conference, but operates autonomously. It has 900 correspondents throughout the world, more than 450 of them in the United States. Many of them are religion writers on local newspapers who provide news for RNS on a part-time basis.

RNS has about 750 clients, including 100 daily newspapers, more than 200 radio stations and well over 350 publications of all faiths. Among them is the All-Church Press, which publishes more than 300 local church newspapers. Officials of the service estimate that their daily offering of 70 to 75 news items and various weekly features, including a "Believe-it-or-Not" style cartoon entitled "Religious Remarkables," reach a total of more than 70,000,000 persons.

Most of the various denominations rely on teams of layman-clergyman publicists, and they are requiring an increasing knowledge of the news media from staff members. Religious journalism is becoming a specialty; the day when the oldest and most decrepit person on a newspaper staff was assigned to the church beat is gone. Priests have turned up in several classes at the Columbia University Graduate School of Journalism and a minister-journalist is on the faculty. A *Buffalo Evening News* reporter who frequently writes on religion also is a Congregational minister. He gathers sermon material in his work.

Stoody became Methodist Information Director after 20 years as a preacher and writer. The Rev. Dr. Everett C. Parker, a recognized authority on radio and television, heads the United Church of Christ's Information Department. A veteran newsman, Charles Hushaw, is publicity chief of the United Lutheran Church in America. A newsman and a minister share the public-relations office of the United Presbyterian Church in the U.S.A.

Priests are in charge of most Catholic publicity, and several of them are former newspapermen. The director of public relations of the Maryknoll Sisters is a nun who worked as a newspaper reporter before taking her vows.

Several church organizations use the services of public-relations organizations. The agency that handles the American Bible Society, Banner & Greif, also is retained by the Methodists and the United Church of Christ for special assignments. The Catholic Hour is publicized by another Madison Avenue concern.

Most religious publicity offices are in New York, but Nashville, Minneapolis and Washington also are key centers of such activity.

Some Protestant leaders complain that the Roman Catholic church receives more space in newspapers than do other religious organizations. But the Catholics see the situation in reverse. They worry about the effectiveness of their publicity as much as the Protestants do.

". . . We who have a Divine Command, who have truth itself, worry about 'dignity' and leave the field open to our competition and to the soap salesmen," said the Rev. Albert J. Nevins, director of public relations for the Maryknoll Fathers. "If mass communications are used to sell soap and breakfast cereals and Protestantism, when are we going to make full use of them in selling Catholicism?"

The National Catholic Welfare Conference, which serves as an information clearing house for Catholic groups across the country, began holding annual seminars on the Church and Communications Arts in 1959. The seminars are attended by "communicators"—nuns, priests and lay persons concerned with publicizing Catholic activities. The teachers are members of the public-relations, advertising, newspaper, magazine and broadcasting professions. They have urged a more vigorous and professional public-relations effort to counteract the "corporate image" of the Church in the minds of many non-Catholics.

". . . The principles of successful public relations that apply to business institutions also apply to the church," one seminar was told by T. J. Ross, senior partner of Ivy Lee and T. J. Ross, which became famous as the firm that helped make the late John D. Rockefeller, Sr. popular.

"After all, the church deals with people, with public opinion. It is confronted from day to day with problems of policy and practices in communications similar to those faced by business institutions in their everyday operations.

"As regards the Catholic Church, there certainly should be no doubt as to the quality of the product or the essentiality of the service which the Church performs."

Ross advised church publicists to study Rome to find out what good public relations is. The Pope is the most available ruler in the world, receiving almost every tourist who visits Rome, he said. His coronation gets more space in newspapers around the world than the crowning of a queen or the inauguration of a president, Ross said, and his every appearance in public is big news.

". . . You have in the Holy Father the perfect exemplar of public relations in its truest sense—authoritative; articulate; unafraid; gentle, yet firm; unerring; ideal and worthy of imitation," he said.

The Church of the Nazarene, miniscule in comparison with the Roman Catholic organization, issued a modest brochure to advise its churches to seek space in newspapers in small towns. About 75 per cent of the Nazarene churches are in small communities, and so ministers of the denomination were advised to read their newspapers carefully, advertise once in a while and awaken to the fact that everything a church does is news.

"If you get a ticket for parking or speeding," ministers were advised, "do not ask to keep your name out of the newspaper."

In other words, to paraphrase an old newspaper saying, it is just as much of a news item when a minister bites a dog as when a member of his congregation does.

11

Architecture: From Gothic to Tepee

A PERSON TOURING America 25 years ago might have been able
to determine just about where he was simply by looking at the
churches. On New England village greens, he would have seen
mainly white-clapboard meeting houses, capped by Christopher
Wren spires. In Chicago, the religious trademark was the massive
stone pile of Gothic design, with buttresses flying. New York
offered Romanesque and Byzantine cathedrals and small churches
patterned after Westminster Abbey. Florida was dotted with
missions of stucco, California with missions of adobe and reasonable facsimiles thereof.

Only in small towns, mainly in the Midwest and South, was
there a native American church style—the little white box, designed and built by the village carpenter.

The scenery has been changing since World War II under the
impact of the new cradle-to-grave concept of church activity,
providing nurseries for infants, TV, hi-fi and soft-drink machines
for teen-agers and golden-year clubs for the aged.

Religious organizations no longer look across the sea for architectural inspiration. A native architecture is being developed to
fill the needs created by the church building boom and the new
role of the church as a community center. Some architects have
found so much business they are specializing in churches. When
the Church Architectural Guild was organized in 1940, it had
38 members, all architects. In 1960, it had 200 architect members,

plus various craftsmen and artisans, and its annual meeting attracted 2,000 persons.

It has been said that religion is declining in civilizations where church building has been completed. England, France and Italy are cited as proof of this theory. Enough churches are available, but seldom are they filled.

The new American churches have caught the eyes of European religious leaders, who are impressed by the vitality they express. In a reversal of the old trend, Europeans are interested in learning more about American church architecture—not the outer design so much as the floor plans. They are amazed at all the uses to which Americans can put a church.

Arland A. Dirlam of Boston, a past president of the Church Architectural Guild, wrote in *Church Management Magazine* that in this sense American churches are a new export. The American concept of a church as a religious home, as contrasted with the European idea that a church is a place of retreat, is drawing attention across the Atlantic, he said.

A large factor in the nation-wide building by all church groups is the now-well-established practice of keeping churches open seven days a week—fellowship community centers six days and houses of worship on the seventh. Recreational or Sunday school facilities often are constructed first and serve as a sanctuary also until one can be built. Jewish community centers, long established among Jewish congregations, were set well apart in the past. Now they are being constructed alongside or even adjoining synagogues, much in the style of Christian churches.

The designers of the new-time church still are groping for a definitive style to fill the practical and aesthetic demands of the modern churchgoer. In the meantime, they are not idle. They are adorning the landscape with hundreds of glass, wood and brick churches built in the shape of tepees or silos or patterned after split-level or ranch-style houses. The structures are surrounded by parking lots, playgrounds, barbecue pits and gardens. One now-popular design, considered shocking when introduced, consists mainly of a sharply pitched roof that dwarfs the rest of the structure. It is more barn than Byzantine.

Houses are being built smaller than they were 25 to 50 years ago, so the church has become an extension of the home. As such, it must offer all the comforts of home—and more. Soft pew cushions, electronic kitchens, bowling alleys with automatic pin setters, air-conditioning and baby sitters all point up the new distaste for the old notion that discomfort and piety are synonymous. A Puritan would have spent a month of Sundays in the stock at the mere suggestion that perhaps the pews could have been softer. Today's church magazines carry many advertisements for the softest cushions yet—for either sitting or kneeling.

About half the money spent on churches now goes into education and facilities outside the sanctuary. New churches are incorporating as standard equipment such things as babyfolds (nurseries) and sometimes even dance floors. Some Roman Catholic churches have crying rooms separated from the main sanctuaries by large plate-glass windows. This permits a mother with a squalling infant to attend mass and tend to the baby, too.

Air-conditioning has become a must in churches in the South and Southwest. Church kitchens are being equipped with stainless steel sinks, wall ovens and dishwashing machines. Large churches have snack bars and auxiliary Pullman kitchens for small groups. New buildings are being equipped with piped vacuum-cleaning outlets, television conduits, built-in public-address systems, radiant heating, indirect lighting, movie screens and projection booths.

The latest rheostatic lighting is being used, with some pulpits being equipped with push buttons so the preacher can raise or lower the lighting for dramatic effect during a sermon. The Westminster Presbyterian Church in Detroit, for example, has a beautiful window that is displayed with striking effect with variegated lighting during services.

Churches are being built for today, not tomorrow; the one-generation church is the goal. Its slogan might well be "not for an eternity, but for a lifetime." Decaying, soot-stained, sparsely attended churches in big cities stand as a practical lesson for the church architect of today. The high costs of construction and the mass mobility of Americans have made the Gothic, Byzantine or Romanesque cathedral both impractical and too formal. The church as an edifice is dying. Ideally, today's church, rather than being an imposing structure, should be an enormous trailer, easily moved along with migrating America.

In the 15 years following World War II, $7,300,000,000 was spent to build new churches. The figure reached an annual record of $1,050,000,000 in 1960 alone. None of these sums includes investments in schools, hospitals, colleges, administration buildings, homes for the aged, orphanages, publishing houses, camping facilities or other projects, which brought the total of religion-sponsored construction in 1960 to $3,000,000,000.

There now are about 310,000 houses of worship in the country. Protestant churches are going up at a rate of approximately one every eight hours. The National Council of Churches expects this pace to continue indefinitely. It will be a long time before the pent-up war needs and the needs of a rapidly growing and fast-moving population are met.

Even the current rate of 1,000 new churches a year is not enough to keep up with the demand—the need is for 5,000 a year. Philadelphia alone should have 400 churches in the next 10 years. Many other cities can match this figure.

The Southern Baptists plan to spend $2,000,000,000 to $3,000,000,000 during the 1960's for church expansion. W. A. Harrell, secretary of church architecture service for the denomination's Sunday School Board, said this would double the present value of Southern Baptist property and amount to about a fifth of all the money spent for church construction in the United States during the decade.

New churches range from modest little prefabricated structures, fitted together by members of congregations on their days off and offering recreational facilities limited perhaps to bowling or shuffle board, to the accordion-pleated Air Force Academy chapel and a huge $2,500,000 religious center built on the "campus plan" by the Wesley Memorial Methodist Church of High Point, N.C.

Wesley, begun in 1958, occupies a 19-acre suburban site. Its planners gave it tennis courts, bowling alleys, a swimming pool, an ice-skating rink, a parking lot and landscaped grounds, in addition to a comfortable air-conditioned sanctuary and the usual meeting and dining facilities. Such trimmings are called "hidden persuaders" by some architects.

Harold E. Wagoner, a noted Philadelphia church architect and president of the Church Architectural Guild, designed the High Point church. He used the "campus plan," on the theory that "worship is a total experience. It is Christian living, a way of life, with integration of worship, music, discussions, recreation and so on. I call it Christianity through Christian fellowship.

"The picturesque white Colonial meeting house, set alone in a grove of trees, and used only on Sunday by a minister who may have had little theological training, preaching to a congregation of uneducated farmers, is a far cry from the complex church plants of today, operated by a staff of 20 or more trained workers, who minister to sophisticated groups of worldly-wise constituents," he said.

Wagoner noted that the new concept presented one great danger —that Christian fellowship would become more fellowship than Christian. He warned against innovations that hide the reason for the church, saying, "Thoughtful, beautiful and acceptable church architecture cannot be obtained unless it is a sympathetic expression of the theology involved. If our churches do not have an atmosphere conducive to worship, they have failed."

In 1900, the traditional American community skyline was dominated by the towers and steeples of churches. Then the churches were dwarfed into insignificance by towers of commerce. The spiritual centers huddled in the shadows of the symbols of materialism—and they went into a decline. Now, with the upsurge, there has come the construction of often spectacular church buildings. They may not tower over commercial skyscrapers, but they stand out on the landscape.

When the Fifth Avenue Association made its biennial awards for good design of New York buildings in 1960, two of the winners were churches—the First Presbyterian Church in Greenwich Village was honored for its new parish house, and the Roman Catholic Church of Our Saviour on Park Avenue for its entire plant. They shared honors with the Guggenheim Museum, a giant concrete cupcake designed by the late Frank Lloyd Wright;

the Corning Glass Corporation's Fifth Avenue skyscraper; Harry Winston's newly remodeled diamond emporium and the Manhattan branch of Takashimaya, a Tokyo department store.

Some church leaders feel there is cause for concern over the heavy investments in new buildings and fine plants. Millions of dollars are being borrowed to foot the construction bills. Churches going deep into debt will be making mortgage payments for many years. There is a fear that individual local churches might become too ingrown, that they might pay so much attention to their own fiscal problems that they neglect their duty to serve the community and the world.

One reason the non-traditional religious groups, more popularly known as sects, have been forging ahead is that they spend proportionately more on evangelism and less on churches. Many of the sects that operate in store fronts gather in comparatively more new and loyal members than do main-line denominations with imposing church buildings.

Elaborate new church buildings are, however, enabling congregations to assume community responsibilities in their everyday activities. The churches are drawing more than just their members; they are serving entire neighborhoods around them. Local churches used to rely mainly on secular agencies for welfare, hospitals and schools or had to depend on national groups for such good works. That no longer is true. Parish house programs are one evidence. Some churches have staffs of social workers, while bowling alleys and bingo tables are the answers to community need in other cases.

The burst of church-building zeal has been accompanied not only by discussions of the role of religion in society but by architectural debates with liturgical backgrounds. There is argument over where the American and Christian flags should be displayed in the sanctuary. There is dispute over placement of the organ and the choir and even the altar.

Congress has ruled that the American flag always is the honored banner, except in church. But differences still prevail on where the Stars and Stripes should be. Some church officials say the symbol of loyalty to God should be in the place of highest honor, on the minister's right in the chancel. Others compromise by putting the Christian flag in that honored position and the American flag on the main floor, outside the chancel, to the congregation's right. But the controversy remains unsolved. It has been suggested that if arguments on the subject continue, both flags should be removed.

Then there is the question of where to put the organ. Some newer churches are using bare organ pipes as part of the décor, requiring that they be placed behind or around the altar. The chapel at the Massachusetts Institute of Technology contains this feature. Some architects prefer to put the organ and pipes in the back of the church, out of sight, but this poses a problem in a church where Elder Jones has donated the organ and likes to have it up front so he—and everyone else—can see it.

Architects also are caught in the middle of the controversy over choir placement. There is a movement toward simplification of churches, to make the minister in the pulpit and the altar the focal points. This increases the likelihood that the minister will have the full attention of the congregation if there are no organ pipes to count during his sermon and no choir singers' faces to study.

In the Gate School chapel in Carpenteria, Calif., for example, the choir hides out in the transept of a long, low church with windows along one side and a solid wall along the other. But most people who sing in choirs seem to want to stand up and be counted by the congregation on Sunday.

Probably the most energetic argument concerns the placement of the altar. Some churches are putting it in the center, in a theater-in-the-round arrangement, which breaks away from the theatrical proscenium arch. Others are using a simple décor to set off the altar. Pulpits are being replaced with communion tables. The Gothic tradition of keeping people either in the dark or behind a pillar is being abandoned in the interest of congregational togetherness.

St. John's Lutheran Church in Midland, Mich., is an octagonal building with an octagonal masonite altar in the middle and a generous display of hanging vines. The new Second Baptist Church in St. Louis is of painted brick and marble, with floor-to-ceiling windows, the organ and choir in the balcony and the cross, communion table, Bible and baptistry in the center. The pulpit is on one side.

The Southern Baptists ran into difficulty finding architects who knew how to design churches fitted to the denomination's special needs. The two main problems were pulpit location and the arrangement of schoolrooms. The Southern Baptists discovered that architects tended to divide the chancel, using an altar and a lectern instead of a central pulpit including both. They also favored large classrooms, rather than a large assembly room surrounded by small classrooms. The Baptists complained further that architects did not know that the baptistry in a Baptist church is a place where converts are immersed, not sprinkled. A program of educating architects in the ways of Southern Baptists was begun to overcome these problems.

There are other concerns involving all denominations: the need for balcony exhaust fans, communion tables with upholstered chairs, Grade A kitchens with safeguards against food poisoning and proper floor coverings and the right mops to use on them.

When the magazine *Protestant Church Buildings and Equipment* conducted a survey to find out what clergymen considered their biggest maintenance problem, 22 per cent replied: proper floor covering. There were at the time of the survey, in 1960, a total of about 798,000,000 square feet of floor space in Protestant church schools alone—a total of 28.62 square miles—for which there was the "sacred duty" to maintain cleanliness, beauty and durability.

Efficient new vacuum cleaners have made it practical to roll red carpets down church aisles that once were covered with broadloom as nearly the color of mud as man could produce. Rubber tile, terrazzo, linoleum and cork also are being used as floor coverings. Ceilings are being lined with acoustical tile, and the First Methodist Church in Lakeland, Fla., was coated inside with an asbestos spray that is decorative, reduces echo and is fire-resistant.

Out of the church building boom have come several notable structures. Possibly the most spectacular is the First Presbyterian Church of Stamford, Conn., designed by Wallace K. Harrison, one of the architects of Rockefeller Center and Director of Planning for the United Nations buildings. His creation is in the shape of a fish, inspired by the facts that often the sign of the fish was drawn on the sand and on the walls of hiding places of the first Christians; that Jesus fed the multitude loaves and fishes and exhorted his disciples to be fishers of men; and that ichthys, the Greek word for fish, had a secret meaning to Christians, the letters being the first letters of a phrase that meant hope to persecuted believers.

The Harrison church, though sharply modern in design, still offers some of the spaciousness and stained glass beauty of medieval cathedrals. It cost a million dollars to build and occupies an 11-acre tract of hilly woodland overlooking Stamford. The pre-cast concrete sanctuary contains pews of untreated African mahogany —"it is honest, as in European cathedrals," an elaborate brochure on the church says. The chancel is dominated by a 32-foot cross from the bombed-out library of Canterbury Cathedral. Embedded in the floor at the foot of the altar is a stone from the castle where Luther hid while translating the Bible. A stone from the Scottish island of Iona, a landmark in modern Presbyterianism, is in the floor by the lectern.

Other stones in the church are from Switzerland, Canterbury and Malta, all places of religious interest. Nails from Coventry Cathedral, destroyed by Nazi bombs in World War II, have been placed at the symbolic points on the cross where the hands and feet of Jesus were pierced. An ancient millstone—symbol of bread—from New England rests in the floor at the foot of the communion table. Five other millstones and stones from former church land also have been built into the church.

The acoustics are so fine that no loudspeaker is needed. Instead of a pipe organ, a custom-built electronic organ was installed. It has enough woofers and tweeters to awe even the most sophisticated hi-fi buff, and its amplifiers, according to church publicists, have the combined output of 1,000 table-model radios.

Almost a third of an acre—30,000 square feet—of the church property is occupied by the parish house. It was designed to serve a congregation of more than 2,000 adults and 1,000 children. There are 15 glass-walled Sunday-school rooms, a babyfold, a nursery and a playground. Studies were provided for the two ministers and the director of Christian education and an office for secretaries. Other facilities include a library-lounge with a kitchenette and serving unit, a small chapel for weddings and funerals and a fan-shaped fellowship hall, with a three-story glass wall looking out at the city. The hall, which can accommodate 500 persons at dinner, has a stage at one end and in wings on each side are a coatroom, a storage room, a large modern kitchen and a serving unit.

Another startling new church building, the work of Frank Lloyd Wright, is the Wayfarer's Chapel at Portugese Bend, Calif. This structure of wooden arches and beams coated with glass overlooks the Pacific.

The Cedar Hills Community Church (Congregational) near Portland, Ore., has been credited with being the first of the tepee churches. When it was designed, there was considerable resistance to anything so radical for a place of worship. Now there are many imitations across the country.

A good example of the "open face" church is the Montclair Methodist Church in Oakland, Calif. One can stand outside and see the full length of the church through a huge glass wall at the entrance. Hope Lutheran Church of Bozeman, Mont., does the reverse—it gives parishioners a view of the outdoors through full-length windows along both sides of the nave. It is described as a house of worship with a "welcome home" atmosphere.

St. Peter's Methodist Church in Louisville, Ky., has an all-purpose recreational area that doubles as a parking lot. Movable concrete slabs were placed over a 40-by-60-foot swimming pool. At the push of a button, the slabs slide back, uncovering the pool. When closed, the floor can be used for tennis or basketball or for parking.

St. Paul's Lutheran Church in Melbourne, Fla., broke ground in 1960 for a round building with a tapered spire in the center, strongly suggestive of the missile age. It looks something like a stylized nose cone for a rocket such as those fired from Cape Canaveral, 30 miles away.

A plastic skylight runs the length of the steeply-pitched roof of Grace Episcopal Church in Massapequa, N.Y. It serves as a sort of vista dome through which the congregation can see the gold cross atop a pole at one end of the roof.

The United Church of Christ constructed a striking modern church in Squaw Valley, Calif., for a relatively modest $140,000.

The church, used for weekend retreats and by vacationists, skiers and year-round residents, has a glass front looking out at Granite Chief Peak. The fellowship room, where young people gather after skiing or mountain climbing, has a sunken fireplace and suspended chimney in the center.

Two softball diamonds, a tennis court and a barbecue pit for family night cookouts are drawing cards at the First Baptist Church of Indianapolis. The sanctuary seats 915, the chapel, 120. In addition, there is a fellowship hall, a gymnasium with stage, lockers and showers, a stainless steel kitchen, 23 classrooms, carpeted parlors and parking for 285 cars.

In 1960, the Mormons had nearly 600 building projects under way. Their architecture follows generally conservative modern lines, but the churches all contain public-address and air-conditioning systems. One new Mormon church building was completed every day of 1960. Each consisted of a sanctuary, classrooms and a recreation-amusement hall with stage, dance floor and kitchen.

Riverside Church in New York met demands for community service by building an eight-story addition to the main Gothic edifice. The Rev. Dr. Robert J. McCracken, minister, said a church open only for a few hours on Sunday was divorced from human needs. The new building serves the weekday world of the neighborhood with a school, child-care centers, bowling alleys and an underground garage. There are kitchenettes and a large, fully-equipped, all-electric kitchen that can serve 750 persons.

The building contains large rooms for parties, recreation and dinners. A roof terrace can be gaily lighted at night. Pathways traced on the floor provide bicycle routes for children. There is a room in which children can be observed at play through a one-way glass window. A gym, a theater, a sewing room and arts and crafts rooms also serve the community.

Not all churches can afford the luxury of a community center such as this or even the price of a new church building. While thousands of congregations have been able to raise the money or to borrow enough for construction projects, others have invested in more modestly priced housecleanings—renovating and remodeling old structures. The work ranges from inexpensive paint jobs to $100,000 face-liftings.

Donald Plouff, executive vice-president of the Studios of Potente, the Kenosha, Wis., branch of an old Italian firm of church beauti-fiers, has participated in the remodeling of about 500 churches since World War II. Plouff, a Lutheran, said he found an in-creasing number of persons were becoming concerned about church buildings.

"They have bought all the new cars they can," he said. "They dress well. They live well. The church came last on their list—and now they've finally gotten to the last thing on their list."

Many churches have been washed or painted in the last 30 to 60 years, but that is about all. Now, with prosperity and a new crop of young ministers, big renovations are under way. Most of Plouff's clients, for instance, are ministers in their late 20's or early 30's. After they left seminaries, they found their first churches in poor condition. Regarding the church as an evangelistic sales tool, they decided to go to work on it. In another ten years, there will be still more young men in old churches that need renovating.

"There is an awakening of the realization that you don't want to live in a $25,000 ranch house and go to a church that looks like a dump," Plouff said.

A renovation job Plouff had nothing to do with was one of the more unusual ones. In Phenix City, Ala., a town known to soldiers and college students as "sin city," Ma Beechie's Place, an old saloon closed during a clean-up campaign, has been turned into a church. The Independent Assembly of God set up Bible classes in former gambling rooms and the main barroom, which once echoed to the bawdy songs of G.I.'s, now rings with hymns.

Rooms formerly used to teach algebra, history and economics in Lake City, Mich., now belong to the Presbyterian Church. The congregation was organized in 1889 in a schoolhouse but for the last 70 years had occupied a church building. Those quarters be-came too small for a burgeoning membership, and when Lake City High School moved to a new building, the Presbyterians bought the old one for $15,175. An additional $13,000 and many hours of volunteer labor brought conversion of the gymnasium into a sanctuary.

A two-in-one building was erected by the Catholics in Norwalk,

Conn. St. Matthew's Church is a church only when it is needed for services. Between times it is a community center and recreation hall. The parish eventually will have a full-time sanctuary, but until then, movable pews are kept in concealed storage spaces. During the week, when it is time for mass, a sanctuary is provided by opening a large wooden folding partition. The altar is rolled out on a track and a drape is pulled aside to disclose the crucifix. A folding communion rail and kneeler are available for fast installation and there are two folding confessionals. When the Stations of the Cross are not in use, they are covered with special doors, as is the choir area. Special lights give worshipful touches during services.

It takes only a few minutes to transform the area back into a recreation hall, complete with basketball court, kitchen and dining tables, which are provided by folding down the backs of the portable pews.

Progress of another kind is responsible for a show-case church in Wilmington, Del. Zion United Lutheran Church was displaced by a freeway. It took advantage of its eviction by retaining Wagoner to design a church with a steeply sloping white aluminum roof and a front wall of glass so passers-by can see through the nave to a large altar cross, which will be illuminated at night. The bells from the old church steeple will hang in an 80-foot tower connected to the church by a porte-cochere. The rest of the building will consist of a one-story square around a patio.

One of the biggest religious construction projects of recent times is Conservative Temple Sinai, in Westwood, Calif. The $3,500,000 synagogue covers a full block. It has an 80-foot-high stained glass Ark of the Covenant and 13 multi-colored pyramids running the length of the facade. The temple is divided into a sanctuary and a community hall, separated by a wall that can be raised into a specially constructed ceiling to provide maximum seating on high holy days. Lighting and cooling units are concealed in the ceiling. The seats are in chevron-shaped rows, giving every person a view of the lecterns. More than 1,000 persons can be seated in the main sanctuary and more than 600 in the adjoining room. A control booth similar to those in broadcasting studios was installed to house public address equipment and the rabbi can reach any official of the congregation with an intercommunications system behind the pulpit.

Religious organizations have not been too busy building to pause to take stock of what they are doing. One of those who oversees construction plans, the Rev. Edward S. Frey, executive director of the department of church architecture of the United Lutheran Church in America and chairman of the board of managers of the National Council of Churches building department, told a conference on church architecture that much of the trouble with new buildings lay in the fact that some builders thought more about the structure than the reasons for erecting it.

"Think before you build," he admonished. "Think about everything, but especially about what the building is going to do for the congregation and what you want it to do. Buildings for the task of the church are both tools and symbols.

". . . We have got to get through to our time. We aren't, you know. And we aren't because we have taken on too many of the gimmicks of the prevailing culture that strikes its highest moments in imitating celebrities, worrying about filter feedback, and dreaming I was a concert pianist or a medieval princess in a Maidenform bra."

Frey complained that "costume" architecture that is imitative or merely novel will not do the job. The first he associated with obsolete symbols of past days; the second he called only a splash on the landscape, "rooted in nothing but a passing fancy.

"I have seen too many church schoolrooms badly built and decorated, utterly inadequate for any kind of thoughtful program with an impact," he said. "For example, I have seen cramped rooms with 'toy altars' in them. From the evidence at hand the altars were used for little more than a catch-all spare table. I have found comic books on them, pickle jars with punched lids for pennies, and, once, an old cigar butt.

"We have been building churches for years as if they were auditoriums with the preacher and the choir as a kind of permanent cast addressing the passive people in the pews. This is a sadly mistaken concept of worship. It has led to some of the weirdest behavior in church history as well as to poor doctrine and surrender to the blandishments of secularism.

". . . I see too much attractive design frankly contrived for sensual effect, demanding attention by strong visual impact and delight, but unable to deliver any meaning beyond itself, once it has captured the eye."

He cited one new church he visited as being filled with visual delight but little theological or liturgical significance.

"Certain sacred symbols, while beautiful in design, were for the most part used illiterately or ungrammatically," Frey said. "Latin crosses abounded ad nauseum. They were even used as door lights."

12

Praise the Lord and Pass the Coffee

"We never close!" could be the slogan of churches across America.

If a sanctuary is filled on Sunday, it is likely that the doors of the fellowship hall will be open and the lights ablaze every night of the week for a wide range of activities from Bible study to gourmet suppers.

By day, the "effective" church offers baby-sitting services, recreation rooms for the aged and TV dens for the teen-age set. Civic organizations are invited to share the church swimming pool, tennis courts or auditorium.

The new-time religion also offers some of the old-time recreation. Arts and crafts still are practiced in church basements; the pot-luck supper is as popular as ever, and nothing has come along to replace the church picnic, with its hot dogs, pop, sack races and baseball.

There are new attractions, too: hot-rod clubs, classes in good grooming, boy-girl discussions, barbecues, garden projects and coffee hours. On the more serious side, the church often ranges far beyond its own four walls with prayer meetings in homes or restaurants, weekend retreats, and summer caravans for young people who visit churches and hospitals to perform much-needed maintenance chores.

The simplest form of fellowship is quite naturally the most popular—the "coffee break" after Sunday service. The Protestant Council of the City of New York conducted a survey to find out

just how important the coffee hour was. It learned that this relatively simple event had become an important missionary tool in
Manhattan churches, which found that their congregations regarded
it as an ideal way to evangelize visitors. The parishioners also
acknowledged that they enjoyed themselves.

The non-denominational, interracial Church of the Saviour in
Washington, D.C., found another kind of fellowship in America's
favorite beverage by opening a non-beatnik coffee house for relaxation, music, art and conversation. The Rev. N. G. Crosby,
pastor of the church, suggested "The Potter's House" after addressing a cold, unresponsive congregation in a New York City
church and then being kept awake half the night by a boisterous
crowd in the tavern below his hotel room.

"I realized there was more warmth and fellowship in that
tavern than in the church," Crosby said.

A thriving hot-rod fellowship was organized by the Rev. Dr.
Paul R. Woudenberg of the Echo Park Methodist Church in Los
Angeles. The son of an auto dealer, Woudenberg became a hot-rod
enthusiast while studying engineering before he decided to become
a minister. He organized boys in his congregation into the Jehus,
named after an Old Testament king of Israel, who is described in
II Kings IX:20—"And the driving is like the driving of Jehu the
son of Nimshi; for he drives furiously."

Horseback riding is a better answer than hot-rodding to the
problems of young people, as far as a Roman Catholic priest is
concerned. The Rev. Lloyd Fortin maintains a riding ring at St.
John the Baptist Church in Hugo, Minn., where he sponsors a
parish horse show every year. A recent show attracted nearly 4,000
persons, whose admission fees were used to expand and improve
parish recreational facilities.

"A boy or girl who rides, grooms and cares for a horse won't
be a juvenile delinquent," Fortin says.

This is specialized fellowship. The National Presbyterian
Church in Washington, D.C., has such an active program, sponsored by its Sunday Evening Club, that the organization probably
should be named the All-Week Club. Hospitality House, next door
to the church, is the group's headquarters for activities each week
that go something like this: Sunday—a speaker. Monday night—

one club group visits the rehabilitation ward of the District of Columbia General Hospital while another entertains children at a home for the underprivileged. Tuesday—the downtown luncheon club meets and in the evening there is dancing or bridge. Wednesday—the midweek discussion group meets for supper and Bible study. Thursday—the luncheon club meets on Capitol Hill. Friday or Saturday—a party or outing.

The bowling and drama groups meet regularly. There are two weekend summer beach trips and a winter ski weekend, as well as two weekend retreats each year for discussion, religious services, sports and Saturday night square dances.

The First Presbyterian Church of Hollywood, Calif., also follows a schedule that could keep a church member busy nearly all of his waking hours. The church occupies a $2,000,000 plant that contains several kitchens, a skating rink, a gym and a fellowship hall. So many adults seek fellowship at the church that they are divided into seven groups according to sex, marital status and age.

"Some of our groups dream up such unusual things that we are always a little bit taken aback," said Richard B. Langford, coordinator of Christian fellowship for the church.

A bus owned by the church is available for all sorts of outings, including visits to recreational spots and camping trips. It operates on a schedule that keeps it in use at least four days a week.

Some of the church classes conduct elaborate programs. For instance, the 35-to-45-year-old group had a series of 12 "around-the-world" parties, each devoted to a different country. The food of the country represented was served along with travel information. One of the men in the class worked for an airline, which provided short films about each country. Either a missionary or a representative of the country ended each party with a devotional.

"We do this not just to entertain the people, but rather to provide an attractive situation in the church in which they will feel free to invite their friends who are not particularly interested in the church," Langford said.

Youth activities include "sermons in magic"—spiritual lessons by a Christian magician—and discussions of Christian dating, courtesy, prayer and the Bible. Outstanding athletes or business or professional people give testimonials and there is a regular Friday "Fun Night in the Gym," with basketball, ping-pong, games and snacks.

An entire building devoted to recreation was built in 1953 by the First Baptist Church of Dallas, which, with 12,000 members, has the largest all-white Baptist congregation in the nation. The church, affiliated with the Southern Baptist Convention, has an average weekly Sunday school attendance of more than 6,000.

A church as large as this needs a recreation building. So they have one structure across the street from the main church, seven stories high—five floors for parking and two for gymnasium, bowling lanes and skating rink. There are automatic pin-setters in every bowling lane. A hundred pairs of skates were bought by the church for the use of the congregation. In addition to sports, the recreation program offers courses in charm and modeling, beauty culture, cake decorating, millinery, Bible study and leathercraft.

The activities are financed with $16,000 a year paid by the concessionaire who runs the parking facilities, which are free only to churchgoers. An additional $10,000 a year is received from a special trust fund. A small charge is made for use of the bowling alleys and other income is received for the sale of candy and soft drinks.

A full-time recreation director—or minister of recreation—was hired to coordinate the many activities. He has a secretary and a number of assistants, most of them young men paid on an hourly basis.

The church itself approved in 1960 what its officials believed to be the largest annual local church budget "in the history of Christendom." The sum was $1,195,000—nearly half of it for missions and the rest for church activities, including the remodeling of a newly acquired 11-story building for the Sunday school and training union.

In a church this size, the Rev. Dan Beam, minister of recreation, said, "Christian recreation" develops the total life of the congregation. "It makes the church more inviting, relieves tension and teaches people to obey the rules," he said.

Social activities in most churches are far more modest and frequently involve the raising of money for various good works. "Think Pink" was the entertainment theme at a Congregational Church benefit in Los Angeles. A woman's group devoted several hours to demonstrating how to make pink the motif for an entire evening's fun.

The Priscilla Society of the First Congregational Church of Geneva, Ill., runs a catering service called "Receptions Unlimited," which raises about $1,000 a year for the church by providing punch, tea, cookies and sandwiches at social events.

Members of Trinity Methodist Church in Stahlstown, Pa., have a good time, preserve a historic ritual and raise money with an annual flax-scutching festival. In May a quarter-acre of flax is planted. In September it is harvested and scutched—an instrument called a scutcher being used to beat the pulp and bark from the linen fibers. The event is turned into a fair, with food and souvenirs sold at booths bringing in a total annual profit of about $2,500.

There is no shortage of ways to raise money through fellowship. A choir robe manufacturer went to the rather great length of publishing a list of "39 ways to help you raise the money for your choir robe fund," including amateur nights, choir concert nights, ladies' aid rummage sales, pot-luck suppers and fashion shows.

Food traditionally is the foundation for church fellowship, whether it is coffee and cookies after church or a full-scale banquet. Grace Episcopal Church in Hinsdale, Ill., holds "celebrity lunches" at country clubs or restaurants, followed by speeches by such persons as William L. Laurence, *New York Times* science editor, or Princess Ileana, daughter of the late Queen Marie of Romania. The First Presbyterian Church in Hollywood serves 2,500 meals a month in its own kitchens, supervised by a full-time cateress and a staff of four. Snacks are served at weekday meetings in many churches and nearly every prayer meeting opens with a meal.

A minister who complained about the accent on eating said his congregation had become so preoccupied with the preparation and serving of food that he felt when he served communion it meant about as much as if he were serving coffee and doughnuts.

Church suppers got their lumps also from the Rev. Donald J. MacCallum, minister of the First Congregational Church of Greenfield, Mass., in an article in *Church Management Maga-*

zine. He complained that the cost of church suppers often was too high and sometimes tended to get out of hand.

"In one church," he wrote, "a faltering men's club concluded that the alimentary canal was the surest route to a man's loyalty and tried to rebuild the shaky organization on a new foundation of monthly steak dinners!"

A woman's club, "in the interests of parish fellowship," charcoal-broiled 29-cent-a-pound chicken to a crisp $2.50 meal and then pocketed a neat profit for a "good cause," he said.

"Must we eat so well? is a question which arises as much from the sensitive conscience as from the sensitized pocketbook," Mac-Callum commented. "Can the church in good conscience lay lavish tables at profitable prices in the name of Christian fellowship?

"Not all church suppers, of course, qualify for a Duncan Hines endorsement, nor do they all bring a price that might adorn a menu at the Ritz, but the trend appears to be in that direction.

". . . The church supper is sacramental in character, an outward sign of an inward reality. . . . In appearance a church supper may be like any other meal, but in reality it is unlike any other meal, for it is the shared experience of a unique community."

There are other criticisms of fellowship programs, one being that they are lacking in one of the most highly publicized, all-time favorite, all-American family ingredients—TOGETHERNESS. While togetherness has become the watchword of nearly every other phase of American life, churches have tended to retain segregation in their fellowship activities. Congregations are broken up by age, sex and interest. The members of a family who go together to the church for fellowship part at the door.

Paul O. Madsen, associate executive secretary of the American Baptist Home Mission Society and secretary of the Division of Church Missions, believes that "churches are doing their best to split the family up. The programming is not for the family."

Among those trying to remedy this situation is the First Baptist Church in downtown Oakland, Calif., which found it could not attract men to Wednesday evening prayer meetings without their families. A church family night seemed to be the answer. The program was set to begin with a supper at 5:30 instead of the usual 7.

After supper, the parents joined in Bible study and the children watched religious movies. This proved to be reasonably successful, although it still was segregated.

Father-son weekend outings and mother-daughter sewing circles have broken down family segregation to a degree. The most successful efforts at togetherness in fellowship have come at picnics, church cookouts and evening parties, however.

"Suburban churches are discovering that the time demands upon their members, especially their leadership, is great," a report on Washington State American Baptist Churches said. "If a church night can be arranged, preceded by a supper and activities planned for the entire family, it may be possible to consolidate all church meetings and at the same time have Bible study, prayer fellowship and vespers.

"To knit together the fellowship of the church membership, it will be necessary to involve them in more than worshipping together."

The same study recommended religion and art festivals during religious holiday seasons, with choir concerts, dramas and lectures. One church had Sunday evening programs dealing with art and Christianity, during which participants studied Christian symbols, the development of Christian art, the significance of morality plays and the Broadway play, "J.B.," about a latter-day Job.

Some churches foster fellowship by quizzing new members on their interests and hobbies and providing them with sponsors, or "buddies," to help them fit into the schedule of activities. Pictures of newcomers are placed on bulletin boards with biographical sketches.

An annual pancake supper followed by movie cartoons for children and a prayer meeting for adults has been found popular at one Baptist church in the Far West. This church also holds a "celebrity series" every year featuring such speakers as Hardy Amies, designer to Queen Elizabeth II of Britain; Gen. Carlos P. Romulo, Filipino diplomat, and Bennett Cerf, publisher, raconteur and television star, who brought a crowd of 600 out in a rainstorm to hear him talk about the TV show "What's My Line?" and tell jokes.

The Rev. Dr. Gerald J. Jud, first secretary for evangelism of the United Church of Christ, has found that people tend to join a church much as they would a social club. Persuading a person to join is the easiest part of the evangelistic job; organizing his sense of values is the difficult aspect. People attend regular "meetings," i.e., the Sunday service, and pay their "dues," i.e., contribute to the collection, he said, but may have no idea what Christianity is all about.

Another minister who has reservations about the value of socializing in church is the Rev. George Barnes Edgar, pastor of the First Presbyterian Church of Fort Pierce, Fla. He believes that when the emphasis is on fellowship, the prime purpose of the church is forgotten.

"For example," he said, "all too many of our church men's clubs ape the civic clubs in programming and get nowhere. That's why they fail. Men want the church to be the church. I've seen two men's groups, one with fellowship emphasis—warm handshakes, good singing, etc.—and the other with recreation emphasis—pool, shuffleboard, darts, ping-pong and bowling—go right down from about 50 to 12 members. On the other hand, when we changed our emphasis from fellowship to a church-centered program, then we began to grow strong, not only in numbers but in effective service to the varied causes of the church.

"People are more interested in constructive activity—activity that makes the church the *church*."

Edgar's church recognizes the need for fellowship, if only on a modest scale, however, in three series of family nights a year involving suppers followed by 45-minute discussions—segregated by ages—of a single study theme. High-school study groups often meet in the church, at homes or on a beach.

"The Christian community must be a community of friends," Edgar believes, "so we try to make opportunity in the life of the church for the development of friendship. But we believe that above all else, the church is the body of Christ. And as the body of Christ our primary mission is that of reconciliation to God. Friendship and fellowship are important insofar as they help us carry out this function."

The Jews were pioneers in the pursuit of religious fellowship. Jewish community centers have been part of the American scene since 1854. First they were social and cultural organizations for older youth. Early in the 20th Century they shifted their main focus to immigrants. Now they cater to the recreational and cultural interests of Jews of all ages.

Before World War II, most Jewish community centers were in heavily populated cities. Since then, the trend has been toward suburbia and the construction of elaborate facilities for meetings and recreation. Nearly every new center has a gym, a swimming pool, kitchens, offices, a nursery school, a workshop and a lounge. Some have steam rooms and exercise facilities. The more modest centers may be built for as little as $300,000, but the new Detroit Jewish Community Center cost about $3,000,000.

Increasing emphasis on social activity surrounding the synagogue was criticized sharply by Rabbi Bernard Lander and his brother, Nathan, in a paper presented at a general assembly of the Synagogue Council of America. The brothers agreed that "the American synagogue is not dominated by the sacred, the major emphasis is not upon prayer and piety, but rather upon the social activity of the Sisterhood, Brotherhood, Men's Club, dances and now the psychological guidance of the parishioner. At best, a large segment of the Jewish community has evolved in our contemporary America a secular religion.

"Our findings suggest that there has been in the last 20 years a remarkable increase in Jewishness but not an equal upsurge in 'Yiddishkeit,' or religious practice. Parents are more interested in sending their children to Hebrew school, Jewish youth are prouder of their identification as Jews. Our youth could even interpret their identity in religious terms, but this pride, identity and increased knowledge has not been translated in the same measure in more frequent attendance at the synagogue, in prayer, in religious practice and in the acceptance of a God who is not only in nature but transcends nature."

A generally moderate view of fellowship in religion is taken by Norman Vincent Peale. He approves of activity programs, but only if they feed the central purpose of the church.

"Any strategy you can employ to get people exposed is all right, provided you expose them," he said. "I have known skillful people to use the tennis court to the glory of God and the salvation of the people.

"The Fellowship of Christian Athletes meets at Estes Park in Colorado every year. It is made up of baseball and football stars and people like that. They bring high-school athletes together so Bob Feller can show them how he throws a ball. He also throws a spiritual ball. The bait put on the hook is to go there and see Feller. But when they leave, they have something besides that."

Peale's Marble Collegiate Church has modest fellowship facilities compared with many churches; he said they are "average" for a big-city church.

"But the church is a swarming beehive all the time," he said. "Everything is pitched to the spiritual. If you can change lives in a church like a barn, that is O.K. If it is a country-club church, like some of those in Texas, that is all right, too, so long as the old spirit is there."

Probably the fastest growing and most fruitful field of church fellowship—and one that has Peale's full blessing—is the prayer group movement. Peale calls it the "new fellowship" of Protestantism, reflecting a growing feeling among churchgoers that they want to carry their religious activities into their weekday lives.

Once a week, for example, a group of well-dressed men gather at a famous university club in New York, but not to discuss business or last night's play. They sit down together for lunch and a prayer meeting. In a Connecticut suburb, a housewives' club that used to hold weekly canasta and gossip parties now meets to pray instead. Factory workers in an Upstate New York community hold lunch-hour prayer meetings. A group of Oklahoma City women set out from their homes early every Monday for a prayer breakfast at a drive-in restaurant en route to their jobs.

Soon after he entered the White House, President Kennedy was the honored guest at the ninth annual Presidential Prayer Breakfast sponsored by International Christian Leadership, Inc. High administration and Congressional leaders attended the breakfast, at which Kennedy had his picture taken with head bowed in prayer while sitting next to Billy Graham.

Similar breakfasts were held in 20 states for local leaders, all under the auspices of the International Christian Leadership, a non-denominational lay organization fostering Christian commitment among national leaders.

In Lena, Ill., many businessmen feel that their morning coffee break has taken on new meaning since the pastor of the Methodist Church has started joining them for prayer and discussion in a restaurant. Businessmen also pray together in Royston, Ga., but at 6:30 A.M., before starting their day's work.

C. Stanton Gallup, president of the American Baptist Convention and the head of a lumber company and water-works in Plainfield, Conn., presides over a prayer breakfast at his home every Tuesday at 5:45 A.M., His wife cooks for the little group of businessmen and ministers. Then they read and discuss the Bible and are at their desks by 8 A.M.,

"We sort of watch our prayers being answered," Gallup said. "It's amazing to see how many are answered."

The prayers are silent at the Presbyterian Church in Tenafly, N.J. Every night at 10, the church is open for silent prayer. The practice was started by the church's two ministers because it was their only time to pray and they decided to share the period with other busy persons.

A Bible study group meets at the Bethel Lutheran Church in Madison, Wis., every Monday night. Members are required to carry their Bible study cards at all times. If one member is challenged by another and is caught without his card, he must treat the challenger to an expensive dinner.

One of the most active organizations in fostering prayer meetings is Faith at Work, with headquarters in New York. It publishes a magazine called *Faith at Work* as a guidebook for prayer groups.

Margaret Peale, one of Peale's two daughters, is a leader of the organization, which recommends programs for prayer meetings and sends teams of volunteers into areas where churchgoers want to begin programs. Teams have gone to 55 communities during a single year, mainly in the Midwest, East and New England. First they held meetings in church, to describe the programs; then they supervised the actual holding of prayer meetings.

In a typical session, 30 men and women may meet in the home of a member. They begin with silent prayer. Then a participant reads from an inspirational book or magazine or from the Bible. Or they may discuss their various personal problems and pray for ways to solve them.

A minister confessed at one meeting that he was in the dumps spiritually much of the time because of dissension in his church. By talking about his problem, he saw a way to solve it. Members of a Detroit prayer group said that by meeting one night a week to discuss their lives they had been able to surmount the fears and anxieties of inflation and the Atomic Age.

There are several small prayer and discussion groups in the First Presbyterian Church of Winnetka, Ill., and a businessmen's group that meets there every week to find ways to apply Christianity on the job. The First Methodist Church of Delmar, N.Y., has a men's Saturday morning breakfast. In the Binghamton-Endicott-Johnson City, N.Y., area, there are 25 small groups that hold an annual joint fall conference. St. Stephen's Episcopal Church in Houston, Tex., has laymen's meetings on Sunday nights instead of vesper services.

Another form of fellowship through Faith at Work is provided by youth caravans. Thousands of young people spurn the luxury of summer vacations to work as volunteers on church-sponsored projects such as digging ditches or teaching tenement dwellers how to sew. Young people of all faiths pay their own way to travel great distances—sometimes overseas—just to work hard for two months, either with no pay or only enough to cover living expenses. Their labors may involve caring for mental hospital patients, painting churches, making toys, building roads, farming or taking children of working mothers on outings.

A caravan sent out by the United Church of Christ was made up of 32 chaperoned teen-agers who traveled for seven weeks. They painted a parish hall in Alma, Kans.; built a barbecue pit at the Crest Community Church in Midwest City, Okla., and sanded and painted chairs at a church in Raytown, Mo.

The American Baptist Convention sends out two caravans each year, one in the East and the other in the West, to travel for a month and help churches, Christian centers and missions. The youngsters carry their own food and sleeping equipment and camp as they travel.

Twelve teen-agers from nine states paid for a trip to Norristown, Pa., to serve part of a summer vacation as members of a Luther League Work Camp assigned to a hospital.

Fourteen New York Jewish children spent seven weeks working under the sponsorship of the Presbyterian Child Welfare Agency in Buckhorn, Ky., a small community in the Cumberland Mountains. They joined young people of other faiths in constructing a building for lockers and showers at a public school. During their weekends off, they exchanged religious services, sang together and discussed mutual problems. When it was over, they agreed they had found a kind of fellowship not available in synagogue or church, whether in prayer meeting or coffee hour.

In some churches, the word fellowship has become a verb. In others, the term is avoided as hackneyed. But whatever the church-related activities are called, they are supposed to point in one direction—toward greater attendance on Sunday morning. A number of ministers and other church officials were asked whether any social activity ever drew more persons than appeared at Sunday services. The reply was a universal "no." In the course of six days of "fellowshipping" the total turnout for prayer meeting, bowling or missionary night is greater, but no single event has the pull of the pulpit and the minister's Sunday sermon.

13

A Cleft in the Rock of Ages

"THE OLD RUGGED CROSS" may not be so rugged after all. It is a favorite song for group singing, but as a hymn it has lost status in many churches as too revivalistic. Songs praising the United Nations, the Home or the Ecumenical Movement are regarded by Protestant leaders as more in keeping with the times than the "religious rock 'n' roll" of "The Rock of Ages" or "The Old Rugged Cross."

Churches have tried to keep up-to-date in their music. Choirs are not singing Bach in a boogie beat yet, certainly, but chorales in a modern style are being heard and hymns are timely in their sentiments. A Protestant Episcopal clergyman has dignified progressive jazz with a syncopated mass and The Methodist Church has recognized the off-beat with a real cool accompaniment of John Wesley's revered "Order for Morning Prayer."

The latest in musical equipment is being built into churches, reviving an interest in the carillon—vibrating with electronic tones nowadays—and revitalizing the organ industry. Some organs are electric but most are intricate modern versions of the old-fashioned piped and wind-blown instruments.

Church notices in newspapers stress music to try to step up attendance. Sometimes "name" soloists are hired by the more affluent churches. Choirs are better prepared than they used to be and many churches have ministers educated in music as well as theology. The old-fashioned practice of accepting just about anyone who volunteered for choir duty has been abandoned wherever possible.

One does not have to look far today for a choir that is without the tone-deaf soprano who used to blight performances every Sunday.

The Methodists have organized a Fellowship of Music. Some churches encourage the teaching of good sacred music to children, instead of nursery-rhyme-type hymns. Choir rehearsal rooms are being included in some new church buildings. Radio and television offer good church music.

There are complaints in religious circles, however, that while the volume of church music has been turned up, relatively little that is new has been added. Some musicologists lament that there is an abundance of new hymns to go with old tunes, but that little original sacred music of quality is available. An era of unequaled religious interest sorely needs a 20th-century Bach.

The hymn, contrary to what some may believe, is the verse only. The music, whether by Haydn or Stravinsky, is called the "tune." The same tune may be used with many different hymns; sometimes one hymn is adapted to several tunes. To keep such repetition to a minimum, the editors of the new *Pilgrim Hymnal* of the Congregational Christian Churches set a limit, stipulating that different sets of words could appear with a single tune only three times.

New hymns have been written on the themes of Christian patriotism, the city, youth, fellowship, citizenship, rural life and the Bible, as well as the Ecumenical Movement. (Fitting the word "ecumenical" into a rhyme scheme is a neat trick indeed.) The Rev. Harry Emerson Fosdick, one of the most famous American preachers, turned hymn-writer with a paean on the home.

A search was launched by the National Council of Churches, through the Hymn Society of America, for hymns to be sung in connection with the 40th anniversary of the Council's Department of Stewardship and Benevolence.

"In the history of Christianity, comparatively little attention has been given to hymn-writing in the field of stewardship," said the Rev. T. K. Thompson, executive director of the department. "Most stewardship hymns now being used were written before 1900."

The Rev. Deane Edwards, president of the Hymn Society, said hymns submitted on stewardship could deal with any one of three themes—"that God is the Creator and Owner of the earth," "that man is the responsible steward of all that God has placed in his hands," and "that man, the responsible steward, must some day render an accounting to God, the Ultimate Owner."

For further poetic inspiration, Edwards cited the definition of Christian stewardship included in the constitution of the National Council:

"Christian stewardship is the practice of systematic and proportionate giving of time, abilities and material possessions based on the conviction that these are a trust from God, to be used in His service for the benefit of all mankind, in grateful acknowledgment of Christ's redeeming love."

In appealing for new hymns suitable for use in connection with a World Order Study Conference of the National Council's Department of International Affairs, the Hymn Society set forth a list of specifications including a requirement that the texts should be "in keeping with the conference theme ('Christian responsibility on a changing planet'), expressing the aspirations of those seeking a new spirit among the nations and a peace founded on freedom, justice and good will." The Society said it hoped to find lyrics to use in churches for "creating a new understanding of the nature of the international situation; and the responsibilities toward it, both personal and national, which spring from the Christian faith."

An appeal went out later for hymns on Christian marriage and family life in a competition held in connection with the North American Conference on Church and Family, sponsored by the Canadian and U.S. National Councils of Churches. The Rev. William H. Genné, executive director of the U.S. National Council's department of family life, said the search was started because of a dearth of such hymns.

"We believe this competition will fill a significant gap in our hymnology," Genné said. "We also believe it will give our hymn-writers an excellent opportunity to give expression to the newer concepts of the relation of Christian faith to sex, love, marriage and parenthood."

Edwards, expressing the hope for new hymns suitable for use at weddings and home dedications, asked for verses recognizing the "fundamental nature of marriage and family life," written in the well-known meters found in standard hymnals.

When the Methodist magazine *Together* announced a contest to find the best hymn celebrating the church's 175th anniversary, it instructed that entries be written to the Mendelssohn "tune" best-known as the accompaniment for the famous Christmas carol "Hark! the Herald Angels Sing." A clergyman, the Rev. Donald Williams of North Andover, Mass., was judged the winner. His verse was designated for alternate use with the original words by Charles Wesley, the "bard" of Methodism and John Wesley's brother.

Whether any of the new anthems praising modern life will ever make the churchgoers' hit parade is impossible to say. But it is a fact that "Onward Christian Soldiers" and other rousing "gospel hymns" have been dropped from most standard hymnals, according to the Hymn Society of America.

"The Old Rugged Cross" and others such as the lilting "In the Garden" have fallen into disuse in many Protestant churches, to the dismay of some old-timers. When the Methodist Committee on Hymnology declared itself in favor of omitting "What a Friend We Have in Jesus" and "Blessed Assurance" from a new hymnal, a Missouri churchgoer wrote a bitter protest to *The Christian Herald*. The editor, the Rev. Dr. Danial A. Poling, replied that he hoped it was just another false rumor.

A short time later, *The Christian Herald* reported the results of a nationwide poll it had made in 1960 asking 30,000 persons to list their favorite hymns. "The Old Rugged Cross" turned up at the top of the list, followed by many other old-time hymns that have been left out of new-time hymnals.

The *Herald* conducted the poll as part of its campaign to encourage families to sing hymns together at home.

After "The Old Rugged Cross" in the *Herald's* top 10 came "What a Friend We Have in Jesus," "In the Garden," "How Great Thou Art," "Sweet Hour of Prayer," "Abide with Me," "Rock of Ages," "Nearer, My God, to Thee," "Amazing Grace" and "Jesus, Lover of My Soul."

The first two were given the same rating in a *Christian Herald* hymn poll in 1953.

The magazine noted that "The Old Rugged Cross," copyright in 1913, is excluded from most hymnals, but said it is nevertheless a favorite of ministers as well as congregations. Ministers polled rated "What a Friend We Have in Jesus" first, followed by "The Old Rugged Cross," "When I Survey the Wondrous Cross," "Amazing Grace" and "How Great Thou Art."

The "long-hairs" among church musicologists were not surprised at these poll results. The songs listed still are "gospel hymns" as far as they are concerned, however, and are not for singing during church service.

Church music authorities are unclear as to the origin of the term "gospel hymn" but they suspect it grew from the fact that the lyrics so labeled had been sung most often at camp meetings and tent revivals, and therefore were associated more with the sawdust-trail school of evangelism than the socially conscious church.

"It is religious rock 'n' roll," declared an official of the United Church of Christ, "and the sentiments are more objectionable than the tunes. When these hymns were sung at revival meetings, it was at a time when group singing was the chief form of entertainment. There were no movies, no radio and no television. People got excitement out of tent meetings. Gospel hymns were part of that excitement."

Edwards agreed with this analysis, saying that "Gospel hymns are ultra-sentimental and inward-looking. Many persons feel 'The Old Rugged Cross' falls in that category. It is popular with many persons and groups, but it is not in most standard hymnals. It is a medium-grade gospel hymn.

"Better ones, in general, are those that have good music and do not have jazzed-up tunes, and that have words that are satisfactory."

The kind of music Edwards frowns upon still is popular with many persons. Nearly 10,000 persons flocked to Madison Square Garden to tap their feet in time with hymns sung at a marathon 10-hour Gospel, Religious, Spiritual and Folk Music Festival. More than 350 performers accompanied by four organs appeared. Among them were three choruses, 12 small groups, a cantor from Israel and Mahalia Jackson, the Negro singer of spirituals.

Members of religious record clubs seem to prefer gospel hymns, too. One club features television's Tennessee Ernie Ford singing a representative selection on a long-playing record. Ford's album

"Sing a Hymn with Me" has a hymnal bound to it so his fans can join in.

Gospel hymns are on recordings by Billy Graham's International Crusade Choirs and are monthly offerings of the Christian Faith Record Club, which features, among others, the Christian Faith Orchestra, the Haven of Rest Quartet and Arnie Hartman on the accordion. One may be either a "hi-fi" or a "stereo" (short for stereophonic) member of this club.

The fact that the gospel variety of hymn is regarded as on the way out by major denominations should be no cause for surprise. Hymnals have been in a state of almost constant revision since congregational singing was introduced during the Reformation. The leaders of the great Christian upheaval objected to having worshippers sit in church and do almost nothing but listen. Joining in singing the liturgy and hymns gave congregations a sense of participation and thus contributed to the success of the Reformation. Part of the secret of this lay in the fact that the words were in the vernacular of the day. Protestantism has held to this formula ever since, seldom hesitating to cast an out-of-date hymn aside in favor of a new one.

In recent years, the Roman Catholic Church has moved in this direction. Under papal decrees, Catholics now are allowed to participate vocally in parts of the mass instead of leaving it entirely to the priests. Some American parishes do not have choirs any more; the worshippers sing those parts of the mass the choir used to chant. There also is a move to put at least part of every service in English instead of entirely in the traditional Latin.

So sharply have sentiments expressed through hymnology changed, that only a little more than half the hymns in the 1931 edition of the *Pilgrim Hymnal* were included in the 1960 edition, and some of those were altered slightly to make them more timely. A reference to a dawning day of brotherhood, written in 1909, was omitted in the new book because such a day still had not dawned half a century later.

The new hymnal includes some of "the better" gospel hymns, but, for the first time, there is no special section for them.

The original *Congregational Bay State Hymnal* appeared in

1640. Only one of its hymns, "O Lord, Almighty God, Thy Works," is in the 1960 volume.

Gospel hymns did not fare well either in the new *Service Book and Hymnal* of the United Lutheran Church in America. Fanny Crosby, who wrote more than 8,000 gospel hymns, is represented by only one—"Pass Me Not, O Gentle Saviour."

Dr. E. E. Ryden, editor of *The Lutheran Companion* and secretary of the group that supervised the hymnal, said a few gospel hymns measured up to the standards set for the book, however. Among those accepted were "What a Friend We Have in Jesus," "Softly and Tenderly Jesus Is Calling," "He Leadeth Me, O Blessed Thought," "I Need Thee Every Hour," and "More Love to Thee, O Christ." Here, again, "The Old Rugged Cross" was omitted.

Hymnals are increasingly reflecting the "one world" aspect of Protestantism. Denominational hymnals are reaching across sectarian lines for many anthems. It is possible to go from a church of one denomination to a church of another and hear the same hymns. Charles Wesley, for example, although a Methodist, is the most popular hymn-writer in the new Lutheran collection, being represented by 17 hymns. The Quaker poet John Greenleaf Whittier led the list of American hymn-writers in the Lutheran volume, with six sets of lyrics. One Negro spiritual was included, along with two hymns that had been introduced at assemblies of the World Council of Churches. Another hymn, "O God of Light, Thy Word a Lamp Unfailing," was written in 1952 by Sara E. Taylor to honor the publication of the Revised Standard Version of the Bible.

Most of the new hymns have been written to go with old music by Haydn, Mendelssohn and others. Four new hymns, "for youth by youth," accepted and published by the Hymn Society were written to be sung with tunes composed in the 19th century. Some modern composers have been drawn upon for church singing, but syncopated hymns have been rarities.

Sometimes a tune in a traditional rhythm will be given a jazz beat, but not often. This is frowned on by those who shun the old-time religion. The native American music form has found more favor in the composition of other church music.

One of the more widely acclaimed modern works for the church is the 20th century accompaniment for the Methodist "Order of Morning Prayer." It was introduced in Texas by a combo in choir robes and received such an enthusiastic response later at a Methodist youth meeting that it was televised by the National Broadcasting Company on an hour-long program entitled "Requiem for Mary Jo," in memory of a child who died of a heart defect in Denton, Tex. The grieving parents of 9-month-old Mary Jo Summerlin had turned to the Methodist Church for comfort. Ed Summerlin, a clarinetist-saxophonist, composed the music as an expression of gratitude to those who had helped him and his wife.

In this endeavor, Summerlin had the advice and encouragement of the Rev. Bill Slack Jr., assistant pastor of the First Methodist Church in Denton, and Dr. Roger Ortmayer, a Methodist minister and professor of Christianity and the Arts at Perkins School of Theology of Southern Methodist University. It was at Ortmayer's suggestion that the music was composed for the liturgy John Wesley had devised for regular Sunday morning services along the general lines of the ritual in the *English Book of Common Prayer.*

Summerlin said he hoped people would realize his jazz liturgy was not just a stunt—that he had sound reasons for writing it and really believed in it.

"After all," he said, "you just don't say, 'I'm going to write a jazz service,' and then sit down and do it. Most of the younger theologians feel that jazz speaks in the language of today and that this is what the church must recognize if it is to meet the needs of today."

Another progressive combo lined out the American premiere of the "20th Century Folk Mass," by the Rev. Geoffrey Beaumont, an Englishman, at communion service at St. Paul's Church on the Green in Norwalk, Conn. Beaumont wrote the mass to put ancient liturgical rituals into everyday language, and he went so far as to test his music in an English pub.

The rector of the Norwalk church, the Rev. Anthony P. Treasure, used it as background for a sermon stressing that religion is part of every phase of life, and as a demonstration to young people that the church is neither "fuddy-duddy" nor out of date.

Priests in age-old vestments stood before the altar, and censer bearers sent their incense wafting as the music rang out, first an "Allelulia" in unmistakable ragtime; then the "Kyrie" and "Agnus Dei" in beguine rhythms; the "Gloria" and several hymns in foxtrot time, and the "Creed," "Sanctus" and "Our Father" in bold jazz.

There are other modern compositions for the church that are not in the jazz idiom. Virgil Thomson, Igor Stravinsky and Russell Woollen are among those who have written outstanding modern choral works. But their music, when played in churches, relies not on orchestras but on the organ, which still is the basic church instrument.

The church building boom has been accompanied by an equally spectacular boom in the organ industry. Every new church "must" have an organ, either electric or pipe. As a result the manufacturers are as much as three years behind in their work and have no idea when they will catch up. The biggest market for electric organs is among smaller churches that cannot afford pipe organs costing up to $100,000, and in some large churches with décors that seem to lend themselves more to electronic tones or that offer no suitable place for pipes.

During World War II, organ makers devoted almost all their resources to defense production, which helped them recover from Depression doldrums. They had gone into a decline in the 1930's after talking movies drowned out theater organ music. Now the industry is thriving as never before. It has trained its artisans to do the exacting work of putting organs together by methods that have changed little through the centuries, although the materials used and the instrument itself have gone through several changes.

The "romantic" organ was developed for silent-movie houses. It was designed to reproduce the actual tones of individual instruments. When played together, the various sounds were supposed to represent an orchestra or band. Now, with the church boom, organs have been restored to their "classical" status, creating tones and chords bearing no resemblance to anything heard from any other instrument.

Despite some architects' objections, organ makers encourage the inclusion of the pipes in the interior design of churches, instead of hiding them behind drapes or in walls. More music comes from an organ if the pipes are exposed, says one of the biggest manufacturers. To encourage this, he provides decorated pipes to enhance interiors.

Organ makers find that churches are willing to spend more money on pipe organs because they have awakened to the fact that they produce a kind of music that contributes to a worshipful atmosphere. There is something about organ music that gives, as no other form of accompaniment can, a full body to the amateur voices of church choirs and the valiant but sometimes off-pitch efforts of congregations, especially now that they have set aside the familiar old gospel hymns and are singing praise of such causes as stewardship and ecumenicity.

There is no question that great sociological themes should receive expression in church music as well as sermons. But there still is room on every church program for a chorus of "Rock of Ages," "The Old Rugged Cross" or any of the other familiar hymns that most persons can sing without opening a hymnal. An old-time song makes a newcomer feel at home, and in fellowship groups, it serves as an ice breaker.

The various excursions into jazz so far have been experimental and may have no real liturgical significance, but they are part of the church going into the world and the world moving into the church. As shown in the *Christian Herald* poll, no amount of this sort of experimentation is going to replace the popular old-time hymns, however. Perhaps there should be a blending of the best of the old and new as a stimulus to churchgoing. The religious leaders most worried about spectatoritis and how to keep attendance at a high level might try putting "The Old Rugged Cross" back in the hymnals and find a lilting new word for ecumenicity.

14

Hollywood, Broadway and the Air

Hollywood is Holy Wood to the churches, but they regard the world of radio and television as being far from a paradise.

Millions of dollars have been spent in the film capital on commercially successful Biblical spectacles featuring the biggest stars. Alongside this great glamour enterprise has grown a religious movie industry that almost matches the commercial studios in the number of films made every year, although on not nearly so elaborate a scale.

The New York theater also is hospitable to religious dramas and to plays worthy of "Christian evaluation." Archibald Mac-Leish's "J.B.," a modern story of Job, won a Pulitzer Prize. Plays based on religious themes have done well in little off-Broadway theaters. Perhaps most notable of all is the return of the play to the cradle of English drama—the church sanctuary.

Radio and television are the desert surrounding these oases. The church has been relegated by broadcasters almost entirely to a "Sunday ghetto." Other than the prayers that open and close each day's broadcasting on some stations, a saccharine TV soap opera with a minister as its trouble-beset hero, and a few children's programs, the principal sacral fare is broadcast or televised at peak non-listening and non-viewing hours, usually Sunday morning. The Sunday morning air is saturated with religious programs at the very hours when most persons interested in them should be in church. They are the hours least likely to find commercial sponsors, so the time is given to religious organizations as a "public service" in a great burst of altruism.

The National Council of Churches learned through a survey that a mere 3.1 per cent of all the broadcast time in a single week was devoted to sustaining programs of a religious nature. The study covered 141 commercial radio and television stations on the air a total of 16,353 hours and 39 minutes a week in 11 major cities. Only 508 hours and 48 minutes of that time were devoted to the spiritual. That came to an average of about 3½ hours a week per station.

Radio gave 3.5 per cent of its time to "public service" religious programs and TV provided 1.7 per cent. In Denver, the five television stations, allocated 4 hours and 40 minutes to religion during the week surveyed. The two Birmingham, Ala., TV stations had 5 hours and 30 minutes of religious programs. Boston's 15 stations gave 24 hours and 13 minutes, while Philadelphia, with the same number of outlets, received nearly twice as much time.

Everett Parker, a veteran of 20 years in the church's struggle for air time, said that TV and radio have downgraded religion at a time when it is receiving increased attention from movies, newspapers, magazines and the book-publishing world. He and others feel that if the TV fare really were good the churches would not have such a strong argument, but they are convinced that what they have to offer the American public is better than much that is being served up in the guise of entertainment.

There are a few isolated instances in which networks have done something special for religious groups. The National Broadcasting Company sponsored a series of 90-minute Bible dramas costing more than $200,000 each, with copies of the films available at no charge to religious organizations for their own use. An N.B.C. crew worked with the Television and Radio Commission of the Southern Baptist Convention in filming the Baptist World Congress in Rio de Janeiro in 1960, and excerpts were carried later on N.B.C. programs.

Such activities are rare. In most cases, religious programs are given to stations or networks by the organizations that make them. Most also are presented without a single "plug" for the sponsoring denomination. They appear to be non-denominational, whether they actually are or not.

Networks increasingly are encouraging non-denominational programs by allocating time equally to Protestants, Catholics and Jews rather than including individual denominations in their programming. Station WABC in New York moved in this direction by cancelling at least seven religious broadcasts financed by various denominations and replacing them with an allotment of 90 minutes a week of free time to Protestants, Catholics, Jews and "evangelicals," or about 22 minutes a week each. One program cancelled was the Calvary Baptist Church Hour, which had been on the air every Sunday morning for more than 30 years. Billy Graham's "The Hour of Decision" was not affected, however.

Sponsorship is a key stumbling block to the presentation of large numbers of religious programs on radio and television. People will pay to see a movie about Ruth and Naomi, Esther, Moses or Jesus in a theater, but commercial sponsors steer clear of the same stories aimed at radio and television audiences. If a program is sponsored by a religious group, the sponsoring body foots the bill for preparation of the show and the network or station donates the time. Churches are limited in the amount they can spend on such projects, and there obviously is a limit to the amount of time commercial broadcasters can give away.

The caliber of the religious programs that do get on the air is remarkably high—often higher than much of the commercial fare. The old bathrobe school of church drama has been abandoned in favor of modern presentations of ancient Biblical themes, often followed by panel discussions of the moral issues involved that are far more interesting than the Sunday afternoon "quiz show" interviews of Congressmen and government officials.

Religious programs are not without the Hollywood touch. The Protestant Episcopal Church recruited Robert Young for a series of radio dramas with such stars as Herbert Marshall and Charles Ruggles. Top-rated radio performers also have been enlisted. Mary Margaret McBride, for example, conducted a series of interviews with family relations experts under the National Council of Churches' sponsorship.

Other popular techniques are used. Cartoon movies with nonsectarian themes have been produced for children, while for their parents there may be modern-dress dramas based on various interpretations of the Ten Commandments. Travelogues with a professional air have been featured, the most notable perhaps being the "Off to Adventure" series prepared by Parker, financed by the Congregational Christian Churches and distributed by the National Council.

Various denominations keep busy in the field, ever hopeful they will achieve a breakthrough in their campaign for a share of what is called prime air time. The Council of Bishops of The Methodist Church took note of the situation in 1954 by declaring an "emergency" in radio and TV and calling on churches to try to use this newest means of mass communication to spread the Gospel to the American people. Two years later, the Council introduced a $250,000, 13-program series called "The Way," billed as the most elaborately produced TV series undertaken up to that time by a religious organization.

The films in the series, which were offered free to 250 stations, dealt with such subjects as juvenile delinquency, choosing a vocation, safe driving, the Christian answer to communism, a mother's problems when her children are grown, a child's need for his father's attention, facing death from cancer and combating prejudice toward foreigners. Forty thousand local churches received materials to help them organize groups to study the programs.

Bishop Donald Harvey Tippett of the San Francisco area of The Methodist Church assured his fellow church members that support of this enterprise in no way implied a lack of faith in the traditional evangelistic procedures.

"Since television is such an effective and versatile medium of communication—perhaps the most versatile—The Methodist Church feels duty-bound to enter the TV field, because it really believes, with its founder, that 'the world is my parish,'" Tippett said.

A similar effort, billed as "Televangelism 1959," was conducted by the Baptists in a 13-week series of "This Is the Answer" films. Local churches sponsored home viewing parties to watch the Sunday series on about 100 stations. Those who attended the parties then discussed the stories, which dramatized some of the moral and spiritual problems of the day.

The National Lutheran Council filmed a $365,000 series called "Light Time" as a public-service program aimed at unchurched youngsters between 8 and 12 years old. The Council received a number of fan letters from parents, one from a mother expressing delight over the fact that her children preferred "Light Time" to the Three Stooges.

Locally produced programs seem to be more in demand than network religious shows. Audiences apparently want to see and hear people who are familiar to them. They also like to find out more about local problems.

A Pittsburgh station, WQED-TV, conducted a program called "Live and Learn" for leaders in Christian education. Directed by the Pittsburgh Council of Churches, the series offered instruction in the psychological and practical aspects of various teaching methods and the use of teaching materials. Groups met in homes and churches to take notes on the lessons and discuss them. Each "student" paid $5 for a syllabus and a reading list.

The Protestant Council of New York offered two popular Bible courses on TV, weekdays from 6:30 to 7 A.M., with college credits available to those who paid $100 per course. The subjects were "Introduction to Biblical Thought" and "Religion and Modern Literature." Materials for church leadership training cost $25; the price of a syllabus, bibliography and text was $5.

Several major religious organizations have well-financed broadcasting divisions. Most Protestant bodies cooperate with the National Council of Churches Broadcasting and Film Commission. Roman Catholic and Jewish groups also have programs, frequently accepting a division of air time with Protestants. The League of Catholic Men has produced outstanding "Catholic Hour" programs on which many controversial subjects have been discussed, including criticism of the Catholic Church and how to fight alcoholism. And, of course, there is Bishop Fulton J. Sheen, whose TV show once gave Milton Berle a run for the ratings.

Some churches have solved the problem of obtaining air time by operating their own stations. St. Mark's Lutheran Church in

Evansville, Ind., has a television station on which it sends its Sunday services over a 60-mile radius. A balcony was built in the rear of the nave for cameras and control panels, and special lights were installed under the roof. Viewers at home follow services without a book, for the words of the liturgy are superimposed on the pictures. Church attendance, surprisingly, increased sharply after the station went on the air.

Riverside Church in New York City built an FM radio station mainly for informational and educational programs, not religious broadcasts. Community service was the aim of the station, which was given an annual operating budget of $125,000. The biggest problem encountered was where to put the antenna so it would not clash with the Gothic architecture of the church building.

The Lutheran Church-Missouri Synod built a special chapel in the headquarters of the Lutheran Laymen's League, sponsor of "The Lutheran Hour," to double as a sanctuary and a recording studio for what the denomination calls the largest non-governmental broadcasting effort in the world, the "This Is the Life" program. The producers say this series of modern-dress Biblical dramas is exceeded in global coverage only by programs of the Voice of America, Radio Moscow and the British Broadcasting Corporation. Why, then, should it not be put on the air in the United States at a prime hour?

Church groups do not stop at trying to get their own messages on the air. They also try to influence non-religious offerings. Clergymen testified, for instance, at the Congressional investigation of the television quiz show and radio disc jockey payola scandals, and an official of the United Presbyterian Church in the U.S.A. called on the networks to share the blame with the individuals who had participated in the "fixes."

Hundreds of Catholic, Protestant and Jewish clergymen in New York gave sermons during the same weekend in 1959 asking their congregations to tell the TV stations and networks how they rated their programs during a given period. This was done to stimulate parental responsibility toward what children watch on home screens.

When James Wine was associate general secretary of the

National Council of Churches, he appeared before the Federal Communications Commission to protest programs loaded with violence and crime; high-pressure "hucksterish" commercials on children's programs "taking advantage of the loyalty and affection of the young"; half-truths, exaggerations and falsifications in ads; mediocrity, and advertising lacking in responsibility.

The Ministerial Alliance of McKinney, Tex., sent a letter to several national denominational groups urging that viewers write letters to the networks protesting the use of profanity on the air as a "total disregard for decency and a violation of the sanctity of our homes."

Criticism has been leveled at religious groups that think they should receive special treatment simply because they represent a worthy cause. One of those who has such fault to find is the Rev. Dr. John W. Bachman, professor of practical theology and director of the audio-visual program at Union Theological Seminary. He reviewed the subject in a book on "The Church in the World of Radio-Television," in which he found that religious leaders often forget that they should be concerned with every program on the air, not just purely religious presentations.

In the past, he said, there has been little awareness of the responsibility of the church toward radio and television, but new interest and concern have been stimulated by the fact that children often sing beer commercials more enthusiastically than hymns and know more about Wyatt Earp than Moses—and that it is almost impossible to draw a crowd to church on Sunday evening when a "spectacular" or "special" is on television.

Bachman called for a definitive church policy toward radio and TV but urged the church to move slowly, taking care to study the entire field and to try to achieve real interdenominational cooperation before pitting its voice against that of the 20th century broadcasting giant.

Organized religion's influence has been felt more in Hollywood than in the broadcasting world, possibly because the film industry is older and wiser to the requests and pressures of the churches. The Catholic Legion of Decency has had a strong voice in judging what Catholic movie-fans should see. Protestants also have spoken out, and effectively, on vice, violence, crime and profanity on the screen. Several religious bodies keep "watchdogs" in Hollywood to look after church interests.

One of the more controversial movies, as far as the churches were concerned, was "Martin Luther," produced by the Lutherans and vigorously opposed by some Catholics. Many Catholic publications printed reviews that Lutherans regarded as both temperate and fair, but the film was put in a special viewing category in which it was neither approved nor condemned. This meant it would be wise for Catholics wishing to see it to consult their parish priests first.

The picture, produced by Louis de Rochemont for Lutheran Church Productions, was notable in becoming a commercial success. Only one other major church-produced film, "Mark of the Hawk," has done well at the box office. "Martin Luther" has been shown regularly in churches and theaters and has been accepted as standard TV re-run material now that a second flurry of Catholic protests has died down.

The Lutheran groups that financed the film were so delighted with the returns on their investments that they provided funds for a second commercial film, also produced by de Rochemont. This one deals with the struggle of the church against communism in East Germany.

In recent years, one of the more remarkable developments in the film capital has been the rise of the religious movie industry, in which no swearing is allowed on the sets and each day's shooting begins with a prayer.

Religious movies are made mainly for TV and church viewing. *The Christian Herald* reported that 227 such films were produced in the United States in 1959—only three fewer than the number of full-length commercial movies made for entertainment purposes.

World Wide Pictures, a result of the merger of Great Commission Films and Billy Graham Films, produces documentaries on Graham's crusades that are advertised as having brought thousands of "decisions for Christ" from those who have viewed them. The Moody Institute of Science and Cathedral Films have produced scores of movies for church use. A major project of

Cathedral was a serialized life of Jesus in 12 half-hour install-ments. Family Films made nearly 400 pictures in 10 years, most of them for church audiences.

Some of the most successful religious film companies operate far from the home of the kleig light. One is Unusual Films in Greenville, S.C., which often does its casting on the campus of Bob Jones University. It also films sermons for TV and produced a short that was exhibited at a Cannes Film Festival. Gospel Films, in Muskegon, Mich., makes dramatic movies for teen-age audiences.

All of these are "independents," meaning they are non-denomi-national. The largest denominational film producer is The Meth-odist Church, with studios in Nashville, Tenn.

The National Council of Catholic Men has sponsored produc-tion of films on Rome, family life, modern art and the history of the scriptures. "Reflections, U.S.A.," was a four-part series prob-ing the psychology, morality and spirituality of contemporary American life. The United Presbyterian Church in the U.S.A. has produced a dramatic documentary on the interplay of church agencies, to encourage greater cooperation among congregations.

American Baptists in Denver have been experimenting with "a new dimension" in evangelism—movie parties at which thought-provoking films are viewed and then discussed. Baptists are urged to take unchurched friends to the gatherings, which have featured such films as "He Who Must Die" and "On the Beach." After seeing the latter movie, one group discussed the questions "Is the world headed for nuclear destruction?" and "What can be done about it?" The Rev. Dr. Elroy Shikles, pastor of the First Baptist Church in Denver, reported two baptisms as a result of viewing parties for "Ben Hur" and "The Big Fisherman."

The other major entertainment field drawn on by churches is the theater, which is the least of the three but possibly the most dynamic. Church drama gives a sense of participation not found in watching TV or movies.

The earliest English drama was the liturgical play, performed in churches by roving bands of actors. Some of the plays produced in churches today are these same ancient dramas, also often presented by touring players. But there are new ones as well. A Christopher Fry drama was produced successfully in a New York City church, and a professional company headed by Uta Hagen and Philip Bourneuf rehearsed in their spare time for five months to perform Henry de Montherlant's "Port-Royal," about a conflict between a group of nuns and a Pope, at Grace Protestant Episcopal Church in New York.

The appearance of the professional actor in a church play is a rarity, however. Most of the Biblically inspired dramas are presented by amateurs looking for new insights into their faith. Ministers hope that this self-evangelization will stimulate attendance on Sundays.

Theological seminaries have introduced drama courses for prospective ministers. A number of denominations sponsor drama workshops, as does the National Council of Churches. The result has been a professionalization of church plays, in which the man who portrays Jesus is persuaded to act naturally instead of walking with his arms outstretched and a benign smile on his face. There are fewer cheesecloth angels, better costumes, more artistic staging and more skillfully written plays to attract audiences.

Lay liturgical drama groups are active outside churches. One traveling troupe gave 477 performances in 43 states in a single year. A Denver liturgical dance company appeared in a number of Midwestern colleges. A survey of 140 colleges and universities disclosed that one-fourth had at least one course in religious drama, one-half had touring drama groups and one-seventh provided supervision for students appearing in local church plays.

Twelve seminaries had organized religious drama programs, with four of them sponsoring companies of touring players who visited churches to perform "Our Town," "St. Joan," "Everyman," "J.B.," "Murder in the Cathedral," "A Man Called Peter," "The Potting Shed," "A Sleep of Prisoners" and "The Lark," most of which had been Broadway successes.

The United Presbyterian Church in the U.S.A. sent a drama caravan on a tour of the South and East to demonstrate the role of the theater in the church. It also has an untheatrical sounding Ecumenical Training Center at Stony Point, N.Y., where an old barn has been converted into a laboratory theater for summer repertory programs that have featured plays based on legends and the Bible stories of Jonah and Noah and Arthur Miller's "The Crucible." The plays, including that by Miller, a Jew, were chosen for their "suitability in communicating Christian philosophy." Students participating in the program come from all over the world, one having been sent by Emperor Haile Selassie of Ethiopia to study Western theater techniques.

Dramas with messages are replacing keynoters at church gatherings. Instead of calling on one person to deliver an oration setting the tone for a national convention, the National Christian Education Committee put its thoughts into a play. A new drama depicting the crucial issues facing the modern church was given its premiere at the 22nd convention of the United Lutheran Church in America. "The Time Is Now," which could have been the subject for a sermon, was the title of a three-act play written for the convention by Dr. Robert E. Huldschiner, feature editor of *The Lutheran* magazine. The plot revolved around a single family, symbolizing the whole church and its struggles to overcome prejudice and outdated traditions.

The appearance of such a new play is cause for jubilation in church circles, for there is an almost universal complaint about a shortage of fresh material—even on old themes. Much of the old-time repertoire is criticized sharply for having unreal, pageant-like qualities and failing to come to grips with any issues.

College students have been urged to try to write religious drama and the Methodist Student Movement held a contest for both full-length and one-act plays about life situations of university students. Another play-writing contest was sponsored by Union Theological Seminary and the National Broadcasting Company, with cash prizes for three winners, and N.B.C. and the seminary claiming first production rights.

Church interest in the drama, whether on stage, screen, radio or TV, is one more evidence of the growing role of the world in spiritual life. The clerical attitude today is that a man's whole existence is his religion, whether he is watching TV, sitting in the movies or praying in church. In the new-time religion, the churches are encouraging writers to create material for or about the church and for use in the church. They are encouraging just as vigorously the production of materials for presentation outside the church for the whole world to see and hear.

Television offers organized religion the most powerful, far-reaching evangelistic tool yet devised, but it is a tool that is being used little and limply. The nucleus for an effective broadcasting program exists in the Sunday ghetto. If these programs were moved to other times of the week, they might serve to influence their audiences to join the parade to synagogue or church. They are unlikely to do more than scratch the surface on Sunday morning.

Many questions are raised, the principal one being: Why can't the churches enlist commercial sponsors to buy prime air time? Religious organizations buy stock in General Motors, U.S. Steel and other companies. Why shouldn't they seek and accept sponsorship by such companies? And why shouldn't such companies give it? Sponsorship on a non-denominational basis or on a rotating basis, with each group taking its turn on the air, certainly would not involve religious bias and it would offer the opportunity for programs of a much higher caliber than some now presented by these same sponsors.

It might be possible for religious organizations to buy prime time once in a while. If some can afford to operate their own stations, others might be able to pool their resources to pay for an hour of their choice periodically. By presenting "sample" programs during peak listening or viewing hours, they might be able to attract audiences large enough and enthusiastic enough to warrant network and sponsor recognition on an equal basis with other radio and TV fare. The churches' initial investment might be considerable, but it would be no more of an evangelistic gamble than they took in underwriting missions to China that were wiped out by communists, or equally risky ventures in strife-ridden Africa.

15

The Bible: Least-Read Best-Seller

THE WORLD'S BEST-SELLER is far from the world's best-read book. The Bible in any of its many versions, Catholic, Protestant and Jewish, has annual total sales well in the millions. There probably is scarcely a family that does not own at least one book of Scriptures in some form. Passages are quoted widely by Presidents and other politicians. Writers borrow from the Bible for inspiration and titles. And yet the United States is called a nation of Biblical illiterates.

Nearly every church sermon is based on a Biblical passage. Children are taught Bible lessons in Sunday school. Movies, television shows and Broadway plays are based on stories from the Bible. The comic book technique has been used to spread the Gospel in some Sunday school lessons. The Good Book has been cited as "must" reading on the floor of the United States Senate for containing "measureless treasures untold."

Publishers reap sizeable profits from Bible sales and never have found any book that has begun to match its popularity. The American Bible Society alone prints and distributes more than nine million volumes of Scriptures in English every year. The new commercially published Revised Standard Version has sold at a rate of about a million copies a year since it was introduced in 1952 with nation-wide fanfare. The Douay Bible and a newer Roman Catholic version have been bought enthusiastically. Special translations of the Old Testament are published by and for Jews.

But, the churches are asking, who reads the Bible after it is bought?

When the Revised Standard Version appeared as the first authorized Protestant text in half a century, it was hailed by President Harry S. Truman as a harbinger of a new religious awakening. Governors of more than 20 states issued proclamations for a Christian Education Week calling attention to community Bible observances coinciding with the publication date, Sept. 30, 1952. Hundreds of similar statements were made by mayors and other local officials, and the new Bible was praised widely in the press. More than 1,500,000 persons attended some 3,400 observances in the United States and at military posts overseas.

Special presentation copies of the new Bible went to prominent persons, including governors, Billy Graham and Trygve Lie, then United Nations Secretary General, for the United Nations prayer room; Jersey Joe Walcott, the heavyweight champion of the world; generals, admirals and Dr. Syngman Rhee, then President of South Korea.

A record first-edition run of one million copies was sold out quickly. The initial printing gobbled up 20,000,000 square inches of 23-carat gold leaf, which was used to stamp the spines of the bindings. Someone took time out from the venture to reckon that the gold was enough to pave a street 24 feet wide and nearly a mile long. Additional computations showed that if the first million copies were stacked in a single pile, they would have stood 24 miles high—equal to 100 Empire State Buildings.

Various denominations marked the appearance of the new Holy Writ with special study courses. In Port Arthur, Tex., more than 7,500 persons celebrated the occasion at a barbecue at which they sang, prayed and ate. In Portland, Me., the new Scriptures were read by six laymen, including a displaced person who recited in German. In Sacramento, Calif., the Bible was read in 10 languages, from ancient Hebrew to modern Japanese, at a special ceremony.

Within five years, the new Bible made history again. This time, it was electronic history. Remington Rand's "selectronic brain," UNIVAC, was used to complete a huge 31,000-entry concordance to the Revised Standard Version. UNIVAC cross-indexed the entire Bible in about 400 hours. It took scholars 30 years to do the same job on the King James Version in the late 19th Century —more than 200 years after that Bible first appeared.

The King James Version still is a best-seller, along with the Revised Standard Version. Both lead all other books. The new version has been put on sale in 115 bookstores of 24 Protestant and Evangelical denominations. An additional 2,500 regular commercial bookstores also have been selling it. Abingdon Press, the Methodist publishing house, has issued a 12-volume Interpreter's Bible, based on the new text. When the millionth copy was sold —to a Presbyterian woman in Spearfish, S.D.—a special announcement was issued and the lucky purchaser received $100, a specially bound 12-volume set of the Bible and the promise of the complete Interpreter's Dictionary of the Bible, in four to six volumes, when it is published.

Interest in the new Bible is part of the new-time religion in America. The upsurge in religious interest has brought with it much talk about the Scriptures. It also has stimulated controversy. Court cases have been waged to fight the reading of Bibles in public schools. Fundamentalists have unleashed bitter attacks on the Revised Standard Version and its translators, calling them heretics, communists and workers for the devil. A Roman Catholic priest precipitated a discussion by predicting the new Bible would be used as the basis for an interdenominational Bible acceptable to both Catholics and Protestants and perhaps lead to the elimination of most objections to the reading of Scriptures in public schools.

Despite some differences of opinion, there are two main points of general agreement on Biblical issues on the part of all but the most rigid fundamentalists.

First, the 300-year reign of the King James Version appears to be coming to an end. Whether it will be replaced by the Revised Standard Version is debatable, but the feeling prevails that the modern American wants a Bible written in *his* language, not that of Queen Elizabeth I.

Second, the Bible is the least-read best-seller in the world, and the average American is indeed a Biblical illiterate.

These are conclusions of clergymen, church leaders and that intrepid army of interrogators who have been traveling up and down America making in-depth studies of what people eat, think, do, read, want, like, dislike, need, don't need, fear and believe. The churchgoer has not been spared this scrutiny, nor has he been spared in reports on survey results.

The Catholic Digest, as part of one of the most comprehensive religious surveys ever made, reported in 1954 that about three million complete Bibles were distributed in the United States each year. It said there then were more than 200,000,000 Bibles in circulation in this country.

Americans do not read the Bible as much as their forefathers did, the survey concluded. What it neglected to say was that in the early days in America there was almost nothing else to read. Abraham Lincoln established a wide and lasting reputation as a Bible quoter and reader, but that was because he had little else to pore over during his formative years. There is doubt today that Lincoln was a religious man, although no one questions that he could quote the Bible, chapter and verse, with greater authority than many a minister.

The Digest survey reported that nearly a third of all Protestants never read the Bible or almost never did; that more than half the Catholics never read it and that an even larger number of Jews did not. Among individual denominations, the Baptists were found to be the most devoted Bible readers; 48 per cent read at least once a week and 21 per cent nearly every day.

Percentages of the total went this way: 34 per cent of those surveyed read Scriptures at least once a week; 12 per cent, every day; 12 per cent, never; 22 per cent, every few weeks, and 28 per cent, almost never.

The National Council of Churches reported an appalling degree of ignorance about the Bible in disclosing the results of the most extensive study of Protestantism ever made. The five-year survey of the urban church brought a report on a Bible quiz conducted in 34 city churches. The council reported that membership scores were poor, and, considering their offices, the deacon and church school teacher scores were even worse. Many of those questioned did not even know that the Psalms were in the Old Testament or which books in the New Testament constituted the Gospels. Membership scores ranged from 4 per cent "good" in one church to 48 per cent "good" in another. In no church were more than half the members able to answer the questions correctly and in only one were 75 per cent of the Sunday school teachers able to do so.

The staff of St. Thomas Protestant Episcopal Church, one of the famous Fifth Avenue churches in New York City, became so concerned over the lack of Biblical knowledge that special Bible-reading sessions were held four days a week at the height of the evening rush hour.

"It has been obvious for a long time that there is a widespread ignorance of the Bible even among professed Christians," said the Rev. Sidney Lanier, assistant to the rector. "Believing that the Bible is the source book of the Christian faith, the source of a great portion of the cultural and political heritage of the Western world, and is filled with stories of insight and beauty, we have sought a way to make it known as well as talked about."

Leading Methodists are among the most outspoken Protestants on the subject of neglect of the Bible. The Rev. Dr. Lowell B. Hazzard, professor of Old Testament at Wesley Theological Seminary in Washington, D.C., has called on Methodists to emphasize Christian education because "We have a theologically illiterate church. That our people know this is evidenced by the wistful question that keeps coming to us: 'Please tell us what we believe.'"

Another Methodist, Dr. Arthur S. Flemming, who served as a Sunday school superintendent while he was Secretary of Health, Education and Welfare in the Eisenhower Administration, called spiritual illiteracy the most serious problem facing the United States today. Bishop Richard C. Raines of Indianapolis called on his fellow Methodists to return to Bible study so Methodism could recover its "outreach, courage and sense of mission" of a century ago.

The Rev. Dr. Robert H. Hamill, pastor of Wesley Methodist Church, Madison, Wis., told a group of Methodist educators that college students had been plodding along with a pedestrian religion, empty of Biblical knowledge. He said the Gospel should be carried into secular studies of art, science, philosophy and history.

"For students," he said, "the Bible is an alien book. In both factual questions about Bible people and places and evaluative questions about Biblical ideas, they reveal their ignorance. We cannot communicate the mind of Christ to students by counting on the Bible to carry its meaning. We have primer work yet to do, and this should cause us soberly to reassess our Sunday schools and youth fellowship studies."

The American Baptist Convention, in issuing a call to its members to join in Bible study, reading and prayer—at home and in church—said that if there was to be a religious renewal, it must be based on increased Bible study. It must be more than a "perfunctory duty performed grudgingly," Baptist leaders said. They called for family Bible reading and set forth a scriptural book-of-the-month program.

"We who call ourselves people of The Book see a generation of Biblical illiterates," Jitsuo Morikawa said. "Even though the Bible is a best-seller, it is not the best read. Every test indicates we are virtually illiterate in the Bible.

"We are summoning our laity to become as serious and as disciplined in Bible study and Christian theology as they are in their study and discipline in pursuit of their professional life, to study the whole Bible as seriously as a scientist studies physics. Until we get to that, we are just playing with religion."

A Southern Baptist, the Rev. Ken Hutcheson, pastor of Lakeview Church in San Antonio, Tex., said he was heartsick that most people were not being taught the Bible. He said Southern Baptist pastors were disturbed over the large number of persons who seldom, if ever, read the Scriptures and did not know what they believed. The average person who attends Sunday school receives less than 20 hours of Bible instruction a year, he complained, and the average Baptist home never has a family prayer.

Sunday school Bible presentations are "domesticated soup, used only for moralizing purposes," according to Dr. Marcus Barth, son of the Swiss theologian Karl Barth and himself a University of Chicago theology professor. He said Bible stories were chopped up so that one had omitted the fact that John the Baptist was beheaded and another neglected to say that the Egyptians drowned. This Barth labeled as "canned food, carefully prepared—but the vitamins are gone."

A fellow theologian at the university, Dr. Victor Obenhaus, professor of the church in agricultural and industrial life, reported to a United Church of Christ Town and Country Convocation that in a study of a cross-section of adults, a high percentage of church people were found who had no idea of the meaning of the Parable of the Good Samaritan. Many persons contend the Bible is a rural book, he said, but because its illustrations frequently draw on rural life that does not mean all of its symbolism is aimed at rural folk.

"The fact remains," Obenhaus said, "that we have not yet grasped a fundamental Biblical concept of the oneness of society."

Still further criticism came from Lutheran Youth Research after a two-year study of young people made in behalf of six Lutheran groups. The survey found a general lack of familiarity with the Bible among both young people and their parents.

"We who see ourselves as a church of the Word have not succeeded in getting our youth into the Word," the report said. "An uncomfortably large number of youth refer to the Scriptures only occasionally."

The report added that young people wanted help in learning to interpret the Bible and were both guilty about their neglect of it and troubled by the fact that they did not understand it.

Despite obvious neglect, the Bible has been dissected and studied in every detail. A sort of informal race through the Scriptures resulted from a Southern Baptist program calling on every member of the denomination to read the entire Bible at least once during 1960. C. G. English, a Barnesville, Ga., Southern Baptist, claimed to be the first person to carry out the program. He said he not only read the entire Bible by Jan. 29 but managed to get through it again before the end of March.

Two other men, Warren Dixon of Jonesboro, Ga., and P. P. Jones, of D'Lo, Miss., finished the project in February.

"The pastor gave such an intriguing study of the entire Bible that I decided I would read it through and try to live by what I read," Dixon said.

During the weeks he pursued his project, Dixon suffered several mishaps, according to a dispatch circulated by the Baptist Press, a denominational news service.

"On Jan. 19, while pushing a stalled car, he was hit by another car," the report said. "Harnessed in the hospital bed, Dixon read one or two books of the Bible each day. On Jan. 31, a blood clot formed in one lung; this kept him under an oxygen tent in critical condition until Feb. 10."

"I read all the names, numbers and hard words to be sure I took adequate time in reading," Dixon related. "When I could not pronounce a word or name, I'd grunt twice."

Among those who have studied the Bible with considerable care is Dr. William Graham Cole, Dean of Freshmen and Professor of Religion at Williams College. He wrote a book on "Sex and Love in the Bible," urging that emphasis be placed on sex where the New Testament put it—"on the inner motivation and not the outer act." He called on parents to use the Bible to combat the "sexual anarchy" of the Kinsey reports in teaching children about sex and concluded that modern man can learn much about the facts of life from the Scriptures.

Cole is convinced there has been a widespread misunderstanding of the Bible, both what it is and what it does, largely because of movies.

". . . Unhappily," he said, "Hollywood has contributed its share to the general confusion by its cinematic treatment of Biblical stories, a treatment which almost invariably stresses the miraculous, the extraordinary, the spectacular."

Many other books have been written on the Bible—on the women in the Bible, the birds of the Bible and the plants of the Bible. There is a Bible cookbook, with recipes inspired by the Scriptures, and a discussion of "Laughter in the Bible," in a volume containing 250 references as part of what its publisher called "a fresh approach to Bible study."

Mass reading of the Scriptures is being encouraged by the American Bible Society as a means of increasing knowledge of "the good news" it contains. Easter and Christmas booklets containing appropriate passages are issued by the Society. More than three million copies of the Easter passage from St. John were distributed in 1960, and ten million booklets containing the Christmas story were circulated the following Christmas.

The Society also has offered suggested Bible reading for vacationists. A fishing enthusiast might read about Peter and John, who were fishermen, or about Jesus and the loaves and fishes. Hunters were directed to the Old Testament stories of Nimrod, of David who slew the lion and other animals that attacked his sheep, and of Esau, "a cunning hunter, a man of the field." Tired swimmers might gain their second wind from reading about the feat of Paul and his fellow prisoners, who swam ashore from a shipwreck. For engineers and scientists there are good professional stories—King Solomon and his copper mines, for one. The tale of Sodom is another; it led geologists to find oil in that section of Israel in 1953.

The Bible Society reported it distributed well over 17,500,000 volumes of Scriptures throughout the world in 1959, in more than 1,000 languages, 60 of them in the United States. This was a record for any year, exceeding the fifteen-million-volume average of the preceding six years, but it did not keep up with the global population explosion. The annual increase in population in most countries has far outstripped the circulation of Bible material, the Society reported. The total number of new Bibles and Testaments circulated throughout the world by 23 Bible societies, including the American, is barely a fifth of the total annual population increase.

Of the more than nine million volumes in English, most of them segments of the Bible, distributed by the society in 1959, 83.2 per cent were in the King James Version and most of the rest in the Revised Standard. Only a few were in the American Standard Version of 1901. Through an intricacy in copyright provisions, the Society is not allowed to publish an entire testament in the Revised Standard Version. It is limited to printing any one book, or all but one book, in a single volume.

The new Bible appeared in 1952, under the exclusive imprint of Thomas Nelson & Sons, a long-established Bible-publishing house. The Nelson contract runs through the year 2008. After that, the text will go into the public domain. The copyright is held by the National Council of Churches, which gains some financial reward from the Bible publication but is less interested in royalties than in preserving the purity of the text and assuring proper presentation of the Scriptures.

Beginning in 1962, several publishing houses authorized by the National Council will join Nelson in printing and distributing the Bible. It was decided to take this step because the wide acceptance and growing use of the Revised Standard Version warranted an enlargement of publishing facilities.

In England, Bible-publishing rights always have been more closely controlled than in the United States. The 1611 edition of the King James Version still is licensed by the Crown throughout the Commonwealth, including Canada. The King James Version has been in the public domain in the United States for a long time, however.

There is a small, hard core of resistance to the increased use of the new Bible, but that has come as no surprise to theological scholars and historians. Every new version has met with criticism, and even cries of heresy, from those who wanted to cling to an older version as "the Word of God."

The new Bible in 20th century language contains the fruits of research not available in the days of King James I. It was prepared by Bible scholars with both the support and the sponsorship of the National Council and financial backing from Nelson & Sons. After a publicity and advertising campaign of vast proportions, the book caught hold as no Bible has since the King James Version. Some authorities have said the new Bible would sell even better than it has if it were available for as little as the 80 cents a copy some complete King James Versions sell for. The cheapest R.S.V. edition now costs $3.25.

There have been predictions that the Revised Standard would supplant the King James within a generation as a principal source of Biblical quotations, although the older version probably never could be replaced as a great piece of literature. No one has been able to improve, for example, on the language of the 23rd Psalm.

The new Bible is used increasingly in churches, for study and for reading from the pulpit. Nearly 40 denominations, with Sunday school enrolments totaling more than 22,500,000, have been using it. Every Protestant denominational hymnal published in the

United States since the Revised Version appeared has adopted its text for responsive readings.

"It is apparent that a Bible which is so widely used in church schools and in public worship is bound to become the Bible of the church, as in a large measure already is true of the R.S.V.," Swaim said. "The R.S.V. is used in colleges and seminaries in courses which employ the English Bible as a textbook."

Swaim, as the National Council's expert on the English Bible, expressed gratification over the large sales of the new book, but he was even happier over the distribution of large pulpit Bibles. Late in 1960, the figure stood at more than 15,000, with the number increasing at the rate of 500 a month. This meant that many congregations had chosen the new Bible for their lecterns. But there were far more R.S.V. Bibles in pulpits. Frequently a small copy has been placed atop a larger edition of the King James Version.

It was a generation before the King James Bible was accepted completely, and against greater opposition than the current version has encountered. The people of the time had been brought up on the 16th Century Geneva Bible and they resisted the change. Opponents maintained that the King James Bible denied the divinity of Christ, but the book took hold anyway. Now the R.S.V. has come along, to the disgust of some older persons and of fundamentalists, who persist in calling the King James Version the "word of God," despite the fact that it attained that status only in 1611. What they do not realize is that the new Bible comes closer to the original manuscripts than any book of Scriptures ever has. They also do not realize that the millions of Bibles read today in foreign countries are in other versions—for each language, there is a different "word of God." The King James and Revised Standard Versions exist only in English.

Hundreds of versions of the Bible have been produced in the English-speaking world. Many of them have appeared in America alone, with some being translated by scholars with special ideas they wanted to get across; and some by groups, such as the one that produced the famous Goodspeed Bible at the University of Chicago in 1943. A New Testament in modern English, presented in narrative style, was prepared by J. B. Phillips, a noted Bible scholar, in 1958. It was designed to supplement formal scriptures. A new Roman Catholic Family Bible published in the fall of 1958 by Hawthorn Press had the personal recommendation of Pope Pius XII. It was the result of many years of international collaboration involving scholars in the Vatican, the United States, England, Italy, Scotland, Holland and Belgium. This elaborate volume is called "The Catholic Bible in the St. Peter's Edition." The Old Testament, except for the Psalms, is in the version originally translated at the English College of Douay at Rheims, France, in 1609-10 and popularly known as the Douay Version. The New Testament and Psalms are in the Westminster Version, translated in England and the United States between 1913 and 1935.

An event of historic importance to Judaism took place in the United States in 1960 with the introduction of the first authorized American edition of the traditional Jewish prayer book in both Hebrew and English. The new Siddur, traditional prayer book for Sabbath and festivals, was the first to appear in the 300 years of American Judaism with a uniform text for all Orthodox synagogues. It also marked the first time the Siddur had been placed on sale in book stores; in the past, it had been available for use only in synagogues.

For 14 years, the Orthodox Jewish community had been in ferment over the new prayer book, which was prepared under the authorization of the Rabbinical Council of America. The need for a uniform text, in parallel pages of English and Hebrew, had been pointed up by an increase in the number of Orthodox Jews and the mobility of the Jewish community. Rabbis felt that if the same prayer book was available in all Orthodox synagogues, worship would become easier and more meaningful.

Dr. David de Sola Pool, Rabbi-emeritus of the Spanish and Portuguese Synagogue, Shearith Israel, in New York, and a recognized Jewish scholar, translated and edited the new Siddur with the aid of a special committee of 15 other scholars and rabbis. The committee members struggled almost daily for 14 years with the problems involved in preserving the spirit and meaning of earlier versions and yet meeting modern needs.

In March, 1961, the Cambridge University and Oxford

University Presses jointly published throughout the world The New English Bible, billing it as "the new translation for which the English-speaking world has been waiting." The date was selected to mark the 350th anniversary of the appearance of the King James Bible.

First came the New Testament, with the Old Testament scheduled for later publication.

The New English Bible was translated from the original language, while the R.S.V. retained some of the flavor of the King James Version.

Another mighty work of Biblical scholarship has been undertaken by Dr. Luther A. Weigle, Dean Emeritus of the Yale Divinity School and chairman of the committee of 35 scholars who produced the new Revised Standard Version. He has devoted years to an Octapla—eight versions of the Bible in one binding. Running in parallel columns are the texts of the Tyndale Bible of 1525, the Great Bible of 1539, the Geneva Bible of 1560, the Bishops' Bible of 1568, the Rheims-Douay Bible of 1582-1610, the King James Version of 1611, the American Standard of 1901 and the Revised Standard of 1952.

The first three were translated by individuals. After that, the task became so great that groups of scholars were required to prepare the others. By the time work began on the Revised Standard Version, the mass of new material and new information on old material was so voluminous that it took all the experts who could be found to do the task.

Weigle explained that the revision was made in the interest of truth and to recover ancient wording and true sense at points where the King James Version had deviated.

The King James translation was based on a few late-medieval manuscripts, which had accumulated the errors of 1,000 years of manuscript-copying by hand. The manuscripts suffered also from a shortage of the kind of knowledge of Bible lands and language available today. Weigle and his associates found more than 1,000 words and expressions that once were considered accurate translations of Hebrew or Greek, but that had become so changed in meaning as to be misleading to anyone without a knowledge of the language and literature of the Elizabethan period.

In the King James Bible, the word "carriages," referring to what Paul took on his trip to Jerusalem, actually meant "baggage." In the Gospel of Paul, "scrip" meant a "wallet" or "bag." "We fetched a compass" now is "we made a circuit." The "nephews" of widows in I Timothy were their "grandchildren." "Coasts" meant "borders." Where Jesus says "take no thought for your life" in the King James Bible, he now says "be not anxious." John the Baptist's head was laid upon a "charger" in the old version and a "platter" in the new. "Lively" has been replaced by "living," "conversation" by "conduct."

Among the Old Testament changes from King James to Revised Standard are: "abhor" to "treat with contempt"; "amazed" to "distressed"; "anon" to "immediately"; "outlandish" to "foreign"; "pitiful" to "compassionate"; "by and by" to "at once"; "denounce" to "declare"; "harness" to "armor"; "furniture" to "saddle"; "sottish" to "stupid"; "wealthy" to "at ease," and "virtue" to "power."

In Luke XXIII:47, "certainly this was a righteous man" becomes "certainly this man was innocent."

Whether the successor to the King James Version will be the Revised Standard Version, the new English Bible or some other translation still remains to be seen. The new American version has been under almost constant study and change, because of new Biblical discoveries and the results of continuous scholarship.

An advantage of the Revised Standard Version is that although it is modern, it retains the language of earlier translations wherever possible. And Weigle has pointed out that its greatest advantage lies in its having sprung from the life of the churches. It is a translation that most of the major denominations in America rightly feel to be their own.

Except for the fundamentalists, who tenaciously cling to often obscure scriptures in a tongue 300 years out of date, Protestants generally agree that the King James Version is being supplanted in the churches and on bookshelves in homes. But will newer versions be read any more avidly? If the past is any clue to the future, the answer will remain that the Bible, in Elizabethan language or modern English, is the least-read best-seller of all time.

16

Raikes' Progress: the Church School

IF, BY SOME CHANCE, Robert Raikes, founder of the 180-year-old Sunday school movement, were to wander into a church class in mid-20th century America, he could not help but marvel at what he had wrought.

Were he to drop into the Sunday school at the Community Church of Almost Anywhere, he would be likely to see little children up to their pinkies in clay, engaging in finger-play, snipping away at Biblical cutouts, smearing paint on paper with dripping hands, rolling large balls or playing house in a corner toy kitchen.

He might see an "interest" table containing such "enrichment" materials as a Bible jigsaw puzzle, the story of Samson in comic-book format and Bible coloring books.

The visitor from another century probably would find a homey atmosphere—children sitting on a carpet around a teacher telling them a story. Near them, within reach on a very low table, would be a Bible and possibly a vase of flowers.

There would be little mention of "the Good Book" to the very smallest children. The progressive Christian educator of today questions whether the Scriptures are proper fare for the pre-kindergarten years. The desire at the outset is to make children feel secure and at home in church. If they like it there, they will want to keep coming back every Sunday. This has been carried to a point in at least one church where a special "tiny tots" Easter service is held at which each child brings a single flower for the cross so that he may be brought into "the big church" briefly on Easter Day.

The Sunday school founded by Raikes bore no resemblance to this one except that it met on Sunday morning. Raikes, a layman, established what came to be known as "the ragged school" in Gloucester, England, in 1780. His aim was to improve the condition of the children of the needy by bringing them together in Sunday classes.

Raikes hired one woman teacher and was able to muster his first class of dirty ragamuffins only by going into the streets and bribing them with money.

He began not by teaching religion, but by instructing the children in reading, writing, arithmetic and cleanliness. At first only a little Bible study was offered. Gradually, he was able to decrease the emphasis on the three R's and pay more attention to the Scriptures.

From that modest beginning, the Sunday school movement flourished. Raikes actually was not the first person to organize a Sunday class, but he was the first to have his work publicized. It was not difficult for him to gain recognition, for he was the publisher of *The Gloucester Journal,* which described his activities.

Most historians credit Raikes with the thrust that put Sunday schools in business in a big way. The movement spread rapidly through much of the English-speaking world. Americans were especially alert to the advantages of the Sunday school as an evangelistic tool. Within a few years after Raikes' first "ragged school" session, Sunday school became the training ground for Protestant children in all "churched" families, not just for the underprivileged. Evidence of its success can be found in the enrolment reported in the United States today—more than forty million. That figure is only about twenty million less than the estimated church membership.

Nowhere else did the movement grow so rapidly as in America. The revivalistic denominations seized upon it as an ideal training ground and developed Sunday schools so avidly that some of the more conservative denominations steered clear of them for a time. Today, however, nearly every Protestant denomination and Jewish congregation has a Sunday or Sabbath school and devotes much of its money and effort to training the young in the ways of religion. The Roman Catholic Church, which probably does more than any other to educate its children in its tenets, does not have classes on Sunday. Catholic children go to mass with their parents on Sunday and receive their instruction during the week, either at parochial school, during released time from public school or in an after-school class conducted by the Church.

The extent of the knowledge of most practicing Catholics about their religion would indicate that perhaps that body may have the answer to how to educate the young. This answer involves almost the total life of the Catholic child, while the Protestant child exposed to a public school education usually has his religion compressed into an hour on Sunday. A solution for the Protestants might be to hold classes on other days than Sunday. Or it could lie in acceptance of Sunday school homework in addition to public school studies, and family Bible study nights in the home.

A pioneer in the religious education movement was the American Sunday School Union, which developed uniform teaching materials for a cross-section of Protestantism. By 1872, the uniform lesson system, as developed also by other groups, was in use for systematic Bible study for people of all ages. In the middle 1930's, graded materials were introduced. Now the churches are in the midst of their fourth major education period—one of restudy and redesign of the school curriculum for the American Christian church.

Since World War II, the American Sunday school has acquired a new look, a new name and a fresh approach to the most ancient of textbooks—the Bible. It is called the church school now, to get away from the idea that religious study should be confined to Sunday. And its program has been modernized and expanded into a lifetime course of study. When religious educators realized that all the hours a child spent in Sunday school actually added up to the equivalent of only two months in public school, they decided that they must expand the courses to extend from the nursery to the grave—not from the nursery through high school.

Many denominations either have revised their curricula or are engaged in doing so to remedy an appalling degree of Biblical illiteracy among churchgoers and to try to stem the tide of teenagers flowing out of churches because they are bored with the educational fare. Young people complain that their questions are not being answered and that they have not been taught much about their religion in years of Sunday school attendance. Many who leave never return. Most of those who do come back wait until they become parents and then rejoin merely to set good examples for their children.

There has been a period in which the clergy and their more devout followers have excoriated young people for straying from church. But they seem now to have awakened to the fact that it was not the young people who erred but the churches. The Sunday schools simply were not teaching children enough and were not geared to the modern age. Jesus, Moses and other Biblical figures were presented as stereotypes. They did not come to life for the pupils. In many classes it became apparent that the teachers were as bored with this lack of vitality as were their students. Sunday school had to catch up with the times or lose out to the many competing consumers of time, particularly Sunday time.

Traditionally, the Sunday school has been a lay institution conducted within the church, but with as little interference as possible from the clergy. But in the new courses of study denominational officials have used their influence to try to put church schools on sounder theological and educational bases. With the help of psychiatrists, psychologists, educators, artists and other experts, they have matched the public school systems in ingenuity and use of the scientific approach.

Church leaders spurn the notion of "progressive education" as John Dewey conceived it, maintaining that this phenomenon of public school education is on the wane. But they nevertheless have become involved in some of its terminology and procedures. The 29 writers, called "contractors," who put into final form a Long-Range Program of Parish Education adopted jointly by four Lutheran denominations decided that in order to draw a curriculum plan, they must examine the various areas of personality growth. They decreed that a personality has 37 pieces, or "Continual Life Involvements." After an examination of each piece, they wrote a description of it in the light of what they regarded as man's relationship with God. They called the descriptions "Continual Christian Learnings."

A description was written for every year from birth through the age of 18. In the first year of life, the contractors decided, the individual learns to distinguish between "me" and "not me." The writers said that the church should be concerned about making sure that this child feels loved and wanted by his parents as an experience that "will form the basis for his later understanding of himself as a child loved by God and received as his child in holy baptism."

By the age of eight, the writers said, a child tends to seek out persons of his own sex. He becomes aware of some of his abilities and limitations, they said, and wavers between independence and a need to depend on adults for guidance and approval.

For this age group, the curriculum planners prescribed a program to help a child understand that he is an independent individual who can rebel against the will of God or accept it. The entire curriculum was designed to emphasize coordination between Sunday school, vacation church school, camp and home. Parish educators had found courses of study overlapping instead of supplementing each other. Now the Lutherans—American Evangelical, Augustana, Finnish and United—are trying to ease the load of the Sunday school and spread the educational program throughout the church's domain.

This progressive program—perhaps better called a program of progression—is regarded as an important stride away from the old-time curriculum. Under the former programs of Protestant denominations, most used the same standard lessons, consisting mainly of the study of a single Bible verse or passage each week in a sort of deadly "march through the Bible." At first, the same weekly lesson was used for all age groups. Then lessons were graded according to age. Memorizing by rote was the standard learning method and there was no homework.

Now the courses are more sweeping. Instead of studying small segments of the Scriptures, thus learning only bits and pieces of the Bible in an incoherent form, church school pupils are being exposed gradually to the Old and New Testaments in courses based on themes, not individual verses. The goal is to teach pupils how to apply their religion to everyday life, not just to be able to recite chapter and verse.

The Roman Catholics, with Vatican approval, have modernized the Baltimore Catechism—also known as St. John's Catechism—as taught in 8,000 of the 15,000 Catholic schools and parishes. This catechism is a standard text used mainly from the fifth through eighth grades. To make it more understandable, the church spent $300,000 and 10 years to produce in dramatized story form the traditional question-and-answer Baltimore Catechism.

A 35-millimeter projector and a phonograph are standard equipment for each lesson. The opening scene of each film strip shows a football game, a snow-shoveling scene, a jet plane streaking across the sky or some other activity attracting the attention of youngsters. The pictures and narrative work rapidly into the lesson for the day, with the pictorial segment taking only 10 minutes. Then questions on what has been shown are flashed on the screen and discussion follows.

The 30 lessons, each with 60 pictures in color, include many portraits illustrating Catholic theological tenets. One such portrait is described in official literature as showing "God the Father in the form of an ethereal cloud leaning over Jesus on the cross and stretching out His arms toward His Son as if to take Him immediately into heaven and end Jesus' suffering forthwith."

This technique—it has come to be known as "audio-visual" in catalogues of theological seminary courses, in churches and in religious publications—is almost universally used in Protestant church schools, too. What used to be called slides have been produced in a more convenient form as film strips, with phonograph recordings providing the "sound track."

The Protestant church school has become a place where potential members are nurtured with as much care as missionaries cultivate converts among the unchurched. It also is serving as a field for recruiting ministers, on the theory that at least once in every generation a local church should "reproduce itself" by offering a clergyman to the denomination.

As demonstrated by the Lutherans, who prepared their new curriculum independently of other denominations, there is a movement away from uniform courses for universal use within Protestantism, and toward the development of individual programs by and for each denomination—although all the new courses may have certain common factors. There is a general accent on the family, for example, with guidance books issued to parents to help them understand their children better and to help the children learn about religion. There is stress on homework. There is an effort to make Bible lessons interesting through toys, books, movies, phonograph records, magazines and the inevitable comic books. And there is a program for carrying educational work into all church activities, instead of limiting it to the Sunday teaching hour. A teenagers' cook-out thus becomes an occasion for Biblical discussion as well as socializing.

This sort of programming basically is as old as Christianity, although expressed in different terms. Christianity is a "teaching religion." Jesus called Himself a teacher and His disciples were teachers. Ministers today are being encouraged to try to become teachers as well as preachers.

It is natural therefore that possibly the most important development accompanying the new courses of study is the fresh approach to teaching them. Denominations are working diligently to train 3,000,000 teachers in more than 250,000 schools in 224 denominations. Nearly all the teachers are lay men and women who volunteer to supervise classes as their contribution to the church. They outnumber public school teachers by about two to one. Their lack of knowledge and preparation for teaching the Bible has been considerable in the past, for many were barely able to keep a lesson ahead of their pupils and often were unable to answer the most fundamental questions.

The average church school teacher has been identified in a *Christian Herald* survey as being 35 years old and most likely a woman with children of her own. The teachers, both men and women, were found to be community leaders, professional people, businessmen, housewives, clerks and public school teachers. Three of every eight were men, some of whom took the time to teach every Sunday although holding two full-time jobs.

Efforts are being made to give special courses of training to teachers, but it is plain that these busy people do not have much time to spare for their own training. As both a supplement to and a substitute for courses of instruction, nearly every denomination has provided its teachers with detailed, well-written manuals and lesson books prepared by authorities in education, theology and psychology, in the hope that the instructors will have time each week to do a little homework.

This closer denominational supervision of church schools has been welcomed by the layman, who is glad to yield some of the prerogatives of his traditional province in the interest of sprucing up the Sunday school.

Changes in curricula have come slowly because it often takes years to develop a single course. The National Council of Churches is only now in the early planning stage of a cooperative inter-denominational church school program that it hopes to put into effect sometime between 1969 and 1974, when many of today's Sunday school pupils will be old enough to be teachers. This delayed action may come too late to be of widespread benefit because the courses developed independently by the individual denominations should be entrenched by then. Smaller bodies that cannot afford the high cost of curriculum revision may be the chief beneficiaries.

The United Presbyterian Church in the U.S.A. was the first of the major denominations to give its Sunday schools a "new look," a task that took about a decade. The program, called "Christian Faith and Life," is graded for different age groups and provides a wide variety of materials for youngsters, their teachers and parents.

"Grading means something more profound than a mere accommodation of vocabulary or choice of subject matter suitable to the limited understanding of immature minds," said the prospectus for the course. "It means . . . bringing a child into a real relationship with Jesus Christ, and not simply instructing the child in facts about Christ."

The denomination, when still known as the Presbyterian Church in the U.S.A., began to study its Sunday school materials in the late 1930's. The program, taking a largely theological approach, was introduced in 1948.

"We wanted to get away from petty moralism, from mere factual knowledge, and other features of conventional Sunday school material," explained Norman F. Langford, editor-in-chief of the denomination's Board of Christian Education.

"We wanted to incorporate into a broad educational scheme,

reaching from the cradle to the grave, the thinking of the scholars who were, by the early 1940's, beginning to give new life to theology in America.

"The general theological orientation could be described, I think, as a swing toward the theology of the Reformation, as developed further by some of the newer theological writers. We also wanted to incorporate the findings of Bible scholarship, where these were essential for the understanding of Biblical passages, and a good deal was done in cooperation with seminary professors."

In a statement on "Basic Principles—Christian Faith and Life," approved by the denomination's governing body, the Presbyterians said two major errors had been made in the past in the content of the church's teaching:

"1. The assumption is that there is a body of objective Christian knowledge which needs only to be conveyed to another person in order to make him more Christian. Learning is thus conceived as a mere storing in the mind of information. There is indeed a very real place in the curriculum for the learning of facts—about the Bible, about Jesus Christ, about the history of the church, about the world in which the Christian has to live—for right thinking is impossible if a person is without the facts or has a distorted or inaccurate knowledge of them. . . .

"2. Too often the pupil has been placed at the center as though the content of the teaching can be determined by examining the needs and problems of the pupil."

The prospectus warned against spending too much time encouraging the individual development of the pupil to the neglect of the Gospel.

"A causal connection can plainly be seen between the inadequate provision for Christian education and the widespread religious illiteracy in Christian circles," it said. "Ignorance of the Bible, of the essentials of the Christian faith, and of the history of the church is common even among those who have attended church school for many years. It is a very serious matter for the church that, in a time when the younger generation is beset on every side by un-Christian and anti-Christian philosophies of life, uncertainty, triviality, confusions, and incoherence characterize so much of the education that is offered in the name of the church."

Among the basic features of the new curriculum were the introduction of parent-teacher magazines to keep the home and church school abreast of each other; of well-bound "reading books" in place of flimsy quarterly papers, and of a three-year cycle of themes, with a year devoted to each.

"We have endeavored to keep the methods suggested within the range of capability of the amateur teacher," Langford said, "for, after all, it is upon amateurs that we depend very largely in the Sunday-by-Sunday process of church school teaching. By the same token, our board had engaged strenuously in a program of leadership education, with a view to training teachers more thoroughly; and in the curriculum itself we have tried to embody sound and advanced but not radical techniques in the suggestions for carrying out session plans in the church school."

For the youngest children—up to age 3—the Presbyterians have prepared a series of nursery books, one of them a simple story of Jesus, another featuring a grace and a third giving assurance that God loves every family. The idea is to provide the children with a sense of security in church.

The primary-grade program offers special children's hymns and stories and "reading books" for the pupils to take home. In the junior grades—9 to 11—children are provided with a simple story of Jesus, to introduce them to the Bible, and a bi-weekly publication containing games, puzzles, stories and other "enrichment materials."

"There is no attempt to shield the junior from any portion of the life of our Lord," the prospectus said. "This means that the junior will be faced with the very real humanity of Jesus and yet, in hearing the whole, will discover also that this man is God Himself. Neither is the junior shielded from seeing how the motives that lead people to reject Jesus Christ at every turn are too often our own."

The junior high age—12 to 14—is regarded as "the time for questioning." The main book for this group is "Men Called Him Master," which portrays Jesus as "the vigorous, commanding figure of all time, who summons and challenges youth."

"New, tried and terrific!" is the way the prospectus announces slick new Presbyterian magazines for young people. ". . . Modern church magazines for youth," they are called. One of them, *Venture,* was described as being read by more "junior highs" in more churches than ever before. It consists of 32 pages "packed to the margins with the best in youth appeal," fiction and articles on science, religion, vocations, manners, grooming and dating.

Hi-Way magazine was described this way: ". . . The fast-growing *Hi-Way* is proving to be one of the *coolest* magazines ever published for youth." Printed in three colors on 32 pages each month, it is published for "older teens" and contains tips on poise, personality and popularity; news about TV, movies, records and books; help in spiritual life and churchmanship; slants on parents, dating, college, jobs and marriage; fun, action and "loads of il-lustrations."

The enrichment reading for the senior high group—15 to 17—includes a chapter-by-chapter discussion of the New Testament. There also is a "youth fellowship kit" containing guidance for discussions of matters such as "What was the good of Jesus' death?" "What's the risk in fall-out?" and "Does God care about outer space?"

In preparing the entire curriculum, the authors took into con-sideration such matters as the muscle development of toddlers, the need for self-expression in the 3-year-old, a desire for responsibility for small tasks in the kindergartner, the incessant questioning of young primary ages and the accident-proneness of the 10-year-old.

A chart was assembled showing the progressive interest in re-ligion, beginning with the 2-year-old's recognition of the Bible simply as a book people respect, through the learning of stories by looking at pictures at age 6, to the beginning of the study of the Bible as one continuous story at age 12.

This elaborate, well-thought-out program is a long way from Robert Raikes' modest effort to link cleanliness and godliness in the minds of potential juvenile delinquents in the slums of Gloucester, England, nearly two centuries ago. The 20th Century Presby-terians are far from alone in taking this radically new look at religious education. They merely were the first.

Among others who have developed fresh programs are the Prot-estant Episcopalians, the Methodists and the American Baptists. All are working with curricula that have been constructed along the same general lines but that have taken into consideration the rituals and beliefs that are strictly their own.

The Episcopalians have a 32-volume curriculum designed to reach every age group. For the nursery child there are "one-a-Sunday, take-home picture cards," with one series depicting the wonders of nature and another showing children the importance of the people who are close to them in their daily lives. Accompanying each picture is a story or verse as an illustration "to provide sound theology for parents."

Later volumes include an illustrated tour of a church by a small boy and a make-believe conversation between a home and the church across the street. For 7-year-olds there are "take-home books" and teaching aids, including a map of the world, Bible verses in several languages, a Nativity scene, a Chinese madonna, a sample of Braille and pictures of the National Cathedral.

The United Church of Christ, formed through a union of the Congregational Christian Churches and the Evangelical and Reformed Church, was among the last of the major denominations to complete a new program, but it was one of the most costly and extensive. It begins with recognition of the fact that there is little in the Bible that a small child can understand. Only two Bible stories are offered to 3-year-olds in this course—the account of Jesus' birth and of Jesus and the children.

Eight years and more than a million dollars went into the preparation of what the United Church regards as a lively, up-to-date and theologically and educationally sound new curriculum. Emphasis on the underlying meanings of the Bible replaces the old-fashioned Sunday school accent on memorization of Bible stories and verses. Just as children do not start out by learning the alphabet in progressive public schools, the churches have abandoned the practice of requiring memorization of the names of the books of the Bible as a prerequisite to studying their content.

"3's in the Christian Community" is the name of the first unit of the new curriculum. Phoebe M. Anderson, author of this segment, has suggested methods and activities aimed at developing Christian viewpoints and at giving children "a personal sense of knowing God." Photographs and attractive art work are important in the format. Care has been taken to provide at least one illustrated story showing children of all races playing together.

"This was not just an accident but a deliberate attempt to say in ways a 3-year-old can understand that his church believes in racially integrated housing," explained one of the new lessons' co-editors, Dr. Robert E. Koenig.

As a further explanation of the curriculum, the Rev. Dr. Oliver Powell, minister of the Oak Park Congregational Church, outside Chicago, said that Christian theology on the 3-year-old level is based on the idea that "God loves you. He knows you, accepts you as you are—mean or fearful, glib or stuttery, neat or messy—understands and forgives your unkindness, your mistakes. Throughout this relation God offers you again and again new opportunities to grow, to learn, to love and to forgive."

The United Church program has six main themes—growing as a Christian; exploring the Christian heritage; Christian living with one another; responding to God's love; belonging to the Christian fellowship, and living in God's world. Each grade, from kindergarten up, studies each theme on its own level, with one theme per term and terms conforming with public school semesters.

More than 80 writers worked on the curriculum with the help of a large group of consultants on the Bible, Christian theology, worship, education, psychology and psychiatry, child study, family life, curriculum construction, communications, design and format.

The experts enlisted by United Church planners worked out courses of study and family resource books for parents to use in guiding children at home. They even came up with a sort of churchly version of Dr. Spock—a basic book for parents, dealing with child development from birth to full growth.

Stories, songs, poems, prayers and finger plays were recommended for the smallest children with the admonition that Sunday school teachers should not use these diversions in such a way as to become mere baby-sitters. Mrs. Anderson instructed teachers to provide children with enough toys and story books to keep them occupied, and with "interest centers" for the very young. The Bible should remain the central attraction, for children to touch and gaze upon, she said, even if they cannot read it. An effort must be made at all times to show children they are in a church, not a nursery school.

Among the concepts taught to the very young is death, which is conveyed by a story on the untimely demise of a turtle named Mr. Red Ears. There are stories also about the first Christmas and about Jesus and the children, in which the familiar King James Version's "Suffer the little children to come unto me and forbid them not: for such is the kingdom of God" becomes "Don't send the children away. Let them come to me. I want to see them and talk with them. I love children, all children."

In this little book, Jesus is drawn in modern style and depicted in garb resembling Bermuda shorts. When newspapers carried an item describing Jesus as being clad in modern attire in a new Sunday school book, there was a loud cry of protest from many clergymen in the United Church. The objections did not die down until the protestors were assured that Jesus had been presented in what might be called Jerusalem shorts—the wearing apparel of the working man of his day. The artist had felt that since Jesus was of the laboring class he should be so presented, instead of in the traditional robe of the nobility.

The decision to present Jesus as he really might have appeared represents an important part of what the churches are trying to do in their Sunday schools. As a Methodist official said, "Sunday school ain't what it used to be in American Protestantism." The Methodist Church, in its modernized curriculum, is emphasizing teaching, with the pupil and teacher exploring together new areas of thinking, feeling and understanding.

This includes much more than merely reading the Bible. It involves developing respect toward all persons, encouraging commitments to spread the Christian Gospel and creating a desire to wipe out crippling and oppressive conditions in society so every person may have a fair chance. This concept calls for good equipment and teachers trained to deal with real theological questions.

The materials used are carefully edited, with much attention given to typography, layout, art work and the use of color—far different from the Sunday school papers handed out a generation ago in a format not much different from that of a high school paper published by students.

One of the larger denominations yet to be heard from in the final adoption of a new curriculum is the Presbyterian Church in the U.S. (South), which is hard at work on a program, due for introduction by 1964, to replace the "uniform lessons" in use since 1872. This will be called "Covenant Life Curriculum," based on the essential unity of the Bible, rather than a few scattered verses each week, thus following the general pattern of the other denominations. Students will receive full-year programs of systematic Bible study, perhaps built around annual themes. An effort will be made to discover a "well-defined ethical position to help the Christian meet contemporary problems."

"We felt the time had come for a re-formation of Christian educational philosophy," said the Rev. A. S. Tippit, director of publicity of the Southern Presbyterian Board of Christian Education and former pastor of John Knox Presbyterian Church in Lubbock, Tex. "To borrow a phrase from I Corinthians, we are in search of a 'still more excellent way.'

"We have found our people do not know as much about the Bible as they should. Particularly, they do not understand the Bible's 'one story.' We feel the church is not making its full impact upon culture and society, so the Christian ethic must be more clearly thought and emphasized."

The Reformed Church of America and the Moravian Church joined in the study of this new curriculum. Pilot studies have been conducted in Presbyterian churches in Hickory, N.C.: North Decatur, Ga.; Pickens and Shiloh, Miss., and Memphis, Tenn., and the armed forces Sunday schools have been using some of the materials already developed.

Teachers being trained in the curriculum at a laboratory school will be encouraged to prepare carefully for each class session, instead of waiting until Saturday night to cram for Sunday morning.

There is another large supplier of Sunday school materials—the non-denominational organization that operates either as a business or a nonprofit foundation. One of the biggest in the field is the David C. Cook Publishing Company in Elgin, Ill., a division of the nonprofit David C. Cook Foundation. It provides materials to about 70,000 churches in 80 denominations and religious groups.

"This is spontaneous ecumenicity—the kind which arises by choice from thinking leaders at the local church level, rather than the kind which is imposed artificially by professional church leadership," said Gilbert V. Beers, executive editor of the company's publications division.

The 80 denominations include a widely divergent segment of Protestantism, he said, with some of them among the strongest opponents of other cooperative church programs.

Beers said the most significant difference between today's lessons and those of past generations is the use of courses of study rather than independent lessons. Today's courses try to "take the pupil somewhere," he said. Another major step forward, he said, is the enlistment of professional educational help and the use of art and visual aids such as a flannel "Storygraph Apron," with generous pockets crammed with suede-back figures that a teacher can affix to the apron simply by pressing them on with her fingers. She turns herself into a "walking flannelboard," free to move among her pupils while telling stories.

For somewhat older children, Cook has published "Sunday Pix," in comic-book style, containing "Our Bible in Pictures"; "Attack That Failed," the story of the battle of Jericho; "Medic of the Jungle," the true story of a medical missionary, and "Tullus," a fictional account of a boy who lived in Biblical days.

The comic book contains two pages of letters from children seeking help or advice. One letter was from "a sad sixth grader," who asked, "Could you please help me to be popular?" Another writer was a boy who said, "I know you're supposed to be like Jesus, but I don't think there's any hope for me. I'm awful bad sometimes. But I'd like to be better. What can I do?" A third letter was from a boy who did not like to play the piano and wanted to know how he could get out of practicing.

Cook materials also include a Bible adventures lesson book about Joseph, Daniel, Solomon, the Apostles and the Disciples. The tales are accompanied by quizzes, puzzles, games and maps. For a nominal sum, a child also can obtain a "Junior Prayer Fellowship Kit," containing recommended daily prayers, a club emblem and a silver ring.

Important to any discussion of church schools is the fact that they frequently pave the way for the formal lay educational experiences of children. A child can go to Sunday school even before he is old enough for nursery school. What happens to him at Sunday school may affect his whole life. If he likes the church school, he will want to go on to nursery school, kindergarten and the first grade. If he does not like it, his first days in public school will be a trial for him, his parents and his teacher.

With that in mind, the churces have tried to present Sunday school curricula that will be instructive and at the same time keep young children happy and older ones stimulated. Whether there is too much emphasis on playing games is a question, despite the fact that psychological research has produced programs designed to fit the attention span of a small child—first a play period, then a story, then more play and finally songs and prayer.

The new programs have as their first goal the nurture of church membership. They are an investment in the future. Churches want to keep congregations in steady attendance throughout their lives. They are relying on the teachers to sow the seeds for a rich harvest—and many of the teachers on whom they rely today are ill-equipped for the job. A generation of Biblical illiterates is being asked to produce a generation of Biblical *literates*. This is quite an assignment and the churches have found no really satisfactory way to perform it. If, by dint of diligence and teachers' manuals that spell out every lesson in detail, the churches are able to keep today's children in church school until they are grown, these children stand a strong chance of being well-educated in religion. Then they will be equipped to educate later generations.

The big problem is how to conduct the classes *now,* especially with the population constantly moving about the country and shifting from church to church.

Church school teachers need a special status. They are volunteers who give their time to the religious education of the young. Their ministers and congregations owe them all the help they can provide, in the form of all the necessary tools and training.

The church school teacher should be treated as a special person in the congregation. He is, after all, helping the minister do his job. As an aide to the minister, the teacher should not be asked to do any other work for the church. He should not be expected to wash dishes after the fellowship dinner or perform other chores.

Education courses conducted in Sunday schools are second in religious importance only to the preacher's sermon. They are, in fact, a training ground for a full appreciation of what the minister says from the pulpit. With that in mind, perhaps the churches should concentrate on teaching the teachers as much as on teaching the children.

17

Reformation U.S.A.

A NEW REFORMATION is changing the church in America—and possibly the world. Whether it should be spelled with a capital R will be for historians to decide, but there is no doubt, regardless of the label, that there has been a realignment of religious forces and a reassessment of their roles, with a growing emphasis on unity and cooperation.

Businesses and industries have gone through a merger era since World War II, and so have Protestant denominations. Bigness has become an ingredient in both spiritual and industrial survival in the 20th century, with its ever-rising costs and keen competition. In completing mergers, industries have sought to diversify as a hedge against changes in the taste of the fickle consumer. Most church mergers have involved related denominations, but at least one was a move toward diversification that could have a far-reaching effect on the fickle churchgoer.

The postwar era has seen the development of the World and National Councils of Churches, comparable to "trade" organizations of business and industry and considered milestones on the road toward real religious unity. An organization representing all three branches of Judaism in America is under discussion. It would operate something like the National Council of Churches. There is a move for a common Catholic and Protestant Bible, with the Jews perhaps sharing in the Old Testament. Pope John XXIII has called for a meeting of representatives of every branch of Christendom to seek a path toward closer Protestant-Catholic cooperation. American missionaries operating overseas are crossing denominational lines in united efforts and are subordinating their own roles to those of the nationals of the host countries. They are more interested in Christianity in general than any variety of it in particular.

The ancient Greek is drawn upon for the word widely used to describe any efforts to make Christianity one global brotherhood. That word is ecumenical, a tongue-twister for which there is no synonym. It is an all-inclusive word, covering all of mankind everywhere. What it boils down to is togetherness on a universal scale.

"Ecumenical" is the label sometimes incorrectly given to unity moves within the United States. These brotherly gestures have come mainly through mergers, which are hardly global in scope. Among the most important have been those of the United Presbyterian Church and the Presbyterian Church in the U.S.A. and of the Congregational Christian Churches and the Evangelical and Reformed Church.

Lutheranism is being realigned through two sets of mergers, one made up of four groups and the other involving three. The Universalists and Unitarians have merged. Preliminary talks are under way among other groups, mainly the Methodists and Episcopalians. Periodically the Presbyterians and Episcopalians make friendly moves toward each other but nothing has come of their talks yet.

The most ambitious merger proposal of all came on the eve of the triennial General Assembly of the National Council of Churches, in December, 1960, when Eugene Carson Blake, speaking as chief executive officer of the United Presbyterian Church in the U.S.A. and a former president of the National Council of Churches, proposed formation of an 18,309,000-member denomination. Blake called for a merger of his denomination with the Protestant Episcopal Church, The Methodist Church and the United Church of Christ to form a Protestant body that still would be less than half the size of the Roman Catholic Church in the U.S.

Christian churches no longer can afford the "luxury" of historic divisions, Blake said, with individual groups becoming competing social forces working to their own advantage.

The several Baptist groups, most notably the Southern Baptists and the American Baptist Convention, have found no basis on which to heal their Civil War wounds, but they have managed to join in some activities. They maintain with other Baptist bodies a Joint Committee on Public Affairs in Washington, D.C., to look after church interests in Congress. Twenty million members of eight Baptist bodies have joined also in the Baptist Jubilee Advance, a five-year warm-up for the 150th anniversary in 1964 of the organization of Baptists in North America.

The Advance, an evangelistic effort reaching into the home, school, factory and office, has involved the 70,000 churches affiliated with the American and Southern Conventions, the Baptist Federation of Canada, the Baptist General Conference of America, the National Baptist Convention of America, the National Baptist Convention, U.S.A., Inc., the North American Baptist General Conference and the Baptist World Alliance.

Most of the major Lutheran bodies, although unable to form one big happy church family, have found an area for cooperation in the National Lutheran Council, organized during World War I to serve as a clearing house of information for and about Lutheranism.

The Church of the Nazarene, a part of the so-called "right wing" of the scriptural holiness movement in the United States, announced with pride that leaders of three other revivalist sects had accepted invitations to a Nazarene General Assembly. Such a thing never had happened before. The representatives were sent by the Wesleyan Methodist Church, the Free Methodist Church and the Pilgrim Holiness Church.

On the interdenominational level, some groups that will not join the National or State Councils of Churches share in activities of some boards or divisions. One principal area of cooperation, a development of recent years, is the interdenominational planning of the location of new congregations. National, state and local councils of churches have staffs of experts who sit down with officials of various denominations and divide territories in a businesslike way, so that each may serve a neighborhood in an individual community effectively without having to worry about competing with a rival organization down the street. Sometimes the new congregations so parceled out are called community churches, but without sacrificing any of their denominational distinctiveness.

The real power in Protestantism lies on the regional level, not in national boards or local congregations, in the opinion of Meryl Ruoss, whose position with the National Council of Churches keeps him traveling from church to church much of the time. The regional office of a denomination or church council is the place for action, he says, so regional church-placement planning on as broadly interdenominational a scale as possible is encouraged.

Southern Baptists will not join the Council of Churches, but in Oklahoma City they have entered into discussions of local church planning. Fifty per cent of the Protestants in Wisconsin are Lutherans and Episcopalians who do not belong to the State Council of Churches, but they participate in regional church planning. No unit of the Council of Churches could be found to fit the geographical planning pattern that was needed in northeastern Ohio, so a special regional operation was set up apart from any Council subdivision. The Missouri Lutherans joined in this home mission effort, although they have refused to enter into membership in the National Council itself and are not even members of the National Lutheran Council.

Planning for church distribution at any level depends mainly on suburban growth. An elaborate program is under way, for example, in the Indianapolis area, where a cooperative 15-year master plan has been drawn that will carry church building in mushrooming suburbs into 1975. The city's Metropolitan Planning Commission is participating in the effort, with church activity being just one of many phases of the entire planning process. A cooperative Protestant office has mapped church locations and assigned them to denominations. Construction dates and costs also have been listed. Each participating denomination in turn has its own 15-year plan carefully plotted.

"There is no rivalry, because there is so much to be done that what is done is just a drop in the bucket," Ruoss said.

Another church planning effort that has attracted national attention is the new concept adopted in the Chicago suburb of Park Forest, a post-war settlement of young families who conceived a sort of "United Nations of Religion." In 1948, soon after the first residents moved in, a group of Protestants polled their neighbors to find out what kind of churches they wanted. The question was whether to establish the usual variety of denominations along traditional lines or build a few united churches to serve the entire community. The result was a landslide victory for the united church.

What followed was the construction of four interdenominational churches, founded by laymen, with financial and technical help from national religious bodies. Each is regarded as a community church although formally it belongs to a single national denomination. The sponsoring bodies are the American Baptist Convention, the United Church of Christ, The Methodist Church and the United Presbyterian Church in the U.S.A. Lutherans, Episcopalians and a Southern Baptist group have small churches. There also is one Unitarian Fellowship, as well as a few Jewish congregations and Roman Catholic parishes. Most of Park Forest's Protestants attend the united churches.

Dr. Gerson S. Engelmann, minister of Faith United Church and the senior clergyman in Park Forest in point of service, regards the community's church system as a landmark in Christian progress. His church alone has 1,660 members who belong to 59 different denominations.

"Here in Park Forest, we have given a practical demonstration that it is not necessary for Protestant Christianity to be severed into innumerable splinter groups," he said. "Christian people from different denominational groups are working together for the kingdom of God effectively and in peace and harmony."

The four churches—Faith, Grace, Calvary and Good Shepherd —are organized into a Council of Cooperating Denominations, which pays for the services of a community chaplain to visit all new members of the community and invite them to join the program.

Dr. C. F. McCall Jr., associate superintendent of the Congregational and Christian Conference of Illinois, has a few reservations about the Park Forest project. He said it was started because of a lack of denominational concern on the part of young people after the war, when they set out to build their own suburbs.

"They were the 'organization man' type," he said. "In fact, about them the book was written. Their idea was to have churches that were inclusive of everybody "

He doubts that the system has been "particularly a triumph," largely because of a rapid turnover of ministers at all but Faith Church, but he regards the community chaplain as a potential help. When a new chaplain was hired, McCall said he seemed to be the sort of person who would work closely with the ministers of the four churches, "but the last man was in danger of becoming the 'superminister of the whole community.' "

The biggest church news along organizational lines is on a national scale, however, not in the Park Forests and Indianapolises. Mergers remain the most important unifying measures within Protestantism. When the Congregational Christian denomination, itself the result of a merger, united with the Evangelical and Reformed Church, another merged body, into the United Church of Christ, it was described as the first time since the Reformation that two major Protestant groups with different backgrounds, practices and forms of church government had found a common meeting ground. It was a case of Christianity diversifying for future strength and possibly opening the way for a further expansion through diversification.

The Congregational Christian Churches traditionally are "free," with each congregation being autonomous. The E. & R. Church operates under a Presbyterian system in which local congregations have certain relationships to regional and national synods—as in the Presbyterian churches. The union has allowed both churches to retain their identities, and so successful has it been that the Disciples of Christ have indicated interest in joining.

The American Lutheran Church is the result of the merger of the Evangelical, American and United Evangelical Churches. The four-way Lutheran merger into the Lutheran Church in America involves the Augustana, United Finnish Evangelical and American Evangelical Churches and the United Lutheran Church in America. The only major Lutheran body to stay away from merger talks has been the Missouri Synod.

While it took the two large Presbyterian groups only three years to form the United Presbyterian Church in the U.S.A., the Methodist Church and the Presbyterian Church of the U.S. (South) have been discussing consolidation off and on since 1888. The 1939 union of the Methodist Episcopal, the Methodist

Episcopal South and the Methodist Protestant Churches was the largest of all the consolidations—establishing a single denomination now claiming more than 10,000,000 members. Efforts are being made to add to this body by a merger with the 750,000-member Evangelical-United Brethren Church by 1964. The two churches have almost identical theological beliefs, disciplines and terminology, thus minimizing unification problems.

In 1958, the Methodists and Episcopalians jointly announced "tentative suggestions" for reaching intercommunion between their churches, possibly within a generation, perhaps to be followed by an actual merger by the end of the century. Such a merger would be a reunion, for The Methodist Church was formed in the middle of the 18th Century when John Wesley broke with the Church of England.

Intercommunion, however, would not mean merger. It would involve merely the participation of clergymen and members of each church in the worship of the other. There was a time during Western pioneer days when the Methodists dropped much of the traditional liturgy because of primitive frontier conditions, but most of the theological frills have been restored and the two bodies are in basic agreement on most tenets. They are not united on certain social issues, however. The Episcopalians have no feeling one way or another about the consumption of alcohol, while the Methodists stand squarely against it; the Episcopalians are strongly opposed to any racial barriers in their churches, while the Methodists are divided on the integration question.

The slow march toward Lutheran unity began in 1880, when there were 70 or 80 small synods in America, each formed by a different group of immigrants from Germany or Scandinavia. By 1959, the number had been reduced to 16, entirely through mergers. By mid-1962, with completion of the four-way merger, the number will be down to 11. Efforts are being made to reduce the number still further, but that will take a long time.

"There are more efforts toward Lutheran unity today than ever before," said the Rev. Dr. C. H. Becker, president of the Lutheran Wartburg College, in Waverly, Iowa.

To this, the Rev. Karl J. Wilhelmsen of Racine, Wis., an Evangelical Lutheran pastor who worked toward the three-way merger, added a prediction of greater Lutheran unity.

"It is simply a matter of history that many mergers precede an ultimate union," he said. "I am sure that, following this merger, there will be other streams of Lutheran life that shall flow together in an even mightier stream."

Bishop Frederick B. Newell, who retired in 1960 as Methodist Bishop of the New York area, believes that all of the world's 40 Methodist bodies eventually will unite. Bishop Stephen C. Neill, of the Church of England, told the Portland, Ore., Council of Churches that the entire Christian world was on the way to union.

"We are caught up in a great movement of church union all over the world," he said.

Reformation is the word used by many—although a leading Lutheran admonished, "If you call it a reformation, spell it with a lower-case 'r.'"

Dr. Henry Pitney van Dusen, president of Union Theological Seminary, is one of those who talks about a 20th Century Reformation, with a capital "R." He has described the Christian church today as the only real world community civilization has ever known. He cites church unions, cooperation and federation as evidence.

In the first 18 centuries of Christian history, there was at least one new major schism of the church in each century, van Dusen said. After THE Reformation, when dissidents broke with Rome and established the foundations for Protestantism, there were scores of schisms in every century until the early 1800's. Then the tide turned, van Dusen said, and in the last 150 years there have been at least 100 mergers of national denominations, with only a few splits.

Van Dusen pointed also to the cooperation and collaboration within the United States in thousands of interdenominational bodies—more than 1,000 of them being local, county and state councils of churches.

In a speech at a Protestant Reformation Festival in Madison Square Garden, van Dusen said that the Protestant Reformation preceded exploration of every continent and the cultivation of the human mind as never before.

"It was creative, but it was also divisive," he said. "It not only split the Christian church into two great branches; it splintered its own branch into 250 diverse fragments.

"The new reformation is no less dynamic. It, too, has been creative; but it has been unifying, and, thus, it is overtaking and redeeming one of the unhappy by-products of the earlier impulse, and is fulfilling the original intention of the great reformers."

C. Emanuel Carlson, executive director of the Baptist Joint Committee on Public Affairs, emphasizes that "reformation" can be interpreted in several ways. It may be regarded as involving changes in institutional structure, basic creeds or other religious patterns, he said.

"Many people have difficulty with the word 'revival' as representing an emotional response of a temporary quality," he said. "If we may take these terms at a deeper level, I would like to say that I believe we have both. There has been a revival of religious faith and a revival of the open mind toward the eternal. The reformation aspect has undoubtedly been more growth than drastic change. Perhaps it is too early to expect far-reaching revision of behavior patterns."

Cooperation between groups has been pointed up in protests of the National Council of Churches against the imprisonment of a Roman Catholic Bishop, James Edward Walsh, in Communist China and Catholic protests against charges that the National Council was being run by a pack of Reds.

The 1960 Presidential campaign also brought a line-up of liberal Protestantism defending the right of a Roman Catholic to be President versus a line-up of fundamentalist and otherwise conservative Protestants declaring the Pope would actually be President if Kennedy won. Neither side in the debate had been so tightly knit before, and the liberal faction never had sided so strongly with Catholicism on any issue. The two remained divided, however, on such a vital matter as birth control.

The Rev. Thurston N. Davis, editor-in-chief of the Roman Catholic magazine *America,* wrote that the religious complexion of the United States had changed to such an extent that it no longer was a Protestant country. He said it was not a Catholic nation either. "Post-Protestant" and "pluralistic" were his terms for it.

Pope John's proposal in 1959 for a meeting of Roman Catholics and other Christian groups found Protestants on more friendly terms with one another than at any other time in the 19 preceding centuries of Christianity. The World Missionary Council was preparing to merge with the World Council of Churches and the Commission of Churches on International Affairs had been formed as a liaison group between the churches and the United Nations. The National Council of Churches had been formed in 1950 and 10 years later represented 38 Protestant and Eastern Orthodox groups with about 40,000,000 members on the books of nearly 145,000 local congregations. The Council was the driving force behind the construction of a skyscraper Interchurch Center on Morningside Heights in New York City, housing the headquarters of some of the largest church organizations in the nation. The World Council, formed in Amsterdam in 1948, is made up of more than 170 member churches in 50 countries with 170,000,000 members. Its North American headquarters is in the Interchurch Center.

There is nothing else like either the National or World Council. Through the National Council, churches of nearly all denominations are working together for the common good and in doing so, for the good of each as well. Groups that once shunned one another now meet together and plan together, with their concerns ranging from great political questions to community matters.

No other movement has spread so far or so fast as the World Council of Churches. It has won the participation and loyalty of approximately a third of the world's population. The United Nations represents a greater proportion of mankind, but on a far different basis. There are those who hope the World Council may pave the way for real brotherhood in a way the U.N. either has not or will not.

This ecumenical movement is cause for excitement in religious circles around the world. At home, the National Council and its ever-growing "outreach" to every corner of the nation is cause for pleasure, if not exactly excitement.

Gradually barriers are falling. When the Southern Baptists and Missouri Lutherans accepted participation in National Council programs, even on limited local bases, it meant that the Council really had been accepted as an integral part of Protestantism.

One of the most heartening moves toward cooperation of Protestantism with Catholicism and Judaism has come through the 33-year-old National Conference of Christians and Jews. The bitterness engendered by the anti-Catholic bigotry of the 1960 Presidential campaign was more than counteracted by the amity that grew among the intelligent leaders of the three religious groups. Even while propaganda lambasting Kennedy as a lackey of the Pope was being circulated, leading Catholic, Protestant and Jewish clergymen were meeting to discuss their differences and finding areas for conversation they never had explored before. The controversy over the question of a Catholic President wiped out an old reticence to discuss religion openly. Questions were asked and answered and understanding was engendered—largely thanks to the bigot underworld, which had inspired formation of the conference with the anti-Catholic attacks of the 1928 Presidential campaign.

In the past, religion in America has been fragmented, probably as nowhere in the world. That is largely because the nation was founded by rugged individualists fleeing religious persecution. These people wanted to live in a place where they could speak and worship as they chose. Americans have been doing just that, but increasingly, in the highly competitive world around them, they are finding that they *choose* to worship together.

Whether, if ever, there will be a complete re-formation in which Catholicism and Protestantism are united is much debated. The Archbishop of Canterbury's decision to call on the Pope in Rome —the first such encounter of the heads of the two religions since THE Reformation—was considered of historic import, even if it turned out to be nothing more than a friendly gesture.

Perhaps the new Reformation, or re-formation, of American Protestantism may turn out to be called Chapter II of one great story—of the Reformation that began 300 years ago. The theme of Chapter II as finally written might be the pulling together of all the Protestant fragments. The big religious question that follows is, Will there be a Chapter III, a grand finale, that will see a reunion of Catholicism and Protestantism achieved in the cooperative spirit of the new-time religion?

Index